And the Clock Struck Thirteen

Lewis O'Brien is a Kaurna Elder of the Adelaide Plains,
Aboriginal Elder of the Year in 1997, Winner of the
South Australian Local Hero award in 2003, and
Honorary Fellow of the University of South Australia.

And the Clock Struck Thirteen

The life and thoughts of Kaurna Elder Uncle Lewis Yerloburka O'Brien

as told to Mary-Anne Gale

Wakefield
Press

Wakefield Press
1 The Parade West
Kent Town
South Australia 5067
www.wakefieldpress.com.au

First published 2007

Text designed by Clinton Ellicott, Wakefield Press
Typeset by Ryan Paine, Wakefield Press
Printed and bound by Hyde Park Press

National Library of Australia
Cataloguing-in-publication entry

O'Brien, Lewis Yerloburka.
And the clock struck thirteen: the life and thoughts of Kaurna Elder
Uncle Lewis Yerloburka O'Brien.

1st ed.
ISBN 978 1 86254 730 8 (pbk.).

1. O'Brien, Lewis Yerloburka. 2. Aboriginal Australian – South Australia – Biography.
3. Kaurna (Australian people) – Biography. I. Gale, Mary-Anne. II. Title.

305.38891509423

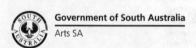

Government of South Australia
Arts SA

fox creek

Contents

To Auntie May and Uncle Lewis Adams,
for their wisdom and generosity.
For Aileen Gale, in admiration.

Foreword

This book is a collaborative effort which grew out of the many requests Uncle Lewis O'Brien had to write a book about his thoughts and philosophies of life. Late in 2001 both Uncle Lewis and I became adjunct research fellows at the University of South Australia. On being given a computer and a desk, Uncle Lewis was told, 'Now you can write your book!' Months later I asked Uncle Lewis how he was going with his book, only to be told that it wasn't going so well; in fact it wasn't really happening at all. Having recovered from the long, yet enjoyable, haul of working with Auntie Veronica Brodie on her life story, *My Side of the Bridge*, I tentatively asked Uncle Lewis 'Do you want some help?' . . . So four years later, after much enriching toil, here is Uncle Lewis' book. No, it is not just a book of his thoughts and philosophies of life, nor is it just a life story . . . it is really a combination of both. After much discussion, debate and trial and error, together we decided the best approach was to weave Uncle Lewis' philosophies of life within the narrative of his and his family's life story, beginning with his great, great grandmother Kudnarto.

Anyone who has listened to Uncle Lewis speak in public will know that he is what one might call a 'talker' who entertains, often with the visual aid of a loop of string. He is also someone who doesn't like to stick to one topic for too long – preferring to digress at regular intervals with little anecdotes from different times and events in his life. So trying to transform the oral recordings of a 'talker' into the written narrative of a 'story-teller' has been quite a challenge. But the words in the text are those of Uncle Lewis, and he has read and re-read the way they have been arranged over and over again, to ensure that any editorial intervention meets with his approval. In the process I have come to respect and admire this 'old man of the sea', Yerloburka, and I sincerely hope he will have a similar impact on you as readers. So I can only trust that our collaborative efforts do justice to Uncle Lewis and his family, and to the wisdom he is so keen to share with us all.

Mary-Anne Gale
2007

Mary-Anne Gale is a research fellow at the University of Adelaide and University of South Australia, and has a strong passion for helping Indigenous people tell their stories. She collatorated with Auntie Veronica Brodie in the writing of her well-received autobiography *My Side of the Bridge*, also published by Wakefield Press. Her PhD, 'Poor Bugger Whitefella got no Dreaming', focused on the writings of the remarkable Ngarrindjeri man David Unaipon. As a linguist and a teacher, Mary-Anne is working with the Ngarrindjeri community to help revive their unique and well-documented language.

Preface

When I was a young teenage boy, living at Kumanka[1] Boys' Hostel in North Adelaide, I quickly learnt that my life was no longer my own and I had to do what I was told – or at least appear to do what I was told. The matron, Mrs Lyndon, soon noticed that I wasn't like the other boys. If any of them didn't want to do what they were told, they would rebel and run amok. One day Mrs Lyndon said to me, 'Lewis, I notice you listen to what people say, but you often do just what you want to do.' And she was right. I did listen to what others had to say, and outwardly I always did what I was told, but then I'd go off and work out for myself what the best thing to do was and then do that. I was lucky because Mrs Lyndon understood me and she often allowed me to choose my own way in that boys' home. Kumanka was actually a home for working boys who had left school but I was allowed to live there even though I was still at school. I was a ward of the state and I had nowhere else to go.

So from an early age I tried to make my own way and consequently I've been out of step with others. In fact I've often felt out of sync with both my own Aboriginal people and the white world and wonder whether this character trait is a throwback to the Irish in me. My Aboriginal grandparents told me that at the age of three I corrected the church minister on

---

1 *Kumanka* is a word taken from the Kaurna language meaning 'together'. It is spelt today as *Kumangka*.

1

Point Pearce mission. He said to me, 'Here sonny, have a picture card of an Indian.' And I replied, 'No, that's a picture of a Red Indian.' The minister immediately told me, 'You'll go far, sonny.' In those days no one questioned the minister on the mission.

My name is Uncle Lewis Yerloburka O'Brien and I am of Kaurna and Ngadjuri descent. Some people call me Kauwanu, which means 'Uncle' in the Kaurna language. Sometimes I use the name Warritya, which means 'second born male'. In more recent years I have taken on the name Yerloburka, which means 'old man of the sea'.

When I returned to live at Point Pearce at the age of nine I was given the nickname 'Prof', short for Professor. My Uncle Tim Hughes[2] gave me that name because he recognised in me an ability to use big words. I used to read a lot and listen to adult programs on the radio and I knew even then that it was important to stay longer at school, which was unusual for Aboriginal people in those days. When I joined the Merchant Navy I used to write letters home to my Auntie Gladys Elphick and cousin Alfie using lots of big words. They would say, 'We got your nice letters, but we don't know what the hell you're talking about!'

Years later I am now an Adjunct Research Fellow at the University of South Australia and have an office down the corridor from Professor Paul Hughes, the son of Tim Hughes, and the nephew of Professor Lowitja O'Donoghue. Paul Hughes still calls me Prof.

So why call my book *And the Clock Struck Thirteen*? The passage my life has taken reminds me of my Auntie Glad's old mantelpiece clock. When I turned eighteen I had to leave Kumanka to make my own way in life. I went to live with my

---

2 In reciprocation, Tim also earned my respect to be referred to as 'Uncle' even though he was my second cousin. He won a military medal in Buna, New Guinea, and an MBE in 1970 (as the first chairman of the Lands Trust).

Auntie Glad at Thebarton, in Adelaide. One day, the family, including my brother and I, were in her sitting room all arguing. Auntie Glad was arguing with Uncle Fred, with Granny Gertie chipping in, and my cousin Alfie and I were arguing about the footy or something, with my brother Lawrence chipping in. In the middle of all this chaos the old clock started to wind up and begin striking. It made us all pause while we counted quietly: ziiip, dong, ziiip, dong, ziiip, dong ... When it reached twelve we were all ready to resume our arguments; but the clock had other ideas. It went on one more time and struck thirteen, ziip dong!

We sat there like stunned mullets, looking at each other in bewilderment. Then Grannie Gertie got up and, pointing to us all, shouted, 'We're all mad. I'm mad, you're mad, and even the bloody clock's gone mad!' And we all burst out laughing.

When I remember that particular incident, it seems like a metaphor for my life – I've always felt as though I was out of step with those around me, just like Auntie Glad's clock. Even now I feel that way. As a small child I accepted the Aboriginal philosophy of life from those around me, from when I lived with my people in short bursts over a long period of time. But I was fostered out during my teenage years so I always felt I couldn't act naturally because I had to do what I was told. I was a ward of the state so my life was in someone else's hands. I coped by thinking about what I wanted to do in life and trying to stick to those goals.

I eventually learnt that if I wanted to be accepted it was best to stay silent, because nobody liked Aborigines in those days and our opinions didn't count, especially if you were a ward of the state. At one stage in my life I even forgot how to talk and communicate. Later, when I joined the Merchant Navy, I was running away from the stigma of being an Aboriginal person, but I eventually realised that you can't run away from who you are.

When I travelled to Japan a customs official asked me what nationality I was. I had a British passport, which all Australians had in the 1950s (because they thought people overseas wouldn't know where Australia was). He read my passport and said, 'British subject, Australian citizen.' Then he said to me in an abrupt way, 'Australian?' Eventually I agreed and replied, 'Australian.' But the ridiculous thing was that I wasn't even eligible to be an Australian citizen at that time because I was an Aboriginal person. My place of birth on the passport was Point Pearce and technically I was a British subject only and not an Australian citizen. I didn't assume Australian citizenship until after the referendum of 1967.[3]

By agreeing with the customs officer I felt like Peter in the Bible denying Christ just before he was condemned to death. I felt guilty, because I should have replied, 'I'm an Australian Aboriginal.' This happened several more times while I was away and when I came home I was so embarrassed and upset about denying my Aboriginality that I never denied it again.

So there it is – I was an Aboriginal kid born on a mission, with blond hair and fair skin, who looked more Irish than Aboriginal. Even the kids on the mission referred to me as the white kid and used to throw stones at me for fun. And yet I grew up for a time with my Aboriginal grandparents as an Aboriginal kid. I'm not a coconut, I'm not brown on the outside and white inside – I'm white on the outside and brown inside. I often wonder what sort of fruit looks like that. Maybe I'm more like a rum ball – with white coconut on the outside and chocolate brown on the inside.

This book tells the story of my chequered life, with all its trials and tribulations, and how I've managed to endure hardship and become a stronger person. Now I don't run anymore,

---

3 This referendum gave the Commonwealth government the power to legislate on Aboriginal issues, resulting in Aboriginal people being counted in the census.

but I still have an affinity with the sea, which is why I refer to myself as *Yerloburka* ('old man of the sea'). I believe that the philosophies of life my Aboriginal grandparents gave me during the few short years I spent with them on the mission have sustained me. So too has the time I've spent with other important Aboriginal Elders during my life, such as Auntie Gladys Elphick. They all taught me to be proud of who I am and not to deny either my Aboriginality or my Irish ancestry.

In writing this book I want to share some of the wise philosophies that my Elders taught me. I also want to share the lessons I have learnt during my own passage through life – especially through the times when I felt out of sync with others. I am in my seventies now and people have been asking me for a number of years to write a book about my life and my philosophies, so here it is. This book is testament to my belief that we can all learn from the Aboriginal Elders and from each other, whether we are black or white, or maybe a bit of both!

1

Padniadlu wadu: Let's walk together in harmony

Kaurna

Martuityangga, Kaurna meyunna, ngai wanggandi,
Marni naa budni Kaurna yertaanna.
Ngai birko-mankolankola Tarndanya meyunnako.
Ngaityo yungandalya, ngaityo yakkanandalya. Padniadlu wadu.

English

On behalf of the Kaurna people I welcome you all to Kaurna country.

I do this as an Ambassador of the Adelaide Plains people.

My brothers, my sisters, let's walk together in harmony.

Our people, the Kaurna people of the Adelaide Plains, have welcomed visitors to our country for thousands of years. We used to hold conferences here on Kaurna land and welcome other Indigenous people to our country, knowing that our visitors would return to their own land at the end of the conference. These gatherings were what you white fellas often call 'corroborees'. So for many years the Kaurna people looked forward to these important social events on the seasonal calendar.

When you non-Indigenous people arrived here on our land we thought you were just visiting, like our other guests. If we welcomed you it was on the understanding that you would eventually go home. But you didn't! We Kaurna failed in our welcome because we forgot to tell you white fellas to eventually go home! So now you are here for good and we have to learn to live in harmony with each other in this special country of ours.

Smallpox came very early to the Kaurna people. I think it came overland across Australia to our group as early as 1789. This was because we ran conferences. There were very few Aboriginal people in Adelaide when the white colonists arrived here in 1836 on the *Buffalo*. They noticed this and thought something was wrong. The colonist John Adams said he only saw one ten-year-old boy, so he knew things were not right. What I'm saying is that smallpox came before the colonists arrived; it came overland via other Indigenous people.

We, the Kaurna people, were the facilitators and we ran the conferences. I don't think many know that. Other Indigenous groups expected us to address various issues at our assemblies and they'd come here to discuss them. The Ngarrindjeri people of the Lower Murray, Lakes and Coorong regions would take part, as would the Permangk of the Adelaide Hills. We were also very friendly with the Ramindjeri from the Victor Harbor and Cape Jervis region. They'd all be called in, as well as the Narungga people of Yorke Peninsula. People even came from the West Coast, including the Wirangu and Mirning, plus the Nauo and Pangkala from Eyre Peninsula. They'd light fires down there on the southern end of Yorke Peninsula and signal all the groups in. But unfortunately, when all these people came together some of them brought the smallpox with them, particularly the groups from the east, and that knocked our mob rotten.

In recent times we have rediscovered the word *Banba-ban-balyarnendi*, in the Kaurna language, which means 'to hold a conference'. So the Kaurna people even had a word to describe these important seasonal events. When you take the '*-nendi*' suffix off the word *Banba-banbalyarnendi* you get *banba-ban-balya*, which means 'a conference'. It was originally recorded back in 1857 by the German missionary Christian Teichelmann in a word list he made of the Adelaide language.[1] He later gave a copy of the list to Governor Grey, which got lost over in South Africa among all his other ethnographic notes and official papers in the South African Public Library. If you look in the old records it's there. So I've only really found out about this word for conference recently.

The Narungga people also held conferences on their own land on Yorke Peninsula. My Uncle Tim Hughes talked about the neighbouring Indigenous groups who used to come together at Port Arthur, in Narungga country. These groups were the Nukunu[2], the Ngadjuri, the Narungga as well as the Kaurna. But Uncle Tim didn't call us the Kaurna then. I should use the exact words he used. He referred to us as the Thura. That's the Narungga name for the Kaurna people. The term *Kaurna* was first recorded by the Protector of Aborigines, William Wyatt, in the late 1830s as 'Encounter Bay Bob's tribe' (who was most likely a Ramindjeri man, not Kaurna). The name *Kaurna* was popularised by the anthropologist Norman Tindale who worked with the Ngarrindjeri man Clarence Long (also known as Milerum). The Ngarrindjeri people referred to us as the Kaurna, probably from their word *Ko:rnar* meaning 'men'. Each group would call you different names and so that's probably what the other Aboriginal groups called us.

Our people attended these conferences that were run by the Narungga on the start of the full moon, when the fish were running, so they could feed the multitudes. The people would come together to arrange marriages, settle disputes of land and boundaries, establish rights of passage through each other's country and to discuss many other important issues.

There is a tape recording of Tim Hughes talking about

1 This was a second list made in addition to the original 1840 wordlist of Kaurna terms, which was compiled and published by missionaries Clamor Schürmann and Christian Teichelmann.
2 The Nukunu – they are the keepers of the law.

how the conferences were run. It was made in the 1960s by historian Betty Fisher. Uncle Tim Hughes remembers the different groups coming together for two moons, which made me realise, heavens, they even did it in more recent times. The different Indigenous groups must have been doing this conferencing into the 1930s, all the Nukunu, Narungga, Ngadjuri and the Thura.

Then years later, in the 1980s, a bloke came from Queensland and he expected me to run a meeting. At first I didn't know what he was talking about and then I suddenly realised it was an old expectation. And so you can see it's in the memory of the people that Adelaide was the centre for meeting and information-sharing. It's interesting, when you start analysing it, because Adelaide is in the centre of this country. It's the shortest distance for everyone to come.

In Aboriginal society individual groups managed their own day-to-day affairs but this system became awkward when it came to managing the whole country. When the British arrived, we were probably going to address the problem through conferencing, but were beaten by smallpox. Aboriginal people lived in isolation from the rest of the world for so many years, we didn't have any experience dealing with invaders. They say that germs, guns and steel[3] conquer the world and these all worked perfectly well in this country for the British.

There are regions across this vast country that are 'free zones'. These are places that are open to each Aboriginal group to gather for particular purposes. One free zone is Mount Barker – no one really owns it, it was a place where Aboriginal people came together. I once heard a bloke talking about how he's found thousands of stone flints and chips on his property

---

3 Jared Diamond wrote a book with this title *Guns, Germs and Steel: A short history of everybody for the last 13,000 years* (1997 & 2005), Vintage, London.

at Nuriootpa. He's taken some to the museum. That must have been another gathering place for Aboriginal people, especially if thousands of stone chips accumulated there. This free-zone idea, a place where everyone can gather, is a bit like an embassy – like neutral territory.

The people always ran these conferences in areas where there was plenty of food, such as near some coastal region, or at Mount Barker where there were lots of kangaroos, emus and possums. And the gatherings were held at different times of the year depending on the seasons. It would be too cold in the Adelaide Hills in winter, for example, so they'd gather instead on the warmer flats. Or in summer they'd come together on the coast. And because they all met on someone else's country, or in a free zone, and for peaceful purposes, they avoided any possibility of war.

Visiting someone else's country is an experience. Traditionally when Aboriginal people had to go from their own country to some other place, they had to learn the other's language. Then they'd come back home happy because they'd been somewhere else, and seen other country and extended their knowledge.

In Australia there were nearly a thousand different Indigenous groups and each one had their own Dreaming stories. These Dreamings explain how we know, understand and come to terms with our own country. The belief system was practical and useful and it made each group respect their own country. They all got to know their own land backwards, so they were proud of themselves and where they came from. It was a nice, fulfilling way to live. They were not envious of anyone else, not coveting their neighbour's ground or property, in fact the opposite. Aboriginal people learnt to respect their own ground and not to want anyone else's. When their neighbours visited, the people took pride in showing their visitors over their own ground, explaining what they knew and how they survived on their land. I reckon it's a lovely idea and way of living.

What I find surprising today – an interesting little twist – is that non-Indigenous people are starting to agree with what we believe. In our own Dreaming stories we say: 'In the beginning the land was flat and featureless. Then the ancestors created the mountains and the rivers and the plants and animals.' Well, I've got a 2001 geology book about the planets, by a professor of geology at Melbourne University, which says: 'When the first surface of the Earth solidified, it was barren. No plants, no animals, no running water.'[4] And I think, that's interesting, it's similar to what our ancestors taught us.

All my life I have found increasing similarities between Aboriginal ideas and beliefs and Western beliefs. I find that these Dreaming stories connect to contemporary times, our timeless Aboriginal way of thinking connects to modern thinking. I am fascinated by how our people developed all these Dreaming stories, and how they seem to be connecting to other people's beliefs.

It's generally accepted that Aboriginal people have been living in Australia for 60,000 years. This is confirmed by archaeologists like the late Rhys Jones. Most people believe that Aboriginal people were the *only* ones living here before the white invasion (or colonisation), apart from the annual visits that the Macassan traders made to the northern coastal areas of Australia from the 1700s to the early 1900s. The Macassans came from the islands of Indonesia to collect and process *trepang* (sea slugs or sea cucumbers), which they then traded with the Chinese.

I believe that Egyptians may have also visited Australia

---

4 See Ian Plimer, *A Short History of Planet Earth* (2001) ABC Books, Sydney, p. 40.

thousands of years ago, well before the Macassan traders came. It was also long before the Dutch explorers landed on the Western Australian coast and before Captain Cook explored the eastern coast in 1770. I also believe Aboriginal people and Aboriginal cultural beliefs influenced the Egyptians. If the Egyptians came to Australia 5000 years ago (that's 3000 years before the time of Christ) they would have seen that Aboriginal people had no idolatry practices and that the people had very little in the way of material wealth. They would also have seen that the people were happy. Perhaps the Egyptians wondered why they weren't happy like the Aboriginal people and questioned their own belief in multi-Gods (polytheism) and material wealth.[5]

Long before the British came to this country, Australia was a spiritual country of a higher order. Aboriginal people were not materialistic and they lived in harmony with the land. But they didn't worship the land or any other kind of idol. They respected and looked after the land, knowing that the land, and all who lived on it, was what sustained them both physically and spiritually.

When the first European explorers arrived here in Australia they saw that we had no idols. Not even the toas, made by the people in the Eyre Basin region of South Australia, are idols. They may look like idols but the people didn't worship the statues. The Kaurna people of the Adelaide Plains actually had a word for a higher creator – *Pingyallingyalla*. They gave this Kaurna word to the missionaries in 1839 when they were asking for a word for 'God'.

One Adelaide colonist, William Cawthorne, wrote a booklet in 1844 called *Rough Notes on the Manners & Customs of the Natives*, and in it he wrote: 'a remarkable feature in the

---

5 If you want to read more about my ideas on the Egyptians and how they could have got here, see Appendix 1.

history of the natives – there is no such thing as idolatry. No gods have they to worship, but their belief is vested in a few imaginary spirits whom they do not reverence, but fear'. I don't believe we Kaurna feared Pingyallingyalla, but we did have other fears and suspicions regarding the many dangers facing Aboriginal people, especially in those very difficult early years of colonisation.

In September 2004 I was privileged to hear the Yolngu man Reverend Djiniyini Gondarra speaking here in Adelaide. He was on a national tour called *Mawul Rom*[6], the title he's given to the 'cross cultural mediation training' that he is undertaking across the country. His plan is to assist the healing between all people from different backgrounds living in Australia and to promote greater understanding between us. What I was most pleased about was how similar his beliefs are to mine, yet he comes from the far north of the country in Arnhem Land, and I am from the very south. In his talk the Reverend explained that Aboriginal people didn't worship idols and weren't pagans before Christians arrived here, that Aboriginal people had sound moral values well before the arrival of Christian missionaries. He believes God was in this country before 1788 and this was in fact 'God's country'.

I also believe Aboriginal people had sound moral values long before white people came. That's not to say, however, that we didn't adopt Christian teachings once the missionaries arrived here as well. Aboriginal culture and philosophy wasn't static, we readily picked up the new ideas the missionaries and colonists brought, including some of their Christian teachings. So whether the values many of us hold now are from before or after the missionaries came, it is hard to say.

---

6 In the Yolngu Matha language and culture *Mawul Rom* means 'place for healing, holy, restricted'; *Rom* means 'law'.

Many of the values that I live by I learnt from my wise old Auntie May, but there were also other wise Elders who influenced me. When we sat down for meals we were always told to be thankful for what we had to eat and not to be envious of what anyone else had. We were also taught to forgo one species of any plant or animal in addition to the rule of not eating one's totem. We were taught to only catch the big fish and to let the little fish go so they could grow bigger. By doing this we soon understood the wisdom of what we were being told. By our actions we could see there would be fish there for tomorrow.

Another philosophy that Auntie May lived by was not to crave for worldly possessions. When I was a boy living at Point Pearce, there were still Aboriginal people living in the Wadjadin scrub on the outskirts of Point Pearce. They had chosen not to live under the rule of the mission. We used to call them the 'old people' and Auntie May always said that these old Aboriginal people living in the bush were happy. They certainly had nothing in the way of material possessions and she used to say that happiness that results from material things or possessions is only momentary. And I think she was right.

One more lesson that Auntie May taught me as a child was to be satisfied with what you've got. I remember she was always telling me that you should leave the dinner table hungry, which didn't really make much sense to me as a hungry, growing boy. Whenever we would visit someone's house, Grandmother Julia would lecture me before we arrived, saying, 'Don't you dare take the last piece of cake on the plate.' I guess she was teaching me not to be greedy and to be content with what we've been given, not to look for more.

In this book I talk about my life and all I have learnt from people like my Auntie May. I also explain my beliefs and understandings about the land of the Kaurna people – the land of the Adelaide Plains and beyond. I invite you to learn from and to respect this land, just as my ancestors did. I hope you will enjoy hearing about my life and the lives of my family, beginning with my great, great grandmother Kudnarto, who was the first Kaurna woman to officially marry a white man in the state of South Australia.

2

Kudnarto of Skillogalee Creek

My great, great grandmother was the Kaurna woman Kudnarto from the Crystal Brook district, which is about 200 kilometres north of Adelaide. Crystal Brook is in the northern-most region of land belonging to the Aboriginal people known as the Kaurna, whose land reaches across the Adelaide Plains and as far south as Cape Jervis on the southern tip of Fleurieu Peninsula.

A few people have written about Kudnarto in recent years but I'm writing about her from my own perspective as her descendant. *Kudnarto* means, in the Kaurna language, 'a girl who is third-born'. If she had been a third-born boy she would have been named Kudnuitya. At the age of around sixteen or seventeen Kudnarto married a white man named Thomas Adams, who was twenty years older than her, and she later became known as Mary Anne Adams. Kudnarto's marriage to a white man was viewed by the other colonists as a news-worthy event because six months before her marriage, the couple's nuptial plans were reported in the colonial papers. In June 1847 the *South Australian Register* reported:

> Thomas Adams, a shepherd in the employ of Mr Ferguson, at his station near Crystal Brook, has wooed and won a native female named Kudnarto, about 17 years of age, to whom he has been long, and as it would appear, sincerely attached: and having resolved to make her his lawful wife, has placed her under the charge of one of the mistresses of the Native School for the

purpose of a four months' initiation into the arts of domestic life and those household duties which she is apparently bent upon learning . . . The future bride is rather personable than otherwise, and her betrothed has been heard to declare that her fidelity, amiability of disposition, and aptitude to learn, are very remarkable, if not unprecedented.

Kudnarto and Tom Adams finally married on 27 January 1848 in the office of the Deputy-Registrar in the Public Buildings on Waymouth Street in Adelaide. Theirs was the first official marriage ever recorded in South Australia between a white man and an Aboriginal woman. It was such a significant event it was again reported in the newspaper the *South Australian*:

Yesterday, the Deputy Registrar-General, [married] Thomas Adams, shepherd, Crystal Brook, to Kudnarto, an aboriginal native girl of the Crystal Brook tribe. This is the first legal marriage to which an aboriginal South Australian has been a party. The bridegroom is about seven and thirty years of age, and the bride sixteen. She has been for more than two years living with her present husband, whose affections have become so strong towards her, that he determined on securing her as his lawful wife. For the past two months she has been in the Native School. Her dress during the ceremony was a neat gown and low boots. She wore no bonnet, but her hair was carefully dressed; and her whole appearance denoted cleanliness and comfort. Mr Moorhouse, Protector of Aborigines, attended and gave her away. She speaks good English, and repeated the responses distinctly. She is, for one of her race, remarkably good looking, and has a pleasing expression of countenance. We are told that the fortunate swain considers he has made an acquisition, as she is a good tempered and very hard working girl. Two other Europeans have, for some time, we understand, contemplated similar marriages, and now the ice is broken, it is probable they will carry their intentions into effect. One of the intended brides is now in the Native School under due training.[1]

I have always been amazed by my great, great grandmother Kudnarto. She must have been a clever woman – she learnt to read and write English in the few months she was at the Native School on Kintore Avenue in Adelaide. I wondered how she did that and then I realised that she would have known the languages of all her neighbours – about seven – so another one would have come easily. Aboriginal people learnt to speak another language quickly in those days. Archdeacon Hale, who later founded the Aboriginal mission Poonindie on Eyre Peninsula in 1850, referred to Kudnarto as an 'educated woman'.

The very first school to be established in Adelaide for Aboriginal children was in 1839 and was actually run in the Kaurna language by the German missionaries Christian Teichelmann and Clamor Schürmann. They taught the children to read the local language and to write in Kaurna in beautiful copybook script. There are still a few letters in the archives that were written in Kaurna by the school children. This school was run at the Native Location, which was situated where the par 3 golf course lies now, just opposite the weir on the Torrens River, not far from the Adelaide Oval.

The Native Location school catered mainly for Kaurna children, while another school was opened in Walkerville for the so-called 'River Blacks' from the Murray River who had moved into the Adelaide area. Both of these schools were

---

1 Another Kaurna woman who was to later marry a white man was Rathoola of Fleurieu Peninsula. She married George Solomon in 1855, settled at Rapid Bay and had four children. The children were eventually sent to Poonindie mission after Rathoola's death in 1858. See Kartinyeri, *Tandanya Souvenir Program* (1989), p. 6. See also Brock & Kartinyeri, *Poonindie: The rise and destruction of an Aboriginal agricultural community* (1989).

eventually closed in 1845 and a new Native School was opened on Kintore Avenue for the few remaining River Blacks and any willing Kaurna children. But all instruction in this new boarding school was strictly in English. It is here that Kudnarto would have attended for her few months of learning how to live as a white woman.

Before Kudnarto got married she was told by the Government Protector that she had to go and learn something about modern ways. She was a minor and a ward of the state and wanted to get married, so the governor had to give his okay, but on the condition that she attend school for a few months where she learnt English and how to do domestic duties. If she was going to get married she had to learn the manners of the people of her day because she was going to live in white society. The Protector of Aborigines, Dr Matthew Moorhouse, made this ruling because it was the first time an Aboriginal was to marry a European. I guess he thought he couldn't just give permission with no conditions. What I find most surprising is that Kudnarto had to go to school yet Tom Adams, her husband-to-be, couldn't even read and write and probably never went to school!

So Kudnarto learnt to read and write in English very quickly which makes me think that she must have had other education. We know that her family had some connection with Bungaree station just north of Clare so perhaps she received some education there and on other properties where she lived and worked.

In the early days of the colony, to encourage Aboriginal people to settle in one place and adopt European ways, some land was set aside by the South Australian governor for use by Aboriginal people. Governor Frederick Robe had made a ruling that if any European married an Aboriginal the Aboriginal spouse could obtain some land. So Kudnarto was offered Section 346 Hundred of Upper Wakefield in the Clare district, comprising eighty-one acres of land. This block of land offered to Kudnarto was just one of a number reserved 'for the use and benefit' of Aboriginal people in South Australia. As outlined in the contract, some conditions applied to the occupation of the land:

To Matthew Moorhouse Esquire, Protector of Aborigines of the said province, and his Successors in Office, and also whom it may concern, Greetings,

Whereas in order to encourage the adoption of settled habits and civilised usages, by the aborigines, certain sections of Land have been reserved for their use; And whereas an Aboriginal native woman named Kudnarto otherwise called 'Mary' hath been married in lawful wedlock to Thomas Adams of the Skylogalee Creek, laborer, and is meet [sic] to encourage the settlement of herself and her lawful Offspring: Now Therefore Know, that I the Lieutenant Governor, in name and on behalf of Her Majesty, by virtue of all powers me thereunder enabling, Do hereby Grant full licence for the said Mary Adams for who during the term of her natural life to occupy, use and enjoy Section No. 346 consisting of eighty one acres more or less, being one of the said Aboriginal Reserves situate on the said Skylogalee Creek; and to clear, enclose and cultivate the said Section, and to build and erect any hut or erection thereon, and to cut, saw, split, and remove timber thereon, Provided always that these presents are granted on Condition that the said Mary Adams shall and do settle and continue actually to reside upon the said land: and shall not, by herself or any other attempt to assign or underlet the same; Provided also that nor possession or occupation under these presents shall give any title whatever to the said Land or alter the rights of Her Majesty, Her Heirs and Successors in respect thereto: And provided that in case of any offence or misconduct on the part of the said Mary or Thomas Adams, her husband, these presents may, at any time, on the report of her Protector of Aborigines, be revoked and determined by the Governor.

Moorhouse had doubts about granting land to Aboriginal women married to white men, because he could see that white men who wanted land could take advantage of the situation. So anyone wanting to marry an Aboriginal woman had to be checked out. Moorhouse expressed his concern in some of his letters. In reply to one bloke he tells him that it would be nice if he actually liked the girl! He saw that this man, who was a teacher, just wanted to marry an Aboriginal girl for her land grant. Moorhouse told him that's not what it's all about. It's really about a proper union. If he only wants to marry for the property, he wasn't going to approve that. I can understand Moorhouse's position.

When Moorhouse viewed Kudnarto and Thomas Adams' case he must have seen that the couple had been living together and obviously Kudnarto loved Adams. So he was in favour of it as a good match. He recommended to Governor Robe that they be allowed to marry, and the governor gave the marriage his blessing. But being the first to marry they had to be asked all these questions, because they were setting a precedent. They had to show that they loved each other.

So Tom and Kudnarto got married and Kudnarto was granted the land at Skillogalee Creek. Section 346 was granted for the term of Kudnarto's natural life and, as you can read in the contract, it was understood that Tom Adams had no rights to sell or sublet the land, and on Kudnarto's death the land was to be offered for lease to her children. It was good land in a peaceful valley and was well watered by a permanent spring and the nearby Skillogalee Creek. It had large gum trees scattered across the flats on either side of the creek. So life was quiet and good to them in the first year of their marriage.

However, their peace was soon broken. They discovered

that the spring in the middle of their property was a popular watering spot for the bullock teams passing through on their way to and from the newly established copper mines to the north, particularly at Burra, but also Kapunda.[2] Their land was located on the eastern side of the well-worn track used by the teamsters passing through with their loads of copper ore on their way to the ship landing at Port Henry near the head of St Vincent Gulf. The town of Port Henry is now known as Port Wakefield. Kudnarto's property was actually between the townships of what are now known as Hoyleton and Auburn.

The teamsters had set stop-overs for their thirsty bullocks on the journey, with seven leagues between each watering hole and the next. The bullocks had to travel a full seven leagues before they got their next drink, which is equivalent to twenty-one miles (or thirty-five kilometres). One league is equal to three miles.

If there was a watering hole for the bullocks, there was naturally one for the bullock drivers as well. After the teamsters watered their bullocks at Section 346, they headed for the noisy and rough bush pub known as the Port Henry Arms Hotel. This pub was on the hill overlooking Kudnarto's block and it tended to attract some pretty undesirable characters. Consequently Kudnarto and Tom experienced a bit of strife from these regular visitors. As well as the teamsters passing through, the Burra mines employed some blokes to camp at Skillogalee Creek to help the bullock drivers get their wagons across the creek, because the wagons would have been heavy laden at times. These men helped the teamsters get their loads safely across the creek and up the hill and on their way to Port Henry where they loaded the ore onto the ships for England.

Having this constant flow of traffic through Block 346

---

2 Kapunda copper deposits were discovered in 1842 and at Burra in 1845, and by 1849 smelters were operating in both centres to refine the ore before it was shipped overseas.

caused considerable problems for Tom Adams and Kudnarto. They couldn't stop the teamsters coming so they thought they might charge the Burra mines for the constant use of their water. They wrote to the appropriate authorities asking for compensation but there were certain conditions set when Kudnarto was granted her block of land. The couple were told they had to live on the property themselves and could not sublease it to anyone else. They were also told they had to develop the property – fencing, clearing and farming the property with stock, or growing crops – but how could Tom work the property when he had no money to get it set up? The only way he could earn enough money to develop their block was by working elsewhere. Tom needed to go off and work as a shepherd to earn the money they needed to put fences up and to do all the other extras necessary. So you can see how these government conditions made the land a burden for those who didn't have any money to develop it. That's why Tom and Kudnarto suggested being compensated for the water the travellers used when crossing their block.

However their request was refused and Tom was told that he had to remain on the block to work and improve the land. But how could he? What was he going to do on the land with no money? He had no sheep, no crops and no money to fence them in to protect them from the bullock teams. It was a big dilemma and Tom eventually had to leave Kudnarto alone and go and find work. Things were rough in those days and Kudnarto was still getting used to living in new circumstances without her family around and with no game to hunt nearby. She had to live in the confines of a house with all these strangers passing across her land – it would have been difficult for her.

Not long after Tom and Kudnarto's marriage there was an unfortunate incident – a murder in the district. This bloke killed another chap in the paddock down the road, not far from Kudnarto's property and she actually allowed the murderer to stay in her house on the night of the slaying. The killer must have left the pub, had a fight and killed this chap, then gone across to Kudnarto's hut and asked if he could take refuge for the night.

Kudnarto was later summoned to give evidence at the murder trial. Kudnarto was highly respected in the local community at the time, as you can see clearly in the reports on the case in the newspapers of the day. You can tell from the way her appearance was reported. It's pretty ironic, when you think about it, because Kudnarto couldn't even swear on the Bible to tell the truth, because she was not only a woman, but an Aboriginal woman. Furthermore she was not a Christian in the real sense of the word. If you're not a Christian you can't put your hand on the Bible and swear to tell the whole truth. That's why the courts were very reluctant to accept evidence from Aboriginal people in those days. They used to debate this point about the legality of evidence given by Aboriginal people when they couldn't take the oath. So Kudnarto gave evidence but not under oath. Even so, everyone took note of what she said and accepted her evidence because she was held in high esteem.

Kudnarto described the alleged murderer, James Yates, in the court and explained how he came to her hut. She knew there had been some sort of trouble because she saw blood on his hands. She also noticed he was a bit cranky, so she didn't want to argue with him when he asked if he could stay overnight, she just let him. That's the sort of thing she had learnt to put up with in her life – to appease people rather than upset them, because she was a young girl and there was no way she could have sent that man off. But her keen sense of observation served her well because she suspected from the time the accused first came to her house that he'd been up to something wrong simply by the way he was acting. So she was very careful to stay out of harm's way that night.

You can tell the court listened to Kudnarto's accurate

description of the murderer and accepted her evidence. The newspaper reports talk about her personal appearance, how she was dressed neatly – they were really obsessed about that – always commenting on her appearance. But it's also obvious in the reports that she was very clear in her statements, even though they reported that she spoke broken English. It's almost like people back then made the assumption that all Aboriginal people spoke like that, but I wondered if she really did speak as badly in the court as they reported in the paper.

On the one hand they talk about how accurately Kudnarto remembered events and how well she was dressed yet on the other they say that she spoke in broken English. It's a bit of a discrepancy. But I must admit that I have even found myself speaking in a simplified way sometimes, despite my educa- tion – particularly when talking to school kids. I don't even realise I'm doing it, so maybe it was the same for Kudnarto.

There's actually not a great deal in the archives about Kudnarto's parentage and relatives. The anthropologist Norman Tindale wrote in his journal that Kudnarto's father was a Ngadjuri man. That's the only written reference I know of about her relatives. I've always known, however, that we've got Ngadjuri connections because everyone in the family used to talk about them. The Ngadjuri group are the north-eastern neighbours of the Kaurna people. I also know from the news papers that Kudnarto was from the northern-most tribe of the Kaurna people, from the Crystal Brook area. Kudnarto was obviously from the Kaurna tribe through her mother, while her father was probably Ngadjuri. So I generally refer to Kudnarto as Ngadjuri/Kaurna.

The Kaurna man Ityamaiitpinna, or King Rodney, married a woman from the Crystal Brook area too, so maybe Crystal Brook was the marriage quarter where many Kaurna women came from. As a result there must have been strong interconnections between the two groups, the Kaurna and the Ngadjuri. You see a lot of Kaurna women from the southern coastal regions of Kaurna country were abducted by sealers but the northern women were in safer territory. King Rodney was actually the father of the famous Ivaritji, or Princess Amelia, the last living so-called 'full-blood' Kaurna person, who died in 1929.

Kudnarto was born in 1831 or 1832, because she was married in 1848 when she was sixteen or seventeen. That means she was born at least five years before South Australia was officially settled and proclaimed a colony. As far as we know, Kudnarto was born in the Clare district on Bungaree Station[3], which is famous for its fine merino sheep. Kudnarto would have grown up knowing the Clare and Crystal Brook district well and she would have been particularly familiar with the land around Skillogalee Creek. That's why she would have chosen to reclaim that particular block of land from the government when she married Tom Adams. She would have known there was permanent water there on Section 346. Our people liked living next to water, so she would have automatically chosen that section. That was her country. She would have known what she needed and it was a good choice. Even the Burra mines didn't want her to be there, because they wanted the water for their bullocks.

A year after Thomas Adams and Kudnarto married, their first son was born at Skillogalee – on 19 June 1849. They named him Thomas Adams after his English father, which seemed to be a tradition for first-born sons in the Adams family. Young Thomas thrived and was joined three years later by a baby brother who they named Timothy Adams. He was born on 11 October 1852. I'm descended from the second

---

3 According to Doreen Kartinyeri, *Narungga Nation* (2002). See genealogy on p. 109.

son, Tim. Unfortunately in 1855 Kudnarto suddenly died at the age of twenty-three, leaving her two small sons without a mother. Tom was six and Tim was three. That meant her marriage only lasted seven years because she passed away when she was very young, which is sad.

I don't know much about the circumstances of Kudnarto's death. I don't even know where she was buried. I gather that Tom Adams senior was away a lot at the time trying to earn an income to develop their property and I imagine Kudnarto would have been battling to survive by herself with two little boys to look after, plus the property to care for. In the archives you can read that she was ill before she died. Tom knew he had to go off and make money so they could buy food and develop the property, so he was not there to nurse Kudnarto. It would have been a hell of a strain on a sick woman to be looking after two kids on her own without any extended family around to help.

When Kudnarto died, Tom was told he could no longer stay on their block of land. You see the land grants were just for Aboriginal women – not for their non-Aboriginal husbands, and Kudnarto's block was granted to her only for the term of her natural life. So when Kudnarto died, the eighty-one acres was immediately reclaimed by the government.

Poor Tom Adams! He was not only grieving over his wife's death, but he was also told he had to leave the property. Of course he wanted to keep it and develop it for his two boys Tom junior and Tim, so he told the government that he wanted to stay on the property. But they told him straight, the land was only given to your wife, not to you. The government gave the land to Aboriginal people with one hand and took it back with the other. I don't understand why Tom wasn't allowed to keep the place for his sons. After all, he had built a house and made a lot of improvements on the place by the time Kudnarto died, but the government just said, no, we can't have *you* making anything out of this. The offer was only to try and help the Aboriginal woman. I suppose because the sons were so-called 'half-castes', and minors, they weren't considered eligible to inherit the land.

And so Section 346 was leased out to white farmers, and Tom Adams had to find somewhere else to settle. Eventually the same block was split up into several sections and sold, so the numbers of the sections have all changed. They later established a pumping station on the place for pumping water from the permanent spring. I know that because I went and saw it once, but it's not there now and there are two roadways cutting right through the property. Skillogalee Creek still runs alongside the property and the spring holds permanent water even today, but that part is not numbered Section 346 anymore – that's Section 400. Ironically, Kudnarto's Section 346 is the only section in that vicinity that was subdivided.

When I went the first time to see this section of land, I remember thinking what an injustice it was. I always mumbled to myself when I was a lad, and I thought, how many times do we have to own this country before we can say it's ours? We're the original owners. My great, great grandmother was given back a piece of her land, only for it to be taken away again from her family when she died. This happened over and over again with land that was put aside for missions. When the missions were closed down, the land got sold to white farmers, rather than being distributed to the Aboriginal people who lived and worked there on the missions. When Kudnarto died her two boys were taken to Poonindie mission to live, near Port Lincoln, on Eyre Peninsula. They resided there for thirty-odd years, yet when Poonindie mission was closed down in the 1890s it was sold off to the white farmers, despite strong Aboriginal protest.

So there are many Kaurna people today who are descended from the remarkable Kaurna woman Kudnarto, either through her elder son Tom or her younger son Tim. Being such a clever woman, she taught her husband Tom Adams to read and write, which was very unusual. Fancy an Englishman being taught by an Aboriginal woman how to read and write! Archdeacon Hale, who founded Poonindie mission and later had a lot to do with bringing up Kudnarto's two young boys, used to always talk about Kudnarto. He used to talk about this 'educated woman' in the after-dinner speeches that he gave to different Adelaide society groups. He was very high up in the Church of England and had much influence in the colony.

Yes, Kudnarto must have been an intelligent woman, because she passed down her talents. She taught her two boys Tom and little Tim as much as she could before she died in 1855. They could both read by the time they were five years old. Both Tom and Tim Adams became prolific letter writers, and Tim's daughter Julia (my grandmother) was also a keen letter writer. Then Julia had my mother who was a very clever woman, and then there is me. The line was never broken. We've always maintained our literacy skills. Our family has always read a lot – we're all avid readers. We must have inherited all those skills of reading, writing and the ability to reason from Kudnarto. She must have been a really smart lady. Kudnarto's talents are embedded in the family. Yes, Kudnarto has passed these abilities on to all her descendants.

3

Who was Tom Adams senior?

For generations my family has remembered the story of how Kudnarto was granted her small patch of traditional land when she married Tom Adams. But who was Tom Adams? I wanted to know more about my non-Indigenous ancestry. Where did Tom come from? Was the rumour that he was a remittance man[1] and from landed gentry in England true? And if so, how did he become the penniless, illiterate shepherd who married Kudnarto in South Australia? These were the questions I was keen to find answers to, but it has only been in recent years that I have been able to unravel the mystery of my great, great grandfather.

My search began back in 1947 when I was still a teenager and I visited the South Australian archives, which were in a building at the back of the museum. I had an idea that Tom Adams had come out to South Australia on the first boat to the new colony, the *Buffalo*, so I asked to see some passenger lists. I was a young and inexperienced kid and I was rather amazed when the archivist asked me which Tom Adams I was after. In my ignorance I thought there'd only be one Tom Adams listed on the *Buffalo*'s passenger lists, but there were three. I was so young I didn't even know what questions to ask. The librarian told me I'd have to come back with some other sort of reference, perhaps a marriage certificate. So then I was stuck.

---

1 Someone who received funds on a regular basis, often from his wealthy family in the home country.

Where was I going to get that from? And then there was a fire and some of the records were burnt, so my search was stalled for a while.

For years there had been a story in our family that we had British landed gentry in our ancestry, and possibly royalty in our blood. Some believed we were connected to the infamous Roger Tichborne, the bloke who ran away to sea for a new life and identity in the colonies. Maybe the name Tom Adams was an alias and my great, great grandfather was the runaway Roger Tichborne. That would really give our family history an interesting twist!

When I started my research into whether this was more than just a fanciful family tale, I didn't really know who the hell Roger Tichborne was. All I knew was that he was possibly royalty and he got lost at sea. Our family had read the countless stories in the paper about the Tichborne Affair and they had always wondered whether our bloke Tom Adams was really the missing Tichborne. You see, there were these strange coincidences that led us to think that this could be true. My family believed that Tom Adams mysteriously received regular cheques of money from England, and later in his life he owned a race horse that was named Tichborne. And my family always referred to each other as the 'Tichborne breed'.

So it was partly this persistent story that got me thinking when I was about sixteen or seventeen years of age and why I decided to look up Tom Adams and this Roger Tichborne in the archives. My family looked at me as this clever kid because I was going to technical school. So when I started asking them all these questions about Tichborne, they told me that I should be the one to go and do the research. But I was no great researcher.

I remember talking to Judy Inglis in the 1960s about Tom Adams. Judy was an anthropologist who worked with the geographer Fay Gale at the University of Adelaide. Judy ended up writing a piece in a book about me saying I was hoping to find riches by establishing this connection between my white ancestor and this man Tichborne. She did some research herself and came up with the information that Tom Adams had red hair, stood six feet three inches tall, was a gun shearer[2] and employed on a regular basis as a shepherd by the station owner Mr Slater, who owned a property between Adelaide and the Clare district.[3] Judy kept getting stumped by the dates; she couldn't make the connection between Tom Adams and Tichborne, but each time I dug further into our family's stories, I'd find anomalies like the race horse called Tichborne.

As the years passed, the family kept asking me how my research was going. I used to just tell them I didn't know yet, maybe it was the same man and maybe it wasn't. I didn't want to upset their dreams of being related to royalty and claiming our fortune!

But the dates don't fit. As Judy Inglis said straight away: 'If there is any connection between Tichborne and Adams, the dates will show it.' Tom Adams was supposedly born in 1810, and Roger Tichborne was born in 1829. So that seems to rub out the possibility. Furthermore, Kudnarto and Tom Adams were married in 1848, whereas Tichborne's journey from England to South America was five years later in 1853; and he was lost at sea the following year in April 1854.

However, every time I thought I'd discovered there was no connection I felt too reluctant to tell the family. I kept thinking that it was a nice dream and we all need fantasies in life, so what right do I have to come along and rub this one out? My family would keep asking me, 'How are you going with your hunting?' And I'd reply, 'Oh, I'm still lookin' into it.'

2 See Judy Inglis, *Aborigines Now: Perspective in the study of Aboriginal communities*, edited by Marie Reay (1964) Angus and Robertson, p. 121.
3 See booklet on Poonindie mission by Bishop Hale, *The Abs. of Aust: Being on account of the institution for their education at Poonindie in South Australia* (1889), p. 76.

I also couldn't tell my family my search was hopeless because I just kept coming across all these tantalising errors that intrigued me. Every time I stopped searching some little twist made me think perhaps there really was a connection. Like when this bloke told me about the horse named Tichborne. It took me twenty years to track down the official race records of this horse. It was actually bred here in South Australia and, according to the *Australian Stud Book*, it was a bay colt bred by a Mr Blackler. I wondered if my great, great grandfather Tom Adams looked after this horse?

Then I even started to think to myself, even though the dates mightn't be right, Tom Adams might have been a son born earlier to some other aristocratic family – someone they sent out to the colonies to avoid some sort of shame being brought upon the family. Those sorts of things did happen in those days, because Auntie Glad always used to tell me that Tom Adams was a remittance man. So next I tried to find out more about remittance men in the colonies. At one stage I found out that most of the remittance men went to New Zealand and then the family told me that Tom Adams went there once. These blokes who travelled the world developed all these survival skills in those days and, coming from gentry, they owned farms and knew all about the land.[4]

But now, looking at the evidence, I think my half-sister Merle has found the true Tom Adams. Merle has a great interest in researching family history and I must admit that she is very thorough. Through her own research she believes that Tom Adams was in fact a convict. She claims he came to South Australia after being transported as a convict to Hobart Town in Tasmania. His grandparents were Thomas Adams senior and

---

4 If you are interested in reading more about the fascinating Roger Tichborne story, see Appendix 2.

Mary Brotherhood who married at Humberstone in England in 1778. They had a total of seven children: Elizabeth, Thomas, Edward, Anna and James, who were twins, plus Sarah and Hannah. The third-born, Edward, became a shepherd and married Ann Mason at St Margaret's Church, in Leicester in 1808. Together they had three children who they named Mary, Thomas and Charles. The middle one, Thomas, or Tom, was born around 1810 in Leicestershire. He was later transported to Australia for stealing bread. Merle believes it is this Tom Adams who is our great, great grandfather.

Merle has written her own (unpublished) history of our family and is aware of other views on Tom Adams' origins, including researcher Luisa O'Connor's. Merle sums up the conflicting accounts of Tom Adams' arrival in Australia like this:

There are differing views of Thomas Adams' arrival in Australia. According to Luisa O'Connor's biography of Kudnarto she says Thomas Adams travelled to Van Diemen's Land on the 366-ton barque Ann, departing London and arriving Hobarttown 30 September 1833. He listed his trade as 'shepherd'. He left Van Diemen's Land and was one of many landless labourers drifting around Australia seeking work. He travelled to Port Phillip Bay then took the 115-ton schooner Hawk, arriving in Port Adelaide on 1 August 1844.

But, according to Merle's research, Tom Adams arrived in Australia not as a free man but at Her Majesty's pleasure, that is, as a convict:

According to convict records, at the age of 16 years Thomas Adams was 5 foot 3 inches tall (about the average height of English men at the time). He had brown hair, hazel eyes and a small scar over his left brow.

Thomas served his sentence in Hobarton under Lt Governor George Arthur, as Port Arthur wasn't built until 1833 . . .

In 1826 Tom was employed as a gardener's boy when he was arrested for stealing bread. He was tried in Leicester on 7 July 1826 and was sentenced to seven years in Van Diemen's Land. He was transported from London on the convict ship Andromeda, departing on 14 October 1826. The ship arrived in Hobarton [later known as Hobart Town and then Hobart] on 23 February 1827.

Merle actually managed to unearth the convict records of the time and found record number 238 for the convict Tom Adams. They claim Tom committed several offences while serving his convict sentence – in fact the records make chilling reading:

September 15 1827 J Balnian [name of Tom Adam's master] / Absconded from his Master. Sentenced to work 4 months in the gaol; and to be returned to his Masters service (P.A.M.)

January 24 1828 Balnian / Feigning sickness for the purpose of getting removed from his Master. Sentenced to work one month in Ch Gang[5] (P.A.M.)

March 7 1828 Balnian / Absconded from the sentence of Mr Balnian of Launceston on Friday last from ? [unreadable] So until apprehended by Constable Swift in Hobarton yesterday Ch Gang 3 months (P.S.)

May 19 1828 P.B. / Gambling in the P.B. yesterday morning. Sentence in Ch Gang extra 14 days. (P.S.)

April 18 1829 T.G. Gregson / Absconds from his Master. Sentenced 25 lashes. Returned to he Master's service (S.A.L)

December 31 1829 Absent from his Master's house and being found in a Dist. House in Goulbourn Street at 11 o'clock

---

5 *Ch Gang* presumably stands for 'Chain Gang'.

lastnight & falsely represented himself as a free man. Received 25 lashes (C.P.M.)

    August 24 1833 F.S. / Charged Revoked ? [unreadable] with breaking and entering here (Dwelling House no prosecutor appearing he is discharged (A.P.M.)

Merle also traced the circumstances of the convict Tom Adams' eventual journey to South Australia:

> After his Tasmanian ordeal, Thomas Adams travelled on the Tamar from Launceston to Port Phillip in Victoria on 5 November 1843, as a free man. From there he travelled steerage to the colony of South Australia, arriving in Adelaide on the Hawk on 1 August 1844.

So the only thing that Luisa O'Connor and my half-sister agree on is that Thomas Adams arrived in South Australia on the *Hawk* in 1844. They both conflict with my theory that he was a remittance man who possibly arrived in South Australia on the *Buffalo*. My version seems a far cry from his supposed larceny offences and convict beginnings, but if he was a remittance man he must have been fleeing his home country for some reason. I must say though that there is further evidence that's starting to prove Merle correct now. I really can't fault her. I think the fact that convinced me in the end was a Royal Adelaide Hospital register that records Thomas Adams as a patient on several occasions in 1881. Those records say that at the time he was seventy years of age, which would mean he was born around 1810 or 1811. It also states that he 'Came to Van Diemen's Land when very young'. They claimed he was a shepherd, his nationality was English and he was born in Leicestershire. His religion was listed as Church of England. Under the section 'relatives' he states that he had '2 sons half-caste living at Poonindie'.

So it seems my half-sister's account is pretty accurate. Perhaps Thomas Adams did come from Leicestershire, and not France or the Tichborne's Hampshire, but does that mean the myth's completely dissolved? I don't think so, because there is yet another funny twist to this intriguing tale. When I looked up further records another thing I found was that our family could possibly be related to the false claimant Arthur Orton, alias Tom Castro, who tried to claim the Tichborne fortune when Roger was lost at sea! So see what I'm saying? History always seems to have these twists and turns when you look hard enough!

When I was perusing the information my half-sister gave me from the church marriage register for St Margaret's Church in England I found something interesting. I was looking up Tom Adams' father, Edward Adams (our great, great, great grandfather), but also found the records of his older brother, another Thomas Adams. The records state that this Thomas married a Sarah Savage in 1803, but they also showed that a Thomas Adams married a Mary Orton at St Nicholas in 1828. Now whether or not this was a relative of the claimant Arthur Orton, or not, I don't know. One of Arthur Orton's sisters was Mary Ann Orton, and coincidently his mother's name was also Mary Orton. So, if we are descendants of the convict Tom Adams, then we could also be related to this Mary Orton through marriage. You see, Mary Ann Tredgett (nee Orton) and Elizabeth Jury (nee Orton) were the sisters who came forward during the Tichborne trial and testified that Tom Castro was an impostor, and that he was in fact their younger brother Arthur Orton.

So it seems we descendants of Tom Adams *are* connected to the Tichborne case, but probably through the claimant rather than through Roger Tichborne himself. But who knows, maybe we are related to royalty somehow because some of the family still believe that Tom Adams was a remittance man because that money he supposedly received from England had to come from someone.

So who really was Thomas Adams? My half-sister Merle sticks by her theory that Tom Adams was the convict from Leicestershire in England who was transported to Van Dieman's Land for stealing bread. The true origins of my great, great grandfather are still a mystery in my mind. Whether he was a Leicestershire convict transported to Australia, or a remittance man, or even Roger Charles Tichborne is still something that my relatives like to speculate on. Maybe the evidence points most strongly to the conclusion that he *was* a convict. And like so many other Australians, I have no shame about having convict ancestry. After all, Tom only stole a loaf of bread, and he was just a mere fifteen or sixteen years of age. But what I know for sure is that a Tom Adams did marry the remarkable Kaurna woman Kudnarto – and she was my great, great grandmother.

4

Tom and Tim Adams of Poonindie

It might seem surprising, but as far as we know all of the Kaurna people living today are descended from just a handful of Kaurna ancestors. That's a couple of thousand descendants from a very small number of people. That says something, doesn't it, about the poor survival rate of Indigenous people of the Adelaide Plains in those early years, particularly the survival of the men and their descendants. That's because the majority of those Kaurna ancestors were women.[1]

Six of these female Kaurna ancestors include: Kudnarto, who married Thomas Adams and had two boys, Thomas junior and Timothy Adams. Tim Adams was my great grandfather. Then there was Lartelare (or Rebecca) who married George Spender from the Needles, a ration station near the Coorong. Lartelare has many descendants, including the respected Elder Veronica Brodie whose life story is published as *My Side of the Bridge*.

Another Kaurna woman married a man named John Armstrong and they had two girls who also have many descendants. Their mother was from the Clare district but her name isn't known, although we do know that she was a sister to Charlotte Tankaira who married Ityamaiitpinna (King Rodney), the Kaurna man well-known among the colonists.

---

1 According to the anthropologist Neale Draper, some of these Kaurna ancestors included: Kudnarto, Father of Charlotte, Father of King Rodney, Nancy Mitchell, Mother of Alice Miller, Rathoola, Mother of Sarah Taikarabbie, Nellie Raminyemmerin. This work, however, needs further research and clarification. (see Kaurna Native Title Claim)

There was also the Kaurna woman Rathoola from the Fleurieu Peninsula who married George Solomon. Rathoola was the only other Aboriginal woman to be granted a block of land like Kudnarto and she settled at Rapid Bay on the Fleurieu Peninsula, south of Adelaide. She had four children and, like Kudnarto, died young and her children were sent to be raised at Poonindie mission on Eyre Peninsula.

And there was also the Kaurna woman Nellie Raminyemmerin who was abducted and taken to Kangaroo Island by a sealer by the name of John Wilkins. He was a Russian Finn and they have many living descendants. Although Nellie Raminyemmerin and Wilkins had more children than any of the other Kaurna women, Nellie had a very hard time on Kangaroo Island. According to oral tradition, when she died her six children were set adrift in two dinghies. One landed at Port Adelaide and the other at Victor Harbor. The children were all sent to be raised at Point McLeay mission on the Coorong, later known as Raukkan.[2] Wilkins must have had more than one 'wife' because he also had children to another Kaurna woman Lizzie, who they nicknamed 'Bumble Foot' because of her deformed foot.

One of the most well-known Kaurna women of the early days of the colony was Ivaritji, the daughter of Ityamaiitpinna of Aldinga. Ivaritji lived until a ripe old age and was regularly reported on in the papers up until her death in 1929. Maybe this was because she was the last remaining so-called 'full-blood' Kaurna person. Ivaritji, however, had no descendants. In fact a lot of our people didn't have any children. I don't think they wanted to bring children into the world knowing how hard life was for Aboriginal people then. My Uncle Lewis didn't have any children and Uncle Charlie didn't have any children, nor did Uncle Bill or Uncle Arthur – which I think speaks volumes.

---

2 Some of this information about the Kaurna ancestors was provided by Doreen Kartinyeri in the *Tandanya Opening Day Souvenir Program* (October 1989).

We had thousands of Kaurna people living here before Europeans came because this was the most plush real estate in the whole of South Australia. Large groups of people all lived here in their clans. We had the Willunga clan and the Cowandilla clan, the Wirra clan and the Crystal Brook clan, Kudnarto's group. From the tip of the Fleurieu Peninsula all the way up to Crystal Brook there were Kaurna people. Even when the colonists arrived they counted about 750 Aboriginal people here. Yet within the short space of about fifty years the numbers were down to half a dozen or so – a handful.

Some people say that the smallpox plague came down the Murray River and wiped out a lot of our people, the Kaurna people, but I don't believe that. I think that's a furphy because there were 1200 Ngarrindjeri living on the river, so why didn't it drastically affect their numbers? If we were reduced to only 750 Kaurna people, and we're sixty miles from the river, why were there so many Ngarrindjeri left? We didn't even go up to the river because we weren't Murray River people – we didn't live near the river.

Smallpox certainly came to the Kaurna people, I'm not denying that, there were pock marks on our people when Europeans arrived here. What I am arguing is that it didn't come down the river. I'm saying it came here to the Adelaide Plains in 1789 via other Indigenous people who came here overland from the east. These people came here because they wanted to talk about the invasion in New South Wales. As I said before, we Kaurna ran the conferences, and these people came here to tell us about the invasion. They wanted us to address these issues, but unfortunately the smallpox beat us, because they brought the disease with them.

These Indigenous groups came to try and meet again in 1829, and again they brought the smallpox, so it knocked us over once more. So we had two whacks of smallpox, and that's why when the colonists landed here in 1836 there were only 700-odd of us Kaurna left. Then our population dropped to 300 and before long there were only a handful.

Kaurna land was plentiful country and the Kaurna had to work very few hours a day to get their food. They had multiple fish in the sea and plenty of animals on this prime real estate. So they had the leisure time to sit down and have intellectual conversations. You can see that by their word usage in Kaurna. You don't get complex words like *yerrakartarta* from people just sitting down talking about the weather. *Yerrakartarta* means 'at random', and that's quite an intellectual idea.

That's what our people were doing, and that's why other Indigenous people wanted to come and chat to them, because they had the time to talk about complex issues. It's not that we're any cleverer than anyone else, it's got nothing to do with that. It's to do with our situation. How can a person sit down in the desert and think about things when all the time he's worried about food, or where the next waterhole is? The desert people have different knowledge. They have singing and all the information about the land and their Dreamings that are tied up in song. I am amazed at the Pitjantjatjara people – you know they even have expressions for musical concepts such as 'singing in harmony' – *jungula inma inkanyi*[3]. So you can see each group has their own area of expertise. The Pitjantjatjara choirs are well-known for singing in harmony.

So Kudnarto was one of the six Kaurna women who survived smallpox, and the other hardships of the early days of the South Australian colony, to have children – the two boys Tom and Tim Adams. Life must have been hard for her, just as it was for the other women, because poor Kudnarto only survived seven years after her marriage. Her husband, Thomas, found her dead on 11 February 1855 and reported it in a

---

3 This expression literally means *tjungula* 'we are together' + *inma* 'ceremony' + *inkanyi* 'singing a song'.

letter to the Protector of Aborigines straight away. She was just twenty-three years old.

Life on her property at Skillogalee must have been difficult all along, both physically and financially. We know this from the regular correspondence that flowed to the Protector of Aborigines at the time, Matthew Moorhouse. It seems Thomas trusted and confided in Moorhouse. In fact he wrote in 1848, before his marriage to Kudnarto, as best as he could, saying: 'You neat not thing that I shall drink Aney more for I have seen my foley in that And it is All over ... [but] I thing pepel shuns me.'[4] Moorhouse at least thought Thomas Adams was worthy, because he gave away Kudnarto at their wedding and approved of granting her land.

However, in September 1848, within a year of settling on the land, Thomas Adams was writing again to Moorhouse requesting a government loan: 'I should teake it A great faver But however if I get No Assistance I Must leve the Section for I Must go where The work is.' And, as I've said before, it seems Thomas did head off to find itinerant work because records show he was employed as a shepherd on the property south of Clare owned by Mr Slater. But the couple's financial struggle continued, and so too did the trouble caused by the constant visits of the bullockies. In October 1849 Thomas felt compelled to engage a scribe to write another letter to Moorhouse on his behalf complaining: '... they are becoming to me and my property a great inconvenience ...' He wondered if he could 'derive some little advantage', by which he meant compensation.[5]

---

4 All letters written by Thomas Adams senior are quoted as they appear in the original form.

5 Much of this detail is held in the State Archives of South Australia GRG24/4. It is also summarised in Meredith Edwards, *Tracing Kaurna Descendants: the saga of a family dispossessed. The family of Thomas Adams and Kudnarto* (c. 1985), self-published booklet.

Adams wrote again on 17 January 1851, suggesting that he might rent out some of the land to help alleviate the financial difficulties he and his young wife were facing. Both Tom and Kudnarto had had to travel to Adelaide for the trial of James Yates the year before and were not compensated, and the bullock drivers continued to use their water and cross their property with no recompense. So by the time their second son, Tim, arrived on 11 October 1852, life was rough. I suppose there was no food and they couldn't just kill their sheep because the livestock was their future livelihood and income. Tom probably returned to his old employer, a Mr Ferguson, for paid work on his station near Crystal Brook. On his marriage certificate Tom had listed his occupation as 'carpenter', but whether he could get this kind of work I don't know, because all his later records listed his job as a 'shepherd'. We do know that he could shear sheep because his sons, especially Tom junior, proved to be top shearers in future years, and Tom had spent some time away with his father working on different properties. Thomas Adams would have taught both of his sons to shear.

At the tender young ages of six and three the two Adams boys found themselves motherless. Grieving for his lost wife, Thomas Adams had no choice but to take his boys with him to the other property where he was working just south of Clare, owned by his other old employer Mr Slater. However, it must have been too difficult for Tom to work and look after two small boys, because three months later in May 1855 they travelled to Port Adelaide and from there took a ship to Port Lincoln on the southern tip of Eyre Peninsula. The boys were destined for Poonindie mission, just north of Port Lincoln – the only mission functioning for Aboriginal people in the state at the time.

Poonindie was started in 1850 by Archdeacon Mathew Hale, of the Church of England. His intention was to convert and 'civilise' his young charges away from the so-called corrupting influences of the city of Adelaide and their own families. He took quite a number of Kaurna kids over to the Eyre Peninsula when he established his training institution. Hale knew that the children were not doing too well in Adelaide because the Kaurna were dying off, and their parents weren't too keen on sending them to school. So Hale thought he'd make an effort to get them educated. He knew they could be educated because the German missionaries running the Native Location school, Christian Teichelmann and Clamor Shürmann, proved that. The missionaries knew Kaurna kids were no different to any other kids, despite all the rubbishing they got about trying to educate them.

Anyway, Hale took the children all the way over to Poonindie, on the south-eastern side of Eyre Peninsula. Actually he whizzed the kids off, so I guess you could say they were the first stolen generation in South Australia. They were taken from their parents, and probably without permission. But it might have been a good thing; if he hadn't there might not be any Kaurna people left. Unless, of course, he had made an effort to keep the children safe here in Adelaide with their families. In my opinion the Kaurna probably wouldn't have had a place to go if Hale hadn't started Poonindie.

Now, when Hale started taking the Kaurna children from the Adelaide School, some of them ran away because they were worried they would be sent to Poonindie. So Hale only took about twenty children, and when they got to Poonindie many of them died from influenza and other diseases, so there was more heartbreak.

Hale took over reserve land there on Eyre Peninsula and got grants from the government to run the mission. They built a church and called it the Church with Two Chimneys. If you look from the east to the west you see that the two chimneys look just like two ears. The same as looking at Mount Lofty and Mount Bonython, and seeing the two peaks, or the two ears (called *Yurridla* in Kaurna) of the red kangaroo of the Adelaide Plains; *Tarnda* is the word for the male red kangaroo in Kaurna.[6] This feature of the church helped the Adelaide children who were taken to Poonindie to feel at home.

The inside design of the church is also interesting. There were two floors and they used to have the dormitories upstairs, which is unusual. That church is still standing and probably still owned by the Anglican Church. I went back there in 2000 and took some photos, but you're not allowed upstairs to look because it's not safe. The woman who lives next door is the caretaker. She has the key and is happy to unlock the door so you can have a look inside. It's a lovely little church called St Matthew's, about twelve kilometres or so from Port Lincoln. They still have services there. Fortunately the church survived the fires in January 2005.

Mathew Hale originally wanted to locate the mission on Boston Island, just off the coast of Port Lincoln, so it would be isolated from the bad influences of colonial life in the 1850s, but they had trouble finding enough fresh water on the island. So they chose the land at Poonindie that was reserved for Aboriginal people. Some land was purchased by the Church of England under the name of the Society for the Propagation of the Gospel. Hale also bought £1200 worth of land with his own funds in order to isolate his mission as much as possible. You see, Port Lincoln has quite a violent history of race relations because the sealers and whalers used to abduct Aboriginal women from those coastal areas. The local Pangkala and Nauo Aboriginal groups were very wary of white settlers when they first arrived. Some of the settlers were ex-convicts

---

6 *Tarnda* is also the root of the words *Tandanya* (the Aboriginal gallery in Grenfell Street) and *Tarndanyangga* (the Kaurna name for Victoria Square in the heart of Adelaide). *Yurridla* is the origin of the name of the Adelaide Hills town Uraidla.

with tickets-of-leave and there were violent clashes between them and the local Aboriginal people.[7]

The German missionary Clamor Schürmann actually moved from Adelaide to Port Lincoln and established another school for Aboriginal children in 1850. He also learnt the local Pangkala language and became involved as an interpreter in many of the violent disputes and court cases that arose between local Aboriginal people and the new white settlers. There was much distrust, often stemming from sheep stealing or issues relating to the desecration of Aboriginal land.

By the time Tom Adams arrived at Poonindie with his two small boys in 1855 the Native Training Institution was well established and comprised a farm of considerable size. The area of land under lease or owned by the institution totalled approximately 6000 acres[8] and from the very beginning the local farmers were envious of the size and success of the farming ventures undertaken at Poonindie. By then Clamor Schürmann's school had been closed and his students sent to Poonindie to join the Adelaide Aboriginal recruits. Poonindie had also become a ration depot for local Aboriginal people who were encouraged to stay and work on the mission.

Hale reflected later on the arrival of Tom and Tim Adams at Poonindie:

> In the month of May, in the year 1855, the man Adams made his appearance at Poonindie, bringing two little half-caste boys. He had come from Mr Slater's property ... for the purpose of asking me to take charge of his little boys.

Tom Adams was keen to stay with his children and asked Archdeacon Hale if he could remain on the mission farm and

---

7 For more detail, see Brock & Kartinyeri, *Poonindie: the rise and destruction of an Aboriginal agricultural community* (1989), pp. 6–9.

8 See Meredith Edwards (c. 1985) p. 14.

work as a shepherd, but there must have been too many others seeking work, because Adams wrote to Moorhouse that same month, on 15 May 1855, saying, 'Mr hales had Nothing for Me To Do.' So Tom Adams had to say goodbye to his two boys and head back to the district of his Skillogalee property near Watervale where he found work as a shepherd on one of the many properties owned by the Scotsman Captain Hughes, a former sea captain.[9]

The letter Thomas Adams wrote in May to Moorhouse, the long-standing Protector of Aborigines, also confessed that he had actually been sub-letting the Skillogalee land for six months (against the terms of their occupation) and there was now eight pounds owing in rent. He asked that the money be sent for the benefit of his two boys at Poonindie mission:

> ... I have seen The man That is on The section And he ows Me eight pounds of The Larst six Months Rent And I have Tould him To forward it To you And you can send it To Mr hales At port Lincoln I shall go To port Lincoln And see The children when I can Turn Myself I ham Now with capt Huges Near watervel Mr hales Tels Me That he will chresen And Babitise The children And send To Adelaide And I hope The section will be give To Them sir ...
>
> I Reman yours Most humble servent
> Thos Adams

Moorhouse recommended to the Acting Colonial Secretary, O.K. Richardson, in a letter dated 26 May 1855, that the rent money be put into treasury but, more importantly, he stated that the two Adams boys had rights to Section 346 when they turn of age: '... the Land should be given over to the children, when they arrive at full age'. On 9 June he confirmed this fact

---

9 Quotes and information from Meredith Edwards (c. 1985), p. 10.

in a letter he wrote to Wm Norrell & Sons of Auburn, who were interested in leasing the Section: '. . . when the children reach 21 years of age they will then have a licence to occupy it'.

Richardson responded to Moorhouse on 7 June 1855, stating: 'I have the honour to instruct you to inform Adams that the Section is now resumed by the Government, it not being considered that he has any claim to it; and that the Government will lease it'. Of the children he said: 'When they are of age a licence to occupy the Section will be issued to them similar to that formerly made out in favour of their mother'.[10]

With this important acknowledgement of their rights to the land, a vigorous and long-running campaign of letter writing began between the Adams family and the government authorities over the boys' right to reclaim Section 346 of Skillogalee Creek once they turned twenty-one years of age. Tom senior was not happy that the rental proceeds from Section 346 were not going to his sons in the meantime. He soon replied from Yorke Peninsula, where he was working as a shearer: 'Sir, I object To The government taking posshion of Section 346 on Skilgee Creek'[11].

Tom senior was aware of the corruption over land dealings in that era and didn't trust the government, so he wrote again, this time with the help of an educated scribe: 'I am informed the Section has been in occupation of a tenant who pays no rent whatever for it. I mention this to your Excellency to know if some benefit ought not to accrue to the children from it. For myself, individually, I neither ask nor wish for anything'.

The plea fell on deaf ears, and the Section was subsequently

---

10 All letters written to the government, whether they be to the Crown Lands Office, The Protector of Aborigines, or the Crown Secretary, are held among the Government Records in the State Archives in Adelaide. Most are held in the file GRG 52/1, but some are in GRG 24/4.

11 This is Tom Adams' misspelling of 'possession' and 'Skillogalee'.

leased out for a period of fourteen years for the sum of £30 per annum. The money went straight into treasury. Any further pleas from Adams were ignored, largely because his ally, Mathew Moorhouse, resigned from his position as Protector of Aborigines in 1856. The responsibility of Aboriginal reserve land was handed over to the Commissioner of Crown Lands, F.S. Dutton, whose self-interest as a large landholder himself must have conflicted with the needs and desires of Aboriginal people.

In the meantime, Tom Adams senior had other concerns. He eventually found work at Green Patch in the Port Lincoln district, where he would have been closer to his two boys and able to visit them at Poonindie on a regular basis. Archdeacon Hale had been appointed Bishop of Perth in 1856 and left Poonindie in the charge of Superintendent Hammond. After the departure of Hale, Tom Adams senior was not happy with the progress his two small boys were making. He again sought employment at Poonindie, so he could be near Tom and Tim, but was refused. Eventually he complained in another scribed letter to the governor, dated December 1858:

> I placed them in the Training Institution at Poonindie then under the charge of Archdeacon Hale, in order that they might have an opportunity of obtaining a little learning but I now find that although they have been there upwards of three years, they might just [as] well have been in the bush all the time for the knowledge they have gained during that time.
>
> During a stay in Port Lincoln district of about sixteen months I have been several times to see them, and on each occasion found

---

12 Letters sent to non-government departments, such as Poonindie mission, are held in the Somerville Collection in the State Library of South Australia. Some copies of government letters are also held in this collection. For this letter, see volume 2, p. 171. 1380.

them as regards cleanliness and clothing worse than the Native children roaming about the bush – finding this the case, and that they have no protector but myself I have taken them away . . .[12]

It seems Adams was so dissatisfied he did actually take his oldest boy Tom out of the care of the mission for a period. A copy of his letter of complaint was eventually forwarded to Hammond himself, who responded by saying that the younger boy Tim was 'studious and well-behaved', but had other things to say about Tom:

Now the truth is that the elder boy has always manifested great carelessness in his habits . . . and the frequent destruction of clothes given to him rendered it necessary to confine him to such as were durable and inexpensive . . . [and of his reading and writing] a large proportion of English children in a similar condition of life would be only too glad to be able to accomplish . . . [his handwriting would improve if] he ever have the desire to do so.

That desire did eventually come, because Tom junior was to become an active letter-writer, particularly regarding his claim to Section 346 of Skillogalee. Tim also became a frequent correspondent, addressing various issues of injustice that he struck during his thirty-odd years living at Poonindie mission.

The boys must have kept in contact with their father because both parties kept writing letters to try and get their Skillogalee property back. It seems like they wrote a hundred letters between them to get some sort of agreement. They had always understood that when Tom and Tim reached a mature age – twenty-one years in those days – they could claim their property back. So both Tom senior and junior wrote letters constantly. In February 1867, twelve years after they lost the block, they received a reply from the Acting Protector of Aborigines, L.B. Scott:

I beg to acknowledge receipt of your letter ... and have the honor to inform you that section 346 of Skillagolee Creek is leased to Mr WG Long, with rent paid up until the 31st December 1867 consequently I cannot entertain your application but at the same time that will not prevent your son from making a fresh application for any unselected Section.

So really what they were suggesting is that Tom junior should apply for some other unregistered land. They had had an understanding, but the arrangement was not built into the leasing agreement of the land. In 1867 Tom junior was nineteen, so he was writing in advance of his coming-of-age because he probably knew how slowly governments work. He was told that they can't get the property because it's leased for another year. The boys were still writing when they were well into their twenties, and they were getting pretty experienced at it by then, but they kept getting fobbed off with comments like 'we're looking into it' from the government. In the meantime the government was changing the Lands Bill. So the Adams' claim was running for an awfully long time.

Over this long period both Tom and Tim grew up to become fine strong men, with reputations in the Port Lincoln district that were surpassed by none. They were excellent farm workers who could plough fields as well as any skilled white farmer, and they were much in demand in the district for their gun-shearing. When Hale made a return visit to the mission in 1872, he was very pleased to hear such positive comments from the local farmers about his former charges. One local landowner 'referred particularly to one of them, Tom Adams, and he said that there was not a man in the district that he liked better to see in his woolshed than Tom Adams (Jnr)'.

The Adams brothers weren't only fine workers, they were also very skilled sportsmen – a trait that they have passed on to many of their descendants, including my boys. I wasn't a bad sportsman myself, but Tom and Tim were fine footballers and regularly played in the Poonindie team that often defeated the local Port Lincoln football team. They were also admired for their cricketing prowess, and were both members of the Poonindie cricket team that played several matches against St Peter's College from Adelaide. The Poonindie team had special uniforms made of white trousers, blue flannel shirts and red elastic belts. They lost the first match, which was held in Adelaide, but won the second which was held at Poonindie. Tom Adams captained the team on at least one occasion, and Tom and Tim both played in the many cricket matches where they often defeated the local Port Lincoln cricket team. Throughout the 1870s and 1880s there were many opportunities for the Poonindie residents to compete in various competitions in the district, and they regularly came out winners, whether it was in shearing, ploughing or athletics. Tom in particular had a reputation for being a very fast runner.[13]

Both Tom and Tim Adams lived at Poonindie until the late 1880s, and it was there that they met their wives and married. Tom married Louisa Milera (nee Roberts) who was a so-called 'part Aboriginal' born at Port Philip in Victoria. Louisa, known as Louie, was a widow when she married Tom and already had two children to her late husband Frederick Milera. Aboriginal people who settled at Poonindie weren't all necessarily from South Australia. Tom and Louie had nine children together, the first seven born at Poonindie. They were William, Maria, Charles, Tommy, Ethela, May, Herbert, Maud and Sydney. With such a large family accommodation was very tight for them in their two bedroom cottage at Poonindie, so in 1878 Tom built on an extra bedroom. He was a skilled

---

13 See Brock & Kartinyeri (1989), p. 46.
14 See Brock & Kartinyeri (1989), p. 61.

53

handyman and did all the building himself, including thatching the roof.[14]

Tim Adams was my great grandfather, the younger son of Kudnarto and Tom. Tim was very unfortunate in marriage because he lost three of his four wives to illness. He only ever had children from his second marriage to Bessie Reeves. Little is known of his first wife, but it is believed she was Fanny from Franklin Harbour, near Port Lincoln. His second wife, Bessie Reeves, was said to be from Kingston, but according to my Auntie Glad she was a sister of Ivaritji, which means she was Kaurna. Together Tim and Bessie had four children – Lewis, Gertrude, Julia and Arthur (nicknamed 'Bishop'). Unfortunately Bessie died in 1878 during the measles epidemic that hit so many Aboriginal people, leaving Tim with a family of four young children to raise by himself. Two years later in 1880 he married Bessie's sister Esther Reeves, who became a much-needed mother to his young children. In Aboriginal society children consider their mother's sisters to be their mother anyway. Much later, in 1907, after Tim had left Poonindie and his third wife, Esther, had passed away in 1901, Tim married Lizzie Sansbury at Point Pearce. Tim died the following year at the age of fifty-six.[15]

The third-born child of Tim and Bessie was Julia, and she was my grandmother. She had to walk with a crutch. She eventually married Henry Simpson and had three daughters. Gladys Simpson was her second-born daughter and she was my mother.

I was saying earlier that both Tom and Tim Adams became keen letter writers to the various government authorities. One of the many letters Tim Adams, my great grandfather, wrote was one saying how his daughter Julia was a cripple and that she couldn't do the heavy work that was required of her by

---

15 See Brock & Kartinyeri (1989), p. 62.

the superintendent of Poonindie mission. You have to read between the lines a bit on what's really going on in some of these official letters. The superintendent at the time had written a letter complaining about how my grandmother Julia was lazy and all the rest of it. What intrigued me though was that Maria Adams, Tom junior's second daughter, was also described as 'troublesome' by the superintendent. That seems a bit much to me! These two girls are both the daughters of the Adams men and both get unfairly criticised by the super-intendent.

Things were pretty rough for people on the missions in those early days. I've read letters written by men who wanted to go off and work to make some money for their family, but the superintendent from Point Pearce said that if they went he wouldn't feed their families. So these blokes had to stay on the reserve so their families would get fed, knowing that they could be making good money by shearing or doing other farm work in the district. They really had no chance to get ahead or improve their position. The superintendent arranged things so that the families were going to be in poverty forever.

Actually there's still game-playing all over the country on this issue, which is not surprising. There is no incentive for people living on the dole these days to go out and find casual work, because if they do it affects their dole money. It takes weeks to get back on the dole if their casual work dries up sud-denly, and in the meantime they're left with no income. It's a sad little game governments can play with human lives, and we're slow to learn, aren't we?

The same sort of game was played on me years later when I became a ward of the state and was living under the authority of the welfare department. I wrote a letter to the government once, when I was still a teenager doing my fitting and machining apprenticeship, and said that I wanted to stay in the care of the department a year longer, so I could finish my apprenticeship. They just told me I had to stop what I was doing and go out and get paid work, but if I did that I couldn't keep up my apprenticeship, and because I was young, I would have had trouble picking up a better-paid job. I didn't want to be a labourer all my life, whereas if I could finish my apprenticeship I would have been better off in the long run. It's a similar issue, isn't it? They're making decisions for people when they're not in a position to judge.

But getting back to Poonindie in the 1880s, these people were cut off from the rest of the world, yet they were supposed to assimilate, and what's more they were put in these vulnerable positions as far as getting fed went. When my grandmother Julia and her cousin Maria were complaining, they were saying the government was responsible for these conditions because they were not paying the appropriate rates. Each family had to be fed on eight shillings a week, which wasn't much, and because some families were bigger than others they found it even more difficult to survive. They didn't even count the children in each family, it was just a standard amount given to each family – eight bob. If one family had five children and another had ten then, as you probably realise, the one with five was better off.

Like many missions in those days, Poonindie had trouble getting suitable staff and overseers. Poonindie was also under particular pressure in the 1880s from the surrounding farmers to hand over the lease of some of their fertile farming land. The white farmers could see how successful they were at Poonindie in farming the land, so they wanted some of that land for themselves. What they didn't realise was that it wasn't all good land. You see, those Aboriginal men working the land were very skilled ploughmen and they knew how to predict the weather. That's why they were so successful. They would plough the paddocks and sow the seed, and then the rain would always come. They knew how to read the signs in the clouds and the stars and moon – they could look at the colouring of the clouds across the moon. When I heard about how they read the weather, I thought, well, I'll be blowed. Obviously, the people who have lived on the land and studied it for centuries knew a lot more than newcomers to this country. The white farmers came from England and Europe, and the conditions here weren't the same as there, so they were confused. The land on Eyre Peninsula was really very poor country, so you had to help it along, and our people knew how to do that.

Before Poonindie was eventually closed down there was one superintendent, J.D. Bruce, who the people particularly disliked. He started as the farm overseer in 1878 and took over as superintendent in 1882, and this is when he really started throwing his weight around. Prior to his arrival Tom Adams was regarded as the most trustworthy and dependable worker on the mission. He was hardworking and very capable, even taking church services when the previous superintendent was absent. But Superintendent Bruce took a specific disliking to both Tom and Tim Adams, probably because they showed too much initiative and challenged his authority. He accused Tim of stirring up any trouble that arose on the place. By 1887 the men at Poonindie had had enough of Bruce's heavy-handedness, so they sent a petition to the Protector of Aborigines:

> Our grievance is that Mr Bruce is to us like a tyrant master. We the undersigned do make it our business to tell you how Mr Bruce is treating us here he just does as he likes with us and when we tell the trustees about our grievances on Poonindie they don't take any notice of us . . .[16]

---

16 See quote in Brock & Kartinyeri (1989), pp. 55–56.

The government authorities just sent the complaint back to Bruce, and he didn't take any action except to accuse Tim of being the instigator of the petition. However, by this stage, in 1884, Tim had had enough of Bruce and the way he ran the mission and had left the place. In a report to the trustees, Bruce wrote that year: 'I do not want him [Tim Adams] back again, I would like to get his brother Tom to join him there it would be a good thing for Poonindie if he was gone'.[17]

Tom did in fact follow his brother, but not until three years of further unrest at Poonindie, during which time he took to the drink, which just brought domestic problems between him and his wife and children. Tom and Louie eventually moved to Point Pearce mission on Yorke Peninsula in 1887, and there they had their final two children, Maude in 1989 and Sydney in 1892.

When Tim left Poonindie he moved around from job to job, mainly in the northern Yorke Peninsula district, presumably with his wife, Esther. He left his kids in the care of the mission, as the younger ones were still at school, but the couple came back regularly to visit them. It was during this unsettled period of Tim's life that the correspondence flowed about his daughter Julia and the work she was being made to do by the superintendent.

The government eventually closed Poonindie down in 1894 because the Aboriginal farmers were too good. They made the land look richer than it really was. A lot of them were good farmers – I can see that by the old records. They did their job too well, and people started asking, what right do they have giving these people higher stations in life? But the local farmers didn't realise that our people had high expectations and high principles from the start. The culture was like that – it was about excellence. It's just that they didn't show it openly.

---

17 Quoted in Brock & Kartinyeri (1989), p. 55.

The Poonindie people's high standards showed up in the end in modern ways, for example if you put your quality wool in a local competition, it's going to win the prize. It was the same with the ploughing and shearing competitions, but they weren't doing it for the prize, they were doing it with the knowledge that they had learnt to do things well over the centuries. Another example is the way the Poonindie people watched the weather, and how they learnt when to put the crops in at the right times because they knew when it was going to rain.

The Nauo people of Eyre Peninsula seemed to know all about the stars – they must have been stargazers and read the weather by the moon and the stars. As I said before, they told the weather by watching the colouring of the clouds as they passed across the face of the moon and the stars. So all the different people who settled at Poonindie mission used their knowledge when they were farming the land, including the Nauo, Barngala and the Kaurna. At Point Pearce mission, the Narungga did it by looking at the plants and insects. So it's very interesting how each group had their own methods.

They used to get such good crops at Poonindie that the farmers in the district concluded that Poonindie must be the best land, so they convinced the church and the government to split it up and lease it to them. This didn't please the Poonindie people, because they considered Poonindie their home. If the land was going to be split up they felt they had some claim to it.

By the time both Tom and Tim Adams moved to Point Pearce they had almost given up on their claim for Section 346 at Skillogalee Creek, but they had not given up on their claim for land, because they made regular claims for sections in the Poonindie area. Records show that over a period of forty years Tom Adams junior continued to apply for his own block of land to farm. In the 1860s he continued the campaign his father was waging with the government for the land at

Skillogalee Creek but after several knock-backs, he changed his tactics and started to apply for some of the land at Poonindie. These applications were made from Point Pearce, but because he had left Poonindie on bad terms with Superintendent Bruce, his requests again fell on deaf ears. In 1888 he wrote:

> I am waiting for your reply about lease of land. There are only 80 acres in the section, but I prefer it to 160 acres anywhere else. I believe Mr Bruce has been trying to prevent me from having land, he makes out it is too close to Poonindie and has been talking to Mr Blackmore ... Thomas Playford offered me land by the harbour, but I didn't take it, I wanted it nearer my neighbourhood.[18]

Tom Adams was eventually granted land in the Poonindie district, but not until 1907 when he was fifty-eight years old. By that stage his family was well settled at Point Pearce and his wife was reluctant to leave. They never returned to Poonindie.

The Adams letter-writing tradition carried on through my grandmother, Julia Simpson. Records show that she made regular requests for land in the vicinity of Point Pearce, her new home. So my ancestors have always sought out land and really tried to get into the system, but everything went against them. When I look at all this now I think, how many times do you have to own the land to be the owner? We were the original owners, then we got a piece back (Section 346), then that was taken away from us. We tried to get it back according to an agreement which was then reneged upon by the government, so it's a very disheartening history.

The same thing happened with the land at Poonindie. This whole business of losing land seems to be a common thread throughout my whole family history. To me, Poonindie is a

18 Quoted in Brock & Kartinyeri (1989), p. 61.

terribly sad story. As I've said, originally Poonindie was leased from the government by the church but Archdeacon Hale also bought a lot of land with his own money and when he left in 1855 he told the Aboriginal people that the land belonged to them. They rightfully should have been the owners of that land, but when some of the farmers and others in the area kicked up about Poonindie being better land producing all the good crops, the government was eventually forced to split the whole property up.

The only successful Aboriginal person to lease any land at Poonindie, on Eyre Peninsula, was Emanuel Solomon, the second son of George Solomon and his Kaurna wife, Rathoola. Like Tom and Tim Adams, the elder Solomon brother, John, had a falling out with Superintendent Bruce, so he was also unsuccessful in claiming any of the Poonindie land. However, Emanuel leased Section 122 in the Hundred of Louth and farmed it until he died at the age of sixty-six in 1922. His brother John inherited the land and stayed on in the district until his death in 1946. John was caretaker of the Poonindie church for many years.[19]

One of the major recipients of the Poonindie land was Superintendent Bruce himself – so you can see why he was so keen to close the mission down. Just as you'd expect, when the local white farmers did get hold of the subdivided Poonindie land they didn't do as well on it as the previous occupants. Then they started saying that the reason the Poonindie mission had been so successful was because of the large size of the place, but the real reason was that the Aboriginal people could read the weather and good farming relies heavily on knowing when to sow crops.

After more than forty years of successful farming on Poonindie mission they closed the place down in 1894. So it

19 Brock & Kartinyeri (1989), pp. 62–64.

didn't last too long, did it? They shipped the Aboriginal residents to Point Pearce on Yorke Peninsula, or to Point McLeay on Lake Alexandrina. I reckon they didn't have the right to do that because the church left the land to Aboriginal people. That's what you find in the law of this country – one law for blacks, another for whites. A similar thing happened at Point Pearce a number of years later, the government wanted to close the reserve down and give it to so-called 'poor whites', but our people protested, saying, this property is only the size of a threepence, why worry about this one little piece of land when there's plenty of other government land?

Back then the same kind of thing happened all over Australia. Aboriginal people would clear the land and get it functioning, then the government would take it off them and give it to white people. I think it's a funny history in this country, we do the hard work, and then the government breaks our hearts. I've read stories about the same thing happening all across the country – Aboriginal people clearing the land, getting farms working and then being kicked off.

So Thomas Adams senior never did get to own his own land and settle down in one spot, even though he was a skilled sheep farmer and gun-shearer. He never remarried after Kudnarto died either, but kept shepherding and trying to eke out a living, always staying near his kids, trying to find work in the area. He wanted to be with his sons wherever they were, but was never able to live on Poonindie mission because he was white.

Thomas Adams senior had a few bouts in hospital in his later years, according to the Royal Adelaide Hospital register. He had dyspepsia in 1864 but really hit rock bottom in 1879 when he had to choose between being admitted to the Destitute Asylum in Adelaide or going to be with his sons at Poonindie. He chose to go to Poonindie but his sons were already struggling at the time to keep their own large families.

So Thomas was admitted to the Destitute Asylum in Kintore Avenue in the city in 1881. He was later admitted to the Royal Adelaide Hospital where he died in February 1882, aged seventy-four. It's interesting that he ended up at the asylum on Kintore Avenue because that is where the Adelaide School was located when Kudnarto went there thirty-five years earlier.

So it was an odd sort of an existence for Thomas Adams after Kudnarto died. I think he was always on the outer of both black and white societies. He must have been very disillusioned as his kids Tom and Tim grew up, especially because he was never able to provide for them adequately. It must have been really frustrating for him to lose Section 346 and to be continually refused work at Poonindie. So who knows, he might have gone back to his old ways of drinking, but he still worked. Some blokes are like that – they drink but they still work.

None of the family were successful in reclaiming Kudnarto's block, Section 346 of Skillogalee Creek. It was eventually split into four blocks by the government. I visited there again recently with Michael Diorio, when he worked at Tandanya, and saw there are two houses now, one with a vineyard – that would suit me! I'm glad I made that trip – it's nice to stroll down memory lane, but it's sad to know that a land claim that spanned three generations of my family was never successful.

5

The Adams family of Point Pearce mission

Point Pearce was established in 1868, and the community still exists today. It is located south-west of the town of Maitland, near the coast just north of Port Victoria on Yorke Peninsula. The two Adams boys had big families and became important members of the community there, but they never gave up trying to claim their own patch of farming land elsewhere.

Point Pearce mission has an interesting history, just like Poonindie. The community is at the top of a smaller peninsula that ends in a point on the western side of Yorke Peninsula. The small peninsula has beds of rocks running along its coastline and juts out from the mainland. Across from the peninsula – or this 'point' – is Wardang Island, where my grandmother Julia lived for a time. It's a fairly large island, about three kilometres across.

Point Pearce mission started as a farm a square mile large (which I always thought was a coincidence, because the city of Adelaide also covers a square mile) and then it quickly grew in size. It went from 640 acres to 12,000 acres, and I think it finished up being 20,000 acres. That includes the island and mainland properties. A lot of that land was leased out later to BHP[1], who used to use the sand off the island in steel production. That's the work that Julia's husband, Henry Simpson, was doing before they closed down the quarry in 1905.

BHP leased much of the land for twenty years for farming,

---

1 BHP is the company: Broken Hill Associated Propriety Limited

which I find odd – that a steel-making company wanted it for farming – but maybe they held onto it for its sand or anything else it had to mine. So a lot of the Point Pearce land was leased out. I find it intriguing that the mission lands were so large, especially seeing as there was water on it. The trust picked one of the prime places for the mission.

The way the Point Pearce mission came about went something like this. The people of Wallaroo said they'd form a trust for Aboriginal people so they could have some place of their own. I think they wanted to compensate Aboriginal people for occupying their traditional land. That was progressive thinking, but I think I know why they really did it. They knew that the Aboriginal man Tom Edwards had found copper at Moonta and Wallaroo. They knew that if it wasn't for the Aboriginal people they wouldn't have known where the copper ore was in those days. They probably would have found it later, but not as early as 1862. The year before, copper had been discovered near Kadina, so Kadina and Moonta mines became the two most important mines in South Australia after 1870.[2] That discovery really helped the economy; the government was broke, and the mines gave people a lot of wealth. The towns of Moonta, Kadina and Wallaroo prospered, while the local Narungga people became beggars.

There's probably another couple of reasons the locals helped establish Point Pearce. They wanted Aboriginal people settled on a place of their own, but out of their way. In 1866 a concerned white woman, Mary Meredith, wrote a letter to the local *Wallaroo Times*:

It is difficult to understand how anyone who has had opportunities of observing the social and moral degradation of the native

---

2 Deptartment of Environment and Planning, *South Australia's Heritage* (1986), p. 64.

inhabitants of this country can really believe that he is not failing in a positive duty when, while enriching himself with the produce of the land, or with its mineral wealth, he leaves the original possessors untaught and uncared for.[3]

So, for whatever reasons, the people of Wallaroo formed a trust and set about trying to lease some land from the government. Captain H.R. Hancock of Moonta Copper Mines was the president of the committee that looked into the leasing of 600 acres on the peninsula at *Bookooyanna*, as it was known by the local Narungga people. I think they must have asked the people which land they wanted, because they chose land associated with the important Dreaming hero *Buthera*. Then the Wallaroo people wrote to the surveyor general about leasing the land. But a man named Samuel Rogers already had the land in this area under lease, and he didn't like the idea and objected. They eventually came to some arrangement, and in 1868 Yorke's Peninsula Aboriginal Mission was established at Point Pearce, thirty-five miles south of Wallaroo.[4]

The Aboriginal people always thought the land was being held in trust for them, but it wasn't really. It was only leased land acquired through the trust. Yet the people always thought they owned it. Well, it was rightfully theirs because they owned the land in the beginning before white settlers arrived, but according to white law, they were only leasing the land for a ninety-nine-year period. They eventually got their land back under the *Lands Trust Act* in 1966 during the era when Don Dunstan was premier of South Australia, which was fair.

The first superintendent of Point Pearce was Reverend Julius Wilhelm Kuhn, who was a Moravian missionary. Eventually he got appointed to be manager of the reserve. Since then

3 Quoted in Mattingley and Hampton (eds), *Survival In Our Own Land* (1988), Wakefield Press, Adelaide, p. 195.
4 Mattingley and Hampton (1988), pp. 195–197.

there's been a long line of superintendents. In 1915 Point Pearce became a government reserve after the Royal Commission that looked into the plight of Aboriginal people in this state in 1913.

The country around Point Pearce is fairly flat – there are no hills, just undulating country that slopes downhill to the coast. The village or township itself is actually built on a saltpan and the point has sandy soil. And there are sand dunes on the coastline. Up from the village though, there's land not bad for farming – they grow good crops there. I'm not sure what percentage of the land is good for farming, but you lose a lot of farming land to sand hills and saltpans. There was scrub at one time but they cut most of it for wood. We had wood stoves back then and burnt a lot of wood. That's why we had to go for miles to get fuel in the end, but in the early days there was the Wadjidin scrub where all the old people lived before and even after the mission was started.

The old people wouldn't live in the houses. I remember Uncle Dasher saying they used to take the meals down to the old people living in their wurlies. They used to be speaking the language, Narungga, but they'd tell the younger ones to speak English. That was before my time there, but I do remember some old bloke getting wild at me when I was trying to learn Narungga, and telling me to go away and learn English. When I found out that they used to say the same thing to Uncle Dasher I didn't feel so bad. See, I thought they were just picking on me because I was fair, but they picked on him too and he was quite dark. I think it was empowering for them to tell us young ones what and what not to do. But they also weren't allowed to teach us young ones Narungga – it was a government ruling and the superintendent enforced it.

As I mentioned before, my grandmother Julia was the daughter of Kudnarto's youngest son, Tim Adams. Even though Tim married four times, he only ever had children from his second marriage to Bessie Reeves. The third child born to Tim and Bessie was my grandmother, Julia Adams. She was born at Poonindie mission in 1876, but was later given a hard time there by Superintendent Bruce, particularly after her parents left her there, along with her three siblings, in 1884. When she was twelve or thirteen she was sent away from Poonindie by Bruce, allegedly for not working hard enough. Her father promptly complained about it in a letter to higher authorities, dated July 1889:

I have written a few lines to you to let you know about my daughter being sent away from Poonindie school by Mr Bruce she is a cripple child all her life she can just manage to get about she was sent away by Mr Bruce because she wouldn't do any work because she wasn't able to do the work

he told me to come and take her away I was living out in a tent at the time working for the Station grubbing for two shillings per acre ... & now I am fishing for a Factory in Port Lincoln ... I am not making my living at it ...

I have no other way of getting my living Sir is it right for Mr Bruce to send a cripple child away from the school & to keep an old white man there doing nothing only feeding one or two pigs ... if Poonindie is a destitute asylum for whites it aught to be destitute for all cripple natives & now I am engage to go shearing & I wish for the child to be at Poonindie and go to school if I were to have my wife at Poonindie while I go shearing I would have to pay seven shillings per week I am still living out in a tent I have been 8 & 20 years on Poonindie and never been treated so badly as I am now

Please Sir will you see into this letter. Yours truly Tim Adams[5]

---

5 Original letter held in the State Archives of South Australia GRG24/4.

Julia also wrote a letter in regard to this claim, saying it was difficult for her to work and get around with this stick. She was expected to carry heavy baskets of clothes and hang them on the line when she needed a crutch to walk. So she wrote a letter defending herself, explaining how difficult it was for her. But then you have to sift between the lines of these two or three letters to see what's really going on between the superintendent and Tim's family. There was a lot of animosity there.

I don't know what happened to Julia's leg. A number of kids had these funny withered legs. I know this Ngarrindjeri man named Garnie Wilson who has one just the same and I think that sometimes it was because of the way they used to set the leg or the bone after it was broken. That's what Garnie told me. They clipped the leg bone on the hip or something – it was bad medical practice. I don't think they knew about knitting bones together then. Aboriginal people knew how to do it, because a bloke named Ted Martin told me this interesting story when I was a kid living at Point Pearce mission. He was a relative of mine through marriage. He told me about how an Aboriginal man out bush set his own broken leg after his horse had fallen on it. The Aboriginal bloke re-aligned the bones perfectly and splinted it with a piece of bark from a tree. When I heard that I thought, well, I'll be blowed. But I think Julia may have had a bad leg from birth.

Julia's parents, Tim and Bessie, seemed to find itinerant work for a while before eventually moving to Point Pearce mission. When Poonindie closed in 1894 they were joined at Point Pearce by the rest of their family, as well as Tom Adams and his many children.

Julia grew up and married my grandfather, Henry Simpson, a white man from Echunga in South Australia. Henry's father was a miner who migrated from Durham in England in 1856 and settled in Echunga, presumably to work in the gold mines there. When Julia married Henry in 1903 he was living in Port Pirie. Two years later they settled on Wardang Island, just off the coast from Point Pearce mission, where Henry worked in the flux quarry.[6] They lived in a small tin hut in the centre of the sheep paddock owned by Point Pearce mission. The rest of the island was sub-leased by the mission to BHP.

Julia and Henry had their first child on the island, Vera Constance Simpson, born in 1904. It was from this hut that Julia commenced her campaign of letter-writing to gain some land for herself and her little family. She wrote on 13 May 1905 to Mr Hamilton, the Protector of Aborigines:

> Sir will you kindly, help me by getting as many acres of land that I am entitled to, as my house is built on the island, & I would like to get the land on the island if possible as I think I would be able to get a living here by keeping fowls pigs and also a garden, I have got one daughter & my husband as [sic] been working in the flux quarry, but the flux quarry is closing end of this month will you kindly let me know. Yours Respectfully Julia Simpson

Julia must have asked Mr Lathem of Point Pearce mission for his support, because he also wrote a letter to Hamilton. Unfortunately, and probably unbeknown to Julia, he wrote:

> ... to give the Simpsons a few acres on the ... island would be a serious trouble to us ... and lead to endless complications, on our behalf kindly squash Simpsons request under the circumstances nothing else is practicable.

Julia came from a persistent family who were not fazed by officialdom's reluctance to grant them land, and she continued to write to all and sundry. When she received a negative response

---

6 The flux mined on Wardang was a sand used in the smelting process.

from Hamilton about her claim for land on Wardang Island, she wrote again in June of the same year. This time she applied for a block of land at Port Victoria, on the coast near Point Pearce:

> I received your letter stating I could not get a block of land at Wardang Island.
>
> Sir would you kindly let me know wether you could get me a block of land near Port Victoria as I want a place to put my house on, so kindly let me no as soon as Possible, as I will have a shift from here as there is no work for my Husband.
>
> Yours respectfully Julia Simpson

Again her request received a negative response – in fact all Julia's appeals for land were unsuccessful. So, landless, and probably penniless, Henry and Julia Simpson moved to Point Turton, on the southern coast of Yorke Peninsula. There they had two more children, including my mother, Gladys Florence Simpson, born in 1907, and the youngest, Ethel Simpson, born in 1916. So my mother was the second-born of the family, which is interesting because it follows a pattern: Thomas Adams senior was the second-born of his English family, and Tim Adams (my great grandfather) was the second-born to Kudnarto, and I was the second-born to my second born mother Gladys. My mother was actually born at Yorketown, which is inland from the coast, but near Point Turton. I assume Julia and her husband weren't able to stay on at Wardang Island and had to seek work elsewhere, thanks to Mr Lathem. Julia wouldn't have been able to stay on at Point Pearce mission because she married a white man.

Tom Adams junior had a large family – nine children. There were five boys: the eldest William, then Charles Samuel, Thomas Frederick, Herbert and finally Sydney. Amazingly, not one of these boys had children, so none of them passed on the family name of Adams. Of the four Adams girls, there was the eldest Maria (Doordy), then Ethela, May and finally Maude Alice. The girls all went on to get married and have children. Maria married an Aboriginal man named Henry Angie and together they had six children, but they all bore the family name Angie. The second Adams daughter, Ethela, married the Narungga man Walter Sansbury and had eight children, but they all bore the Sansbury family name. May Adams married the Aboriginal man Joseph Edwards and together they also had eight children, who all took the Edwards family name. And Maude Alice Adams married a Ngarrindjeri man from Point McLeay called Robert Wilson Junior, and together they had three children who took the Wilson family name.

As I mentioned before, Tim Adams had four children to Bessie Roberts, including two boys and two girls. The eldest was my great uncle, Lewis Adams, who married May Edwards. These two people became important people in my life as a child at Point Pearce mission, maybe because they never had children of their own. Tim Adams' youngest son was my great uncle, Arthur, who was nicknamed Bishop. He married a Mary Simms, but they never had any children who survived. Of Tim Adams' two daughters the elder Gertrude married William Williams from the west coast and had four boys, all taking the Williams family name. And my grandmother Julia's three daughters took on the Simpson family name, including my mother Gladys Florence Simpson.

So it's interesting isn't it, how such a large family as the Adamses of Point Pearce, despite there being so many boys, can lose the family name of Adams in just two generations. As I said before, I think some of my great uncles felt the hardships and prejudice of the era they were growing up in and chose not to bring children into the world to face similar trials.

I remember one day getting into a taxi when I was about

twenty, and as soon as I got in the taxi the driver burst out crying. I thought, what the hell is this all about? Eventually he said, 'Sorry lad. Sorry, sorry.'

I didn't say anything because I was out of sorts and thinking, what's wrong here? Anyway, he explained to me. He said, 'Look lad, when you got into the taxi I thought there and then about my life. I've been through a depression, and later in life I made up my mind that I would not have any kids so they wouldn't have to go through the nonsense I went through. So when you got in the taxi, you looked just like the sort of kid I would've had if I'd had a child.' Then he said, 'I've made the wrong decision, and it hit me when you got in the car. It was like, here's my son that I could've had.'

He explained to me that a son of his *could* have had twenty years of good living and not the misery he thought he'd have. It just hit him at an emotional moment. I said to myself, hell, it's an uncanny thing how people get caught by their own decisions sometimes. I never forgot that.

Those sorts of decisions people make have long-term effects. I've seen a lot of Aboriginal men make those same decisions. When that taxi driver confided in me like that I suddenly thought of my own grandmother's brothers – Uncle Lewis and Uncle Arthur – because neither of them had children. Perhaps it was because they were Aboriginal and they were treated in a certain way and they didn't like it. I know that feeling because I have been through certain unpleasant situations myself.

So that's why there are no people carrying on the Adams name today. Instead there are only descendents of Adams women.

Just as the Aboriginal residents of Poonindie became accomplished farmers and sports people, so too did the Aboriginal residents of Point Pearce. I should tell you some of the stories about sport at Point Pearce, particularly football. As you probably know South Australians are pretty keen on their Aussie Rules football, and the people of Yorke Peninsula are no exception – both the white and Aboriginal population. For many years there were regular football competitions between Point Pearce and the teams from the local towns like Maitland and Wallaroo. Following the First World War they actually stopped the Point Pearce team playing for a short time. I reckon that was because they were too good, and the reason they were good was because Point Pearce used strategies, and the strategies they used were later copied by other teams in the South Australian football league.

It started back in 1912 when Point Pearce was playing Maitland. The Aboriginal team knew Maitland were pretty good so they had to develop some tactics to beat them. What they worked out is something that I think has been built into Australian culture – and that's to always respect the opposition. See, that's why we're different to British culture – respect. When we're playing sport against someone, we recognise they're good and say that they're good and realise that we have to do better. British culture doesn't say that, they say, we're better than everyone else, so we'll build on that strategy. Maybe that's why the English have been going so badly on the world sporting scene these days. They know they're not doing too good, but they keep telling themselves that they are the best. I suppose they did prove themselves to be the best when they won the Rugby World Cup in 2003 though – but it took them thirty-seven years. Similarly it took them sixteen years to win back The Ashes from Australia in Cricket in 2005.

Believing that you're the best is only good for defence. If you want to attack it's better to know what the other team is like – what their strengths and weaknesses are. You've got to adopt a better strategy. I think that this Aboriginal idea of respecting your opponent has had an effect on Australian culture. If you respect the other bloke and say, he's pretty good, so we've gotta be pretty darn good to beat him, you've got more chance of winning yourself in the end.

My father-in-law, Eddie Sansbury, told me that back in 1912 the Point Pearce football team knew the Maitland team was the champions of the year, so they sat down on a Friday night and asked themselves, how are we gonna beat these people? They're pretty good. Even though they had a pretty good team themselves, they knew that Maitland had more good players, and that's what they learnt to look at. They knew that they probably had four good players themselves, but they knew Maitland had six. You can only build on the good players you have, and when I say good players, I mean *champions*. Many footballers are good players, but all good players are equal – equal skills – they can run fast and pick up the ball, they can mark well, all of that. But it's the champions who give you the extra boost – they can tap the ball when they're being tackled, grab the hard balls and mark one-handed.

The Point Pearce team had a meeting the night before the grand final and devised a plan. They thought that during the game they would shout, 'Over here!' but confuse the opposition with what this really meant. This call was straightforward in the first half, but in the second half of the game the Point Pearce team shouted, 'Over here!' but really meant 'Over there!' every time they punched or kicked the ball in the opposite direction. As expected, in the first half Maitland was showing their ability and was leading by five goals, so they were going easy. Then in the second half Point Pearce changed their tactics to kick and pass in the opposite direction to where they were calling, and they won by a goal with 5000 people watching! Well, maybe it was 500, I don't know. You know how exaggerated these figures get for the sake of a good yarn. It was a big crowd anyway, for a country game.

Everyone in the district was pretty upset that the champion

team was beaten by this lowly Point Pearce team – all except the Point Pearce mob that is. They were so pleased they even wrote a poem about it that was published in the *Maitland Watch* on 20 September 1912:

The Football Shield
by Hilda Stuart, 1912
A Lay of a Modern Mission

Attend all ye, who list to hear
Our grand old Mission's praise,
The story of a victory
Which made a thousand gaze,
With wonder and astonishment
At fortunes tables turned,
When the Mission met the Maitland team
And victory, dearly earned.

From Moonta's copper mines they came.
To see the glorious sight;
Urania's farmers left their ploughs
To cheer the glorious fight;
Ardrossan's cliffs deserted were
By all who love the sport;
Victoria's motors, trap and carts
Drove from their royal port.

The umpire Sanders, dropped the ball,
And started was the game,
Which was to test, which team was the best,
And which was worthy fame;
Should Maitland still the honour claim
And gain the silver shield?
Or should the Mission strong enough
To win it on that field?

Like tides at springtime, Maitland's men
Fell full upon the Mission,
Whom back they bore, and fast they score,
Five goals were their addition,
Then Barbary shone like Arab stead
All o'er the slippery ground,
Maloney, Oatey, Sellars, Hill,
Showed they sportsmen sound,
When o'er the field half time was called,
And loudly rang the bell;
It seemed to sound to Mission hearts
Like a funeral knell.

Hope springs eternal in the breast
Of every noble heart,
Inspired by this, the Mission men
Went out to do their part,
When once again the battle joined
To try from dire defeat,
To snatch a victory more bright
Because they were thought 'beat'.

Then like a torrent, Rivers rolled
O'er Smith and Doctor Betts,
And Varcoe kicked a lucky goal
Such as one seldom gets;
And fickle fortune smiled upon
Dan Wilson's splendid marks,
Which drew from many Maitland throats
Some most discordant barks;

On wings of wind the Milera boys
Descended to the fray,
And Stuart's princely blood was stirred
To turn the doubtful day,

Then Edwards placed his men anew,
No longer, 'Poor old Joe',
When he saw the tide of battle turn
On their exhausted foe.

And victory smiled on Sansbury's face
As with the ball he ran,
And Angie kicked with confidence
As well we know he can,
Fred Graham, Hughes and Wanganeen,
Alike they do their best,
To drive the ball through Maitland's goal
And so did all the rest.

At last the bell rang o'er the field,
Proclaiming time was gone,
And by a goal the umpire said
The Mission team had won.
Five hundred hearts were light as air
Five hundred hearts were sad,
Five hundred hearts danced gladly there,
And just a few were mad.

Fair Maitland's maids now hang their harps
Upon a willow tree,
And Tiddy's store reopened now
Is busy as a bee.
It was a victory worthy of
A poet or a seer;
And e'en the ranks of Tuscany
Could scarce forebear to cheer.
By campfire and in cottage home
They talk of that bright field,
When native boys – test match won
Brought home the silver shield.

The Point Pearce team used to come and play the winning league teams here in Adelaide at different times. They played the South Adelaide premiers at Woodville Oval in 1935 – I've got a copy of the program with the team listed. All the Point Pearce family names are there: Hughes, Wanganeen, Sansbury, Williams, Graham, Newchurch, Warrior, O'Loughlin, Edwards, Varcoe, Weetra, Stuart, Lansbury and Buckskin. Even in the 1950s when I was playing football, Point Pearce used to come and play Norwood. They used to do this criss-cross short passing, and I noticed later that Norwood adopted that same sort of strategy. Old Jack Oatey came from the Peninsula and I think his father played for Maitland. So they brought that method over. That Point Pearce team knew about team playing so well that Norwood learnt from them. When Jack Oatey moved to coach Sturt he passed on all these team tactics to them. That's why they had so much success in the 1960s. They developed this '180 degrees strategy' which I think copies the techniques of the Point Pearce team. It was really a clever tactic – you got everyone to run over to the one side, and then you'd kick the ball to the opposite side. They also learnt to handball to their team-mates a lot more.

Aussie Rules footy is like a traditional game played by Aboriginal people. The Kaurna people used to play a game called *parnda* with a ball made from a stuffed possum skin (*parnda* is the Kaurna word for 'this ball'). They used to kick it in the air and mark it just like modern football. That's why there are so many champion Aboriginal football players I reckon. Aboriginal people were made for football, and they knew the marking and kicking techniques because they'd practised them for years.

Once when I was playing football for the North Adelaide colts, the champion footballer Hayden Bunton (senior) came and showed us this special method of training that we found very difficult to do. Bunton showed us how he could roll a ball from one end of the field to the other, end over end[7]. You try and do it – it's very difficult! But if you manage to do it, you get to know where the ball is going to bounce and where the ball is all the time. All champions devise their own special training methods. The champion cricketer Donald Bradman used to hit a ball against a tank stand with a cricket stump, which gave him a keen eye for the ball.

The Point Pearce men were also champion cricketers. The old blokes used to always tell me about this fellow from Point Pearce by the name of Rivers. When Rivers played, he'd say, I'll make sixty runs without moving. That meant he thought he could stay at the crease and hit fours and sixes without having to make any short runs. Well, usually you hit ones and twos and just the odd four or six. But he could really play a full game without moving – hitting all fours and sixes. After he'd made his sixty runs, he'd just hit whatever was bowled to him and make a few runs to the other wicket just for some physical activity.

One day I told this story about Rivers to Bernard Whimpress, the curator of the Adelaide Oval. He looked up the oval records and checked the scores of past matches and found that this Rivers fellow did make hundreds, which confirmed he was a very good cricketer. But they didn't put his scores in the local paper, the *Maitland Watch*, so there's no record of his local achievements.

Quite a few Point Pearce blokes were also very good athletes. Eddie Sansbury was a champion runner over 200 yards. Bobby Wilson played on the wing for Point Pearce football team, and he was such a good sprinter he won the famous Bay Sheffield footrace one year. It's held here in South Australia every year, and run over a distance of 100 yards, down at Glenelg on Colley Reserve. In the early days of the colony

---

7 This means the ball didn't roll on its side, but from its pointed end to the other pointed end.

Colley Reserve was an Aboriginal campsite. They camped there until they were all sent off to live on the isolated missions. A number of Aboriginal people have won the Bay Sheff – Bobby Wilson, Kenny Hampton and Bobby Ware – and a few have won it more than once.[8]

Once I came across a runner whose name I will always remember – Fooks, or Fooksy, as everyone used to call him. He was a white fella who once played for the West Torrens Football Club on the wing. Fooksy ran one year at Stawell in Victoria, which is famous for its annual sprint race known as the Stawell Gift. Fooksy won the pre-run at Stawell and the judges came over to him after the race. When he saw them walking towards him, he thought they were going to disqualify him. But instead they came over and congratulated him. They told him he was the fastest man ever. The race was run over 120 yards and his was the fastest *ever* recorded time at Stawell over forty yards. He passed the whole field of competitors just forty yards into the race – an incredible effort. He was one of the best starters they'd ever seen at Stawell, just unbelievable.

One year I decided I was going to run in the West Torrens Football Club picnic race. I said to myself, alright, I can't run too fast, so I'd better do something about it. I'll see if I can find out something to increase my speed. So I went up to old Fooksy – we worked together then – and asked him what to do and he told me this special method. What he did was practise every day. That might not sound very special today, but he did this in the twenties and thirties, so he was far ahead of his time. These days all athletes practise every day.

I've witnessed for myself how fast Fooksy was. One time there was this bloke who kept goading Fooksy saying, if you

---

8 The name 'Bay Sheff' comes from 'the Bay' plus the name 'Sheffield' (probably named after the family that donated the shield for the race). Glenelg is commonly referred to as 'the Bay' by South Australians.

give me ten yards, I'll beat you, Fooksy. He kept at him. Eventually Fooksy got wild and said to him, I've had it with you. I'll bet you five pounds that if I give you ten yards in twenty, I'll still beat you. The other bloke just laughed, and said he was silly, but he did take Fooksy on. He was thinking – like I was – that he could almost walk to the line and still win with such an advantage. Immediately after the starter bloke had clapped his hands, Fooksy was past the other bloke! He'd made up ten yards in the clap of a hand. He was so fast you could hardly follow him with your eye. It was mind-boggling to watch. He took off like a *rocket*!

I won that Torrens picnic race in the end, thanks to Fooksy. The coach said I was the slowest bloke in the B-grade team so I was a hundred to one to win. He wasn't too pleased when I won the race! I had made up my speed by ten yards just by practising every day for three months. On the day of the race I was on the front mark and my competitors never passed me.

The next year I was favourite for the hundred metres in the A grade, and, being cheeky, and knowing I'd improved since the year before, I said to my aunt, do you want that silver tea service? (That was the prize.)

Anyway, I was the favourite that year for the higher race, and the starter told me where to stand. I said, I'm not standing there, there's water there.

He told me that if I didn't stand where he told me he'd disqualify me. Which made me think, hello, they're playing games here, but never mind. I'll jump this puddle. The bookie must have had a word with the starter.

When the starter gun went off, I forgot about the puddle, took off like a rocket and ended up falling over in the mud. So I had to pick myself up and chase the rest of the field down the track. I still ran second but my aunt didn't get her silver tea service. Fooksy later admitted to me that he wasn't the fastest runner over the distance, but because he was a fast starter and ran an even time, he could pass the field in forty yards and they would all give up. He was beating them with his tactics.

You learn to talk to the blokes who know all this stuff. That's our Aboriginal way – we ask the old fellows. People living in modern society don't always do that. They think we've got modern methods today, but the old blokes have life experiences, and there's a lot we can learn from them.

Aboriginal people were naturally geared for excelling at sport. Their way of life taught them how to strategise. Some people think Aboriginal people were aimless wanderers, which always tickles me because they weren't at all. Aboriginal people had to be very astute and smart in their food gathering and survival. If they wanted a feed, they had to work for it. For example by digging for little potatoes for hours or gathering berries. They had to be active and move about the country, or go out in the sea to spear a fish. Circumstances made them learn all these different skills – to get food, defend themselves and manage their affairs. I think our prowess in sport has since proved our considerable tactical skills.

6

Treasured memories and lessons from the mission

I was born at Point Pearce mission on 25 March 1930 and was named Lewis William Arthur O'Brien by my mother, Gladys Florence O'Brien (nee Simpson). She headed back to live on the mission just before I was born. I remember someone telling me that when my mother named me one wise uncle quipped, 'That's a hell of a burden to put on a kid, naming him after three kings!' But I was actually named after three of my maternal great uncles: Uncle Lewis Adams, Uncle Arthur (Bishop) Adams and Uncle William (Bill) Adams.

My father, Ernest Patrick O'Brien, was one of the Barwell Boys who came to South Australia as part of the immigrant boy apprenticeship scheme. He was one of 602 boys who came to South Australia on the ship the *Balranald*. He was to work as an apprentice to a farmer, and arrived on 29 May 1923. The scheme ran from 1913 to 1929 and brought out over 1700 British boys to work in this state. They were called the Barwell Boys because Barwell was the premier of South Australia at the time the scheme was begun.

I never met my father because he must have left my mother before I was born. He went back to England in 1935, remarried and had another family over there. So I didn't grow up knowing much about him, but according to my half-sister Merle's research, his mother followed him out here to South Australia. They returned together to England on the ship the *Moreton Bay* on 30 May 1935.

People look at me sometimes, see how fair I am, look at my

name and then tell me that I must have Irish connections. And I guess that's true, but you can't identify with that unless you grow up with some knowledge of your Irish ancestry and culture – and I didn't. That's why it can be confusing when it comes to my identity. When I spoke to an Irishman once about my Irish connections, he summed it up by saying, 'Very tenuous!'

For much of my early childhood I grew up on an Aboriginal mission and spent time with Aboriginal people. They were the people I knew, so my reference point is being Aboriginal. I feel privileged, to be honest, spending all those early years of my life with Auntie May and Uncle Lewis Adams at Point Pearce. They were actually my great aunt and great uncle, because Uncle Lewis was the older brother of my grandmother Julia Simpson, but I called them Auntie May and Uncle Lewis. Sometimes we get lucky with the strong beginnings we have.

See, when you're born in a place and you live in that place, you're connected to it, so I always felt that I was connected to Point Pearce, or Bookooyanna[1], as it was always called. When I was growing up I thought that I was Narungga[2] because I didn't know anything different. I learnt about my family's Kaurna ancestry a bit later.

Being born at the beginning of the Depression years wasn't easy for anyone, but life was particularly difficult for my mother. Here she was, a deserted Aboriginal woman with a

---

1 The term *Bookooyanna* is said to be derived from the name of the oil bush that grows in abundance in the Point Pearce area. If you look up the Kaurna dictionary (a closely related language) the term *Bukkiana* means 'ancient ancestor'. The Point Pearce mission took its name from the Point Pearce peninsula opposite Wardang Island, midway up the western coast of Yorke Peninsula in South Australia.

2 The word *Narungga* is also in the Kaurna dictionary and is spelt *Ngurrungga* and is said to mean 'behind, at the back'. This makes sense because the story about the Buthera Dreaming ancestor is set at the back of the mission.

young baby and no income. The obvious place for her was with her family on the mission. I often returned there throughout my boyhood, sometimes with my mother and sometimes without her. I always stayed with Uncle Lewis and Auntie May, maybe because they never had children of their own. I remember staying with them once with just my younger half-brother Lawrence.

You know, it's funny how life turns out for some, because my younger half-brothers and half-sisters don't relate to Point Pearce mission at all. They didn't have that early connection like I did. Merle told me once about how she had seen a fortune teller in Spain. See Merle was a bit like me in that she felt she needed to go away to sea when she was older, so she went as a stewardess on a ship. The fortune teller told her she was the seventh child. Merle said, 'No, I'm the sixth.'

So then I had to tell Merle the truth. 'You are the seventh.'

Merle said, 'Hang on: first there's you, then Lawrence, Joy, Angelina, Angelo and then me. I'm the sixth.'

'Yes,' I said. 'But we had an older sister called Patricia, and she died when she was quite young. So she makes you number seven.' Merle didn't know about the passing of our oldest sibling Patricia but I was older and I remembered. As the eldest I can remember certain facts that helped explain things that happened in our family many years earlier. I often wonder whether our older sister Patricia's early death was the cause of the break-up between my father and mother. Patricia dying so young would have upset the family a great deal. She was only eighteen months old when she passed away. The family didn't have any records then, but I used to hear her name mentioned by my grandparents, and by Uncle Lewis and Auntie May. I used to think I was pretty good to hear them discussing things with my mother. I'd pick up on things by listening intently.

I didn't always live at Point Pearce. My mother and us

older kids were coming and going all the time. I know I was born there, and I was there again when I was three, and again when I was nine. I remember that time because I went to school. What stands out so clearly in my memory was being at Point Pearce school in 1939 when the anthropologist Norman Tindale from the South Australian Museum in Adelaide visited. He came to take photographs and to measure everyone living at Point Pearce. If you look at the photos in the museum today you can see that none of us looked too happy – they look like mug shots. We all had to line up in the school and have our heads and bodies measured with callipers. We didn't know what was going on, but I remember feeling out of sorts about the whole business. I guess Tindale wanted to know if we had skulls and brains the same size as non-Aboriginal Australians. The irony is that they have since discovered that brain size has nothing to do with intelligence. And I've read about a Nobel Prize winner for literature, Anatole France, who actually had a smaller brain than most other people.

But getting back to my mother and us kids being on the move all the time. I guess my mother moved around a lot in the 1930s because it was the time of the Depression, and everyone was poor. Mother didn't want to wear out her welcome anywhere. I think we were on the move the most when I was aged between two and five. At one stage I think we all moved to a house in Moonta, because I remember going to school at Moonta, which is about forty kilometres north of Point Pearce. It was during our stay at Moonta that my mother had two more kids to two different partners. So before long she had three kids in tow, and that was a few mouths to feed. There was me, my younger half-brother Lawrence and my younger half-sister Joy. At another time we moved to Wallaroo and stayed with my grandmother Julia Simpson. She had half a house in Wallaroo, which is another seventeen kilometres north of Moonta, still on Yorke Peninsula. I remember though that we were always coming back to Point Pearce, and that we always stayed with Uncle Lewis and Auntie May.

I kept returning to Uncle Lewis and Auntie May on the mission, even after my mother got a house in Adelaide. And later on in my teens when I was fostered out, I went to Point Pearce during the school holidays. I'd usually go back by myself, because to me it was home.

I learnt a great deal about my culture and the stories attached to the land around Point Pearce when I lived with Auntie May and Uncle Lewis. They had more skills and knowledge than anyone else I have ever met in my life. They complemented each other. Auntie May had the talking and story-telling ability that many of our women have, while Uncle Lewis had the non-verbal teaching methods. I was privileged to have lived with them, because I know Auntie May was a psychologist and a philosopher, and both of them had spirituality beyond belief.

When you live in a place you learn all the stories of that place, so I learnt a number of Narungga stories from Point Pearce, or Bookooyanna. One story I learnt was about the Dreaming ancestor Buthera, who lived at Wardang Island, just off the Point Pearce peninsula. Now Buthera was the big man who often had arguments with this little bloke Ngarna. They would fight each other but Ngarna was clever and he used to hide behind rocks. One day Buthera threw this waddy, or fighting stick, at Ngarna, but it missed him and hit the rocks instead and broke in two. Today you can still see the head of the rock, there on the other side of The Point, which was formed by the club end of the waddy. On the other side you can still see the impression left by the tail of the waddy.

Sometimes the Elders would mix up traditional stories with modern stories. Just by translating them into English they would change. It's pretty darn good, you know, the way they took their own stories and put them in different settings, mixing and matching. That's the way oral story-telling works in many cultures. So I'd be listening to a story and suddenly I'd realise that what they were telling me was actually about me or someone else, and not just Buthera. See, with that story, what they're pointing out to you is very subtle: even though you're a big strong man, the little man who's cleverer and agile can out-smart you.

The Buthera story is a funny one really, because this Ngarna, who Buthera has an argument with, is really Madjitju. Now *madjitju* is the Narungga word for 'bat', and when Buthera fights this bat, at one stage he grabs him and cuts him across the stomach. I went to the museum once to check out a bat from this area to look at the markings on the stomach, and found that they had rolls of skin on the stomach that looked like lines. You can also see the bat has little short legs, just like the man Ngarna in the story. So it's actually a very intricate story about the bat.

It's really about positioning, which is getting to the heart of Aboriginal thinking. There's this little man Ngarna, who's really a bat, Madjitju. But when does he become the man and when is he a bat? This is really philosophical thinking that is common to Aboriginal stories, which makes them different to many other nation's stories. See, it's not like Hollywood's batman that's both man and bat. No, it's a man *or* a bat – a transformation of forms. I don't think people fully understand the difference. Some may think you can't have the two characters together in the one story – instead they think it has to be like in Greek mythology, where you have the centaur, which is half horse, and half man. But that's not the case in Aboriginal stories. Within our stories you are one or the other, but not both at once.

That's what our Elders did – they told stories about ordinary, everyday themes, but they told them through our

Dreaming ancestors like Buthera and Ngarna. I always look for the story behind the story. I think that's because I had the luxury of being with Auntie May who used to point out the philosophy behind it. Most people in life just listen to the story, whereas when you're with people who understand the philosophy, you pick up more. See, she taught me why they do things, and why things are there. So then you start looking deeply at the meaning. But not all the Elders told stories like Auntie May. The other gran of mine, Grannie Gertie, she didn't do this. She used to just tell the story and that was it.

Buthera lived at Wardang Island and the Elders would talk about how Buthera had campfires there and how you could gain some of Buthera's strength if you rubbed your body with the ashes of Buthera's campfires. There was an emphasis on strength among the men in the community. Some of the Narungga men were very strong. Uncle Dasher said that one day Captain Hughes came to the mission and they were digging an underground water tank, and he said to the other blokes he brought with him, 'Watch these Point Pearce men dig if you want to see shovellers. These are the best shovellers you'll ever see.' It was true; they could handle a shovel really well, probably because of the strength in their arms and wrists.

I would often hear stories about the strength of Susie Hughes who was a resident at Point Pearce. Apparently she tossed her six-foot husband, Alfred Hughes, over a fence once! So that's a hell of a lot of strength. You could see the strength in the sheer build of some of the people – they were very powerful. Even my Auntie Glad was pretty strong – she's my mother's first cousin. I saw her one day at the horse races at Cheltenham, because she used to make sandwiches for the canteen there. Suddenly I saw her take off after someone at a great rate of knots. She was chasing after a Chinese man, and she nearly knocked him clean over. I asked her what she was doing and she told me, 'Don't you know you gotta touch a Chinaman for luck?' Touch him alright – she nearly knocked him rotten! She was behaving like a ruck-rover in the local football team. She was probably strong because she milked forty-five cows a day by hand. It's incredible what some people used to do in those days.

I used to go out into the bush with Uncle Lewis in the horse and cart to pick up stones that were used to build the houses on the mission. I was only a little kid of about five years at the time. He didn't talk much to me and I used to find it bewildering, because a kid expects to be talked to, and I'd sit there wondering why this old man was taking me out into the bush if he wasn't going to talk to me. But looking back, there was a lot to learn from non-verbals, and I did learn a great deal from him. On other occasions, I'd be riding along in carts with some of my other uncles and they'd be rattling off the names of the different bushes to me. At one stage I thought, I don't wanna do all this. It's too difficult. I guess I realised I couldn't take in all this information so quickly. With my coming and going a lot from the mission, it was like living in two worlds. I'd go off and then I'd come back. I'd go to school for a while, and then I'd leave, and then I'd come back again.

As I got older I recognised my unusual situation. I suddenly realised that I couldn't pick up on all that I was being taught, so I decided to pick up just three subjects: I made up my mind that I'd learn the psychology that Auntie May was excellent at, and the philosophy that she talked about, and finally the educational things that I saw Uncle Dasher do with string. To this day I can still do those tricks with string that Uncle Dasher taught me. I do all these manoeuvres on my hands with a loop of string, passing the string around my fingers and over my palm, and between my thumb and fingers. Then eventually I pull the bottom of the string and it comes free from my hand. I wasn't just learning all these fancy manoeuvres from Uncle Dasher. I was fine-tuning my skills of observation. I was learning how to learn. So then I could transpose those learning skills to anything I wanted to learn. Once I understood the concepts they were both trying to teach me, I was right.

Recently I visited a waterhole on a property on Yorke Peninsula with two Narungga men, Lester Rigney and Dookie O'Loughlin. The waterhole is known in Narungga as Gardi-Mulka, which comes from the words *gardi* for 'emu', and *mulka* for 'face'. The water gathers in a depression – the surrounding rock is a funnel and the water collects in this hole in the middle. Anyway, the Narungga people have a Dreaming story about this place Gardi-Mulka. The emu came to this waterhole, looked into it, and could see his reflection. He was fascinated by his own face, so he just stood there admiring himself. His ego was so big that he would just gaze down at the water and get captivated by his face. I guess it was like what we call narcissism today – self-worship. That word actually comes from Greek mythology, and the youth Narkissos who fell in love with his own reflection in the water. Anyway, the ending is that the emu is condemned for his pride, and forever more has to drink from the water holding his head level. So now when he drinks he can no longer look at the water. If you watch an emu drinking, you'll see that he puts his head level to the water and then lifts it up to swallow. He sort of scoops the water up.

They had caves at Currimulka (which is the English spelling) as well, but you can't go into the caves now because they've quarried a lot around there and they're becoming dangerous. The Elders used to tell a number of stories about these places 'south' of The Point.

One of the stories they used to tell me was about catching fish. When they caught a lot of fish, rather than let it go to waste the Narungga would invite other groups to come in and share. They signalled by lighting fires. I think they'd light three fires, which was a sign that invited the other groups to come. So when they'd come, they would feed them on all this fish. But if too many people came they wouldn't have enough fish, so they would wrap a bit of bark around one of the fish and send this wrapped-fish back out to sea. They used to send it out to round up the other fish, so then they could feed the multitudes, as it were. When the wrapped-fish came back it was bigger. So when they sent it out again, they had to put a bigger bit of bark on it before they sent it back out again to round up more fish. Then when the wrapped-fish came back again it was bigger still, so they would wrap an even bigger bit of bark around it and send it out again to once more come back with more fish. But when the wrapped-fish came back for the last time, on seeing its size they all jumped back in fear and exclaimed, '*Paitya!*' a word that means 'watch out!' (or 'something to be feared') in the Narungga language.[3] They even used to call out *paitya* as a warning when policemen were about.

When you hear that fish story, on one level it's very practical in that it's telling you how to feed many people by getting assistance from a fish. But really there's a lot more to it than that. There's a message in there, but they don't spell it out when they're narrating it. So you are being taught to arrive at the conclusion yourself. If you arrive at that conclusion or message yourself it's far better, because you'll retain it and it's yours, whereas if I tell you, it still belongs to me – you'll forget it in time. That's the funny thing about learning.

What I draw from that story about the fish is that if we go to a meeting, it'd be far better for all of us to speak with one

---

3 According to the Kaurna dictionary (a closely related language) *paitya* means 'vermin; reptile; monster; any dangerous or disliked animal; expressing wonder or admiration'.

voice than a lot of little voices. So there's a lot to be learnt from stories. That's what the Elders show you all the time. They don't go into depth, they just tell a story and say, 'What do you make of that?' What I often wonder about that fish story is if it actually foretells the arrival of strangers coming to our land from the sea. Just as Europeans arrived, and then more and more came.

I smile when the Elders don't do the second step of analysing parts of the story. See, the actual story is clear, but what about the other hidden story – the one beneath the story? What you need to ask is, have you looked around the mountain? What's on the other side? What's beneath the story? What's between the lines? What else can you gather? Many of these stories are teaching you the same thing. They're saying, look at what's going on around you, and then you'll be able to govern and manage your own life better. They teach you to be the manager of your own affairs.

Some stories may even sound like nonsense, such as the Kaurna story of Pootpoberrie and Muldarpi[4]. But you can learn from nonsense as well as sense. You can see there's this balance in stories, just as there is in life. Sometimes you have to have bad experiences to gain the necessary knowledge to develop as a person. You don't just learn from the good things in life, or from the good stories. It doesn't matter if the stories are true or false – you can gain from both.

You know there's one thing that annoys me about Europeans. When you're with some Europeans they'll say, only tell me the facts! I think to myself, that's a bit silly. They just want to stick to this one step, or one line of thinking, all the time, and it starts to annoy me. They don't realise that

---

4 *Muldarpi* means 'nonsense' in the Narungga language, but *Muldarpi* is also the word used for 'bunyip' by some Aboriginal people of southern Australia, or sometimes *Mulyawongk*. The bunyip is a creature that haunts waterholes, and children are taught to fear it.

you can gain from two ways of looking at things. You need to look at both sides of the argument, and look at the many angles – then you can see how Aboriginal people look at things. If people are limited in the way they view things, they can't move on. They think things have to be true or false, right or wrong. You have to vote for this way or that way, and not both.

But I think you can waste your time doing that all your life. We often have to deal with many viewpoints, or ways of doing things that make it difficult to go just one way or the other. Take for example the evolution versus creation debate. Many Christian people don't know how to come to terms with these two alternative views of creation, thinking you have to go one way or the other. Our older people say, accept both! It's quite possible to accept two ways of viewing the world. With the creation versus evolution debate, you just say, things were created and then they evolved. If you accept both, you can then move on.

The alternative is to debate the issues forever, with no end or solution to the contradiction. You see, with some debates, there are just too many arguments either way, so you have to put them in the two-way box. If you think about it, the creation issue is just like that – you have to put it in the two-way box. There are many contradictions in life.

The way I see it is, why argue about something that you'll never solve? The best way is to accept both – we were all created and evolved. There. You've solved it! Aboriginal people believe in our creation stories that tell of our Dreaming ancestors who created the land, yet we also understand Western science and geology and other explanations of how the world could have been formed.

Do you see what I'm getting at? Accepting two ways makes for easiness in life if you think about it. You don't have to make sense of everything, so why worry about it? You can only go so far with your logical debates and arguments. I find all this very interesting and I really think this two-ways philosophy is how we have to start thinking – both how we think, and what we think about.

Some people in life will try to find the clear cut road, but I've learnt that life is not all clear cut. Just like nature, life is unpredictable and sometimes inexplicable. Take for example this particular place in Papua New Guinea where I went later in life. We couldn't predict the tide there. In most places around the world, you can tell what the tides will do – but not here, the tides were unpredictable. Well, life is a bit like that. Ninety-nine times out of a hundred you can be sure about things, but it just takes one person or one thing to prove you wrong, or to cause a hitch. But that doesn't matter. You just say to yourself, I've got to be satisfied with the ninety-nine per cent.

Another example happened when I was working in a cement factory. For 364 days of the year I could fix this one particular pump – yet why couldn't I fix it on the 365th day? So you can see there's no point worrying about it too much. You'd like to know the answer, and everyone comes along and thinks they can tell you why the pump's not working, but still the pump doesn't work. See life isn't all laid down neatly for us, and it isn't all clear-cut. Just like those unpredictable tides they get in Papua New Guinea, you can't make assumptions about life or nature. There are some things that act differently to what you expect, and you've just got to accept that.

Another thing that I find intriguing about the Western way of operating in the world is the lack of consensus. In the Western system there seems to be no compromise – you're either with me or against me. When there is disagreement it's the majority that rules and the minority gets out-voted. By contrast, the Aboriginal system that can be learnt from the Elders is the importance of consensus. They begin from a different premise – they start by stating all the good ideas that the group puts into a barrel (so to speak), then they debate, and sometimes disagree over things, but in the end they choose an idea from the barrel that suits them all. They see it as important to negotiate and come to a compromise so that everyone in the group is happy with the outcome. With this system there is no unsatisfied minority. I find this is a more conciliatory way of coming to a final decision.

So over the years, I have learnt to appreciate such alternative views and ways of operating in the world. I have also developed my own philosophies on life. I first learnt such ideas from my own people, particularly from my Elders at Point Pearce mission. I think they knew I was listening and learning from them because they started calling me 'Prof' from a very young age.[5] It wasn't just Auntie May and Uncle Lewis who I listened to, it was also Tim Hughes, Uncle Clifford (Dasher) Edwards, and my Auntie Gladys Elphick. They were all very wise people and taught me a great deal in the time I spent with them, for which I am still grateful.

When I talk about Aboriginal views (or my own views) on life, I do not mean that all Aboriginal people follow the same philosophies. It's actually quite the opposite. Many of our younger ones aren't following the philosophy of the old people, which is a big problem. What I talk about is what I learnt from my Elders, and what I have learnt myself over the years through my many experiences. I have developed a view of life, largely by comparing how the rest of the world thinks and acts compared to what I learnt from the Elders many years ago.

I think it is important for this philosophy to be passed on, otherwise it will be lost. We need to pass the wisdom of the Elders on to our kids, so that one day they will have the

---

5 I was also called Lew Billy by Auntie May to differentiate me from her husband Uncle Lewis.

wisdom and strength to cope with the many and varied challenges that they will face. When I was a kid on the mission, for example, I learnt to listen and when I asked questions the Elders would say, tut, tut, tut. Then they would walk away. So I soon learnt to shut up and listen carefully, and not to interrupt. This I believe is the first step needed in accelerated learning.

Because I learnt to listen intently, and I was very quiet, they would forget I was in the room, so I would pick up on things they were talking about, which sometimes wasn't for my ears. Then they'd notice me there and say, 'Get that kid out of here!' I think they thought I was learning too much too quickly. I even got to the stage where I knew what people were going to say and I could predict it, which was annoying for them, and boring for me. My cousin Alfie Hughes was clever like that too – he could predict things. It must be a trait that Aboriginal people learn, because he wasn't the only one who could predict what people were going to say.

But I didn't only learn by listening to the Elders. Later in life I became an avid reader, beginning in my teenage years. I learnt from reading books and I still read books from every section of the library – maths books, psychology books, philosophy books, physics books, astronomy books, books on evolution, biographies about famous people. You name it, I read it. I learnt a great deal about the world, and life, by reading books on the great thinkers, such as Pythagoras, Archimedes, Newton and Einstein. One of my favourite examples is the lesson on relativity from Albert Einstein. He tells us that time is all relative. 'You sit with your girlfriend for an hour and it seems like a minute. Yet you sit on a stove for a minute and it seems like an hour.' He was a wise man, Einstein.

So I learnt from Elders such as Einstein as well as from my Point Pearce Elders. The wisdom of the Elders on the mission was often profound. Auntie May used to say to me, 'Lewis, you see that bird on the tree at the corner?' So I'd look out to see if I could spot the bird she was talking about. But she wasn't really asking me if I saw the bird. She actually wanted to know if I was watching and observing and listening to what was going on around me. It was the same with Grannie Gertie's advice when she told me I shouldn't marry a girl with big feet. She didn't really expect me to measure the length of all my girlfriends' feet. She was trying to teach me to be more evaluating, to weigh up situations and to assess things on their merits. She was teaching me the important message that men in particular need to look beyond girls' beauty. They need to analyse the girl they fancy and assess whether they are compatible. Girls usually do this automatically, but we men don't. Grannie Gertie wanted to teach me not to be naïve – and to go beyond good looks.

The irony of this story is that I ended up marrying a woman who has really small feet – she takes a size three shoe! When I look at my wife's feet now I think Grannie Gertie would have smiled in approval. Especially because at the time she gave me that advice I was going out with a girl with very large feet! But Grannie knew more about me then than I realised.

The most profound philosophy I learnt from our people is this idea of seeing the world differently – in two ways, or in doublies (as I like to call it). This was what I was talking about when I gave the example of people accepting both creation stories and evolutionary theory. This two-ways idea is complex, but if properly understood, I think it could affect the way we all think about the world and life. See Westerners tend to split everything in life, plus their belief systems, into dichotomies, which forces people to take sides. It is the basis of the political system of European democracies, as well as the basis of the adversarial system of Western courts of law. Everything is left or right, black or white, guilty or not guilty – there is no in between. There are no grey areas, or fence sitters.

You have to make up your mind one way or the other in the Western system – you just can't have it both ways – otherwise the system doesn't function properly.

I follow a philosophy of life that allows people to shift between multiple systems of thought, or to follow contradictory belief systems, or to sit on both sides of a fence all at the same time. This system doesn't only allow you to have it both ways, but even *requires* you to have it both ways, so to speak.

Aboriginal people are known to be great story-tellers, and I often get asked to talk to kids in schools, so I invariably tell them stories. I tell them about Ngarna and Buthera, and the story of the fish, and a number of others. But when I finish the telling, the kids will often ask me whether the stories are true. I find this question annoying, embarrassing and even bewildering. To me these kids shouldn't be asking such questions. They should be looking at the story for its own sake and what lessons they can learn from it, and not worrying about whether the story is 'true' or made-up. These kids were asking me, a stranger, a question that they shouldn't be asking. They should be thinking about the story itself, and working things out for themselves.

All stories have levels – first the story itself and then the different levels of meaning we can glean from the story. The lesson we Aboriginal people get taught as we grow up hearing these stories is 'don't believe anyone', and 'you must work out truth for yourselves'. We are also taught that there are multiple truths: there is truth in the story, and there is the truth of the story, and there are the other truths of why the story is being told, and what we can learn from it.

So I hope and trust I have been able to share some of the truth and wisdom I have gleaned from the Elders over the years. The philosophies on life that I myself have developed are not all necessarily taken directly from traditional Aboriginal belief, but there is definitely that influence there. My own life has taught me much on the way. It should be said too that my Elders were also inevitably influenced by the mission system they were brought up in, so what they taught me incorporated some of their Christian upbringing as well as their own beliefs. But whatever the origins, we cannot ignore the wisdom of the Elders.

7

My difficult childhood

When I turned six my mother managed to get a house at Ethelton in the north-western suburbs of Adelaide. Life started to settle down for us then. Maybe that was because my mother met an Italian bloke named Damiano, who worked on the wharf at Port Adelaide. My mother had four children to Damiano, so my four youngest half siblings have Italian ancestry. They include Angelina, Angelo (who has now passed away), then Merle and finally Lee. Merle is the one who has done a lot of research on our family's history and genealogy.

It's funny how life can do a full circle because I've come back to live in the same suburb after all these years. I first lived in Willimott Street in Ethelton in 1936, and then I came back here again in 2000. So now I live in the same street in the same suburb, and I'm in my seventies.

The first house my mother rented was a little weatherboard home – it was only just demolished in 2003. Then we moved just round the corner to Russell Street into another weatherboard home – that one is still standing. Even though we were a little less on the move once my mother got her own place, that didn't mean life was much easier.

I was a pretty sickly kid, and I remember going to the Adelaide Children's Hospital a lot as a young boy. See I was born yellow and jaundiced. Sometimes I was admitted to Mareeba Hospital at Woodville as well. For years I was as weak as a kitten. Other kids could push me over with a feather. I had to take all these pills and odd concoctions every morning and night to treat the jaundice. I remember them clearly – a whole row of bottles and cans on my bedroom window sill. I was on medication for ten years I reckon. The pills tasted horrible. I also had to take codliver oil, castor oil, malt, and goodness knows what else. There were so many I've forgotten them all now – probably because they were all so terrible. It's funny, because now I can swallow nasty tasting things with ease; maybe I became accustomed to bad-tasting tablets as a young fella.

It wasn't until I was ten that I gained any strength. The teachers used to get fed up with me because I was always away sick and missing out on school work. But I always managed to catch up, when I sat down to really nut it out. They used to complain about us Aboriginal kids and our 'walk-about' ways – especially since my mother moved around a bit. I don't think they realised how hard it was for someone like her to support all of us children by herself. They also didn't realise that I was often away from school because of my illness. You know there's a funny twist to all this, because my half-brother Lawrence was never sick as a child, yet he died relatively young of a heart attack in his early sixties. My half-sister Joy had diphtheria, and Merle was sickly as a child too, so a number of us were pretty unwell at times.

When I was younger I used to stutter. There were some words that I just couldn't get my tongue around, like 'shoulder' and 'shin-bone'. My mother used to send me to the local butcher's shop, and I used to ask him for 'a soldier of mutton' or whatever it was she wanted. And the bloke would say to me, 'Do you mean "shoulder"?' When I asked my mother why I couldn't say these things, she told me my tongue was tied. Other people would tell her that she should have had my tongue snipped when I was younger.[1]

---

1 They were referring to that thin flap of skin that holds the tongue to the bottom of your mouth. Sometimes it holds the tongue too tight and needs to be snipped a bit.

Mine wasn't a nervous stutter, more a physical impediment. I had a top front tooth that was bent ninety degrees back into my mouth. I was always embarrassed about that tooth and used to pull my upper lip down to hide it. At first my tooth was slightly bent, then when it hit my lower teeth it just got forced back further and further into this odd shape. We couldn't afford to go to a dentist to get it fixed, so it just got worse and worse. So my tongue had to get around this tooth as well as cope with being 'tied'.

I never did get my tongue snipped. I eventually learned to overcome my speech problem, but it took a while. My teachers would tell me to put my tongue up or put it this way. So I'd go through all these lessons, but then get bewildered, because I was trying to do this and that, but my tongue just wouldn't do what I was trying to get it to do. It's just one of those peculiarities, stuttering.

I didn't overcome my stutter by practising the words I couldn't say, because I just couldn't pronounce them. I had to adapt in other ways, by using different words and by slowing down my speech. I had to learn to think about how the words sound, and try to choose words I knew I could say.

It was an embarrassing time, especially when I had to read out loud at school. When you read you have to follow the exact words in the book, so I would have to miss some words. Then the other kids would stare at me. I knew what the words were, but I just couldn't say them. I could say the words that started with vowels okay but the words that started with *th* and *sh* used to really stump me.

So I had all these little difficulties in my childhood. My problem with my teeth wasn't fixed until years later when I was a ward of the state after my mother died. I think my problems with my speech led to other little traumas in my early life such as bed-wetting. So I had to overcome that problem as well as often being sick with yellow jaundice. I always remember my younger brother Lawrence used to pick on me. He would sit on top of me and pin me down, and just laugh. He used to do this for years – and the other kids used to push me over too, because I had no strength at all. This went on until I finally started to get a bit of strength in my body when I was about ten years old.

One day Lawrence was sitting on top of me and I told him to get off, but he just laughed and sat down heavier on my arms. I was getting jack of this, so I started to get a bit wild, and yelled at him to get off me. He laughed again. The third time I told him if he didn't get off I'd throw him off.

As expected, he just kept laughing but I can tell you he soon stopped laughing when I threw him three foot high into the air! I pushed him off with every bit of strength I could muster. He ran away and I picked up an orange and I threw it as hard as I could at him. It hit him in the middle of the back and dropped him. I was that wild that I threw the orange with as much power as if it were three times the size.

From then on Lawrence never picked on me again. He always remembered that incident and told me never to lose my temper like that again! It scared the hell out of him to think that I could suddenly go from this little weakling to this strong man when I was angry. It made me realise suddenly that you can gain amazing strength from sheer willpower. Almost like you're gathering it up from the strong man Buthera, our creation ancestor from Point Pearce. I guess I had had enough of being picked on and bullied. Everyone gets tired of being the underdog.

I was a bit older and stronger by the time we moved around to Russell Street, in Ethelton. We used to get up to all sorts of capers in that house because we were left to look after ourselves a fair bit. We used to dig holes in the backyard because the Second World War was on, so we used to make our own bomb shelters. We would entertain ourselves all day, all us kids together. This was when my mother met Damiano, the Italian wharfie, and had her last four children. I was the oldest, so I used to help look after the little kids. There was always a baby in the house, so I was kept pretty busy. Lawrence was like the father, because he used to cook the meals, while I was like the mother looking after the baby. That's how we seemed to live for a while – which was an unusual thing really, but we managed.

To tell you the truth, I don't know what my mother did during the day, but I know she wasn't working. She was a very wise woman, and a lot of other women used to ask her for advice. She was also an expert at knitting and crocheting, and she would often be asked by friends to finish off difficult patterns. She had lots of friends, and I know she used to visit them and spend a fair bit of time playing cards to earn a bit of money. She liked playing cards.

My mother would always come home in the evening, and we'd eat our meal together and be looked after by her. Damiano was also there at night. I think my mother was pretty unwell around then. She married Damiano when she got very sick. I think she was worried about who would look after her children if she could no longer care for us all. She wanted him to be the legal father. She hadn't married earlier because there was a lot of prejudice against the Italians during the Second World War, which worried her. She didn't want the family to suffer the discrimination that would come with having an Italian surname.

But she finally married Damiano in 1944 and took his Italian surname. This was just before she got *really* sick. I remember that Damiano used to take all us kids around because he had a motor car. We used to go to the trots and all over the place. But really we were pretty limited in how far we could go, because there were seven kids in tow by then. And he had a dog.

I lost a chunk of my childhood when I was left at home to look after the younger ones. I was forced to grow up before my time and missed some of the experiences I needed as a youth. I had the responsibility of looking after children, when I should have been mixing with kids my own age.

In mid 1942, when I had just turned twelve, my mother became very ill with a severe kidney infection and had to go to hospital. So Lawrence and I were left to our own resources to look after the rest of the family. I'm not sure where Damiano was, but he wasn't around looking after us kids. We were all on our own for a number of days. Eventually it got to the stage where we were really in a bad way, because the youngest was just a baby, and it was pretty hard for me and Lawrence and Joy to manage. The neighbours would have known what was going on, so maybe they let Welfare know. While there was an adult in the house at night the neighbours thought we were alright, but when they noticed there was no parent turning up at night, they realised we were living on our own. So they started watching a bit closer and thought they better tell Welfare – which was good, I suppose. You've got to watch out for the well-being of children.

When the welfare department heard they came and picked all us kids up. I don't know how all the legal stuff worked out, because when you're a kid a lot of the detail goes straight over your head. But I do remember going to court and the judge asking me questions. I was the oldest, so I had to answer. He asked me how we managed and what we ate. He asked me, 'What did you have for breakfast?' and I replied, 'Weet-Bix.'

'What did you have for dinner?'

'Weet-Bix.'

Then he asked, 'What did you have for tea?'

'Weet-Bix,' I said again.

So that's what we lived on – Weet-Bix. You know the

funny thing is that even now I still eat Weet-Bix for breakfast every day!

There was even a piece in the daily newspaper about us, saying that seven kids had been picked up by Welfare in a really bad state. The headlines said: 'Family of 7 Neglected, Port Court Told'. The reporter must have attended the court hearing because he quoted some of the things I told the judge.

> Some bread, jam, and butter were on the kitchen table. In a cabinet was a decayed cabbage, and the remains of a meat joint which was green with mildew.
>
> The eldest boy, 13, said that on the previous day they had cereals at every meal.
>
> He said his 11-year-old brother [Lawrence] did the cooking adding, 'He's a pretty good cook: he made a cake last week.'

After that the family was all uprooted. They took us away from my mother because they said we weren't being looked after. In the court I was charged with being 'destitute' and some of my half siblings were on the charge of being 'neglected and under unfit guardianship'. See, in those days it was common for Aboriginal kids to be taken away by Welfare. My mother probably didn't let anyone know we were on our own because she wanted to keep us all together for when she got better and came home. She probably thought she wouldn't be in hospital for too long. But as it turned out, all seven of us kids were taken away anyway.

What stands out most in my memory of this period in my life is always being on the move, and always feeling unwanted. No one wanted to take on seven kids, so Welfare had to place us with whichever foster family would take us. Welfare had also told Damiano that he couldn't work and look after seven children. It proved particularly difficult for them to find anyone who wanted a teenage boy like me, who supposedly 'ate like a horse'. Initially Lawrence and I went to Glandore Boys' Home, also known as the Industrial School. Joy, Angelina and Merle were fostered out with a woman in Richmond called Mrs Bigley[2], but eventually all three girls were fostered out to different places. My brother Angelo went to the Woodville Hearing Centre because he was deaf. My youngest brother Lee, who was just six months old, went to Seaforth Orphanage, south of the city at Brighton by the sea.

Legally I became a ward of the state and therefore in the care of Welfare until I reached eighteen years of age. Altogether I lived with three different families and in two institutions for boys between the ages of thirteen and eighteen. Lawrence and I were always on the move because of the different emotional problems we had developed. We'd find ourselves continually being returned to the boys' home when things didn't work out with the different families. It seems the fifteen shillings a week that the Children's Welfare Department paid the foster families to keep me just wasn't enough incentive.

After spending some time in the Glandore Boys' Home, Lawrence and I were fostered out to a Mrs Haddock[3] at Klemzig. Fortunately Joy was placed with Mrs Haddock's sister, who lived relatively close by, so we got to see a bit of her. I had a bit of a problem with bed-wetting, so Mrs Haddock sent me back to the boys' home at one stage. But poor Lawrence got so upset about being separated from me that Mrs Haddock agreed to take me back again. I often wondered whether I should have shown more emotion and cried like Lawrence used to. Maybe that way I would have been placed in a home where I felt more wanted and settled. At one stage, in despair at my bed-wetting, they sent me to a doctor, and he recommended that I get circumcised. So there I was, an Aboriginal kid getting circumcised at

---

2 I am using this name as a pseudonym.
3 Again I am using this name as a pseudonym.

an age when most other Aboriginal kids in remote communities go through the law and get circumcised. I'm not sure if it solved my bed-wetting problem.

There was one time when Angelo and our half-sister Merle were placed together with Mrs Bigley at Richmond, but that was just for a short time. Mrs Bigley must have taken a shine to Merle, I guess, because she was younger and cute looking. Anyway, she always got to live in the front of the house with the rest of the Bigley family, but when her two older sisters Joy and Angelina were with them they had to stay out the back, as did Angelo when he stayed there. So even though they were living together in the same household, they were mostly isolated from each other. Later Merle and Angelo were together again with Mrs Bigley, but this time they were living at Semaphore. During this period Angelo went to LeFevre Primary but he was ridiculed because of his disability. Not long after this Angelo went to live at Townsend House, which was a home for deaf children at Hove in the southern suburbs.

So, as kids we didn't get to spend much time all together once we were taken in by Welfare, which was pretty difficult for us to cope with at times. In fact we didn't connect up as a family until forty years later, because it took that long to find Lee. That was at his wedding when he had turned forty.

A while after we were put into care, my mother was released from hospital, but she was still weak with high blood pressure and an advanced kidney condition. As soon as she got out of hospital she started enquiring after us kids. Despite her illness she fretted for us and went to Welfare and asked for us older three (me, Lawrence and Joy) to be released back into her care. She said she couldn't cope with the younger four as well. Welfare was pretty strict in those days, so she had to prove that she was well enough to look after us older three. She had to fill in this form that described what sleeping arrangements she had for us, and prove we'd each have our own bed. She also had to put down a ten shilling deposit on a bath so we could adequately wash ourselves. I think my mother felt us older ones would manage between us, and we could help her too.

The official reason she wrote on the Welfare form for wanting us older ones to be 'released' into her care was 'Mother's love: am fretting for them'. When I first read that in my Welfare records recently, I thought what she wrote was really moving. In retrospect, I think they let us older ones go back with her because they thought that my mother didn't have much longer to live.

According to the Welfare records, the Probation Officer wrote about my mother:

> Mrs O'Brien frequently and persistently enquires regarding the welfare of her children. Although careless of their upbringing in the past she has a genuine affection for them, and the action taken by this Department appears to have made her realise her responsibilities as their mother. According to her doctor, providing the utmost care is taken, she will be able to carry on the home and the care of these three children ... Mrs O'Brien is not strong enough to cope with the little children.

Unfortunately we were only back with my mother for a short while before she started to get weaker and weaker. Her kidneys were failing. She couldn't look after us properly, and we couldn't really look after her. So I went to stay with this lady down the end of the road, and Lawrence and Joy went to stay in their foster homes. I suppose my mother was happy about me being down the road because she could still see me. But I really only have vague recollections of all the details about this difficult period of my childhood. I'm not quite sure how often I saw her at this stage. I was struggling to deal with my living arrangements.

My mother was never a very strong woman because she

had scarlet fever as a kid. A lot of people had scarlet fever in those days. She had very thin hair – that's one of the repercussions of having scarlet fever. After we were put into care again my mother just got weaker and then she had a haemorrhage. She eventually died on 2 November 1944, nearly two years after she first got sick, at only thirty-seven years old.

It was inevitable that us kids would end up being wards of the state – and with my mother's passing our fate was sealed. Damiano didn't look after us after my mother died. In fact he wanted us to look after *him*, later on, which was funny. He used to come out to Kumanka Boys' Home when I was living there. The woman who ran it used to try to run him off. She told me, 'This bloke wants you to look after *him*!' She wasn't going to allow that, so she told him to get going. He was a funny bloke, he wasn't bad to us or anything, but he just wasn't there much for us when Mother was around, nor when she was gone. He'd be on the wharf working, and coming home late at night. He did provide us with some money and food, but even then it was irregular – at his whim and fancy. I remember fainting in the school yard once, and hearing the teacher say, 'Give him some air – he's fainted with the heat.' I remember wishing that I just had something to eat. We went without food a lot, even though we were supposedly living in a family. But I shouldn't talk too much about Damiano, and what he didn't do. He was a funny bloke, and I really don't know how to sum him up.

Once my mother was gone, us seven kids were permanently separated. My half-brother Lawrence and I eventually got fostered out to these people at Felixstow, north of Adelaide. This bloke had a property out there and we used to look after his chickens and fruit trees and gladiola flowers. I must have been a bit older by then, getting close to fourteen. So I could work for my keep.

I went to Payneham Primary School when I lived there – for

the end of grade seven. I always remember going to that school because I was going to Ethelton Primary before that for some of my final year of primary school. One teacher at Payneham used to mumble at me because the teachers were worried about us kids passing our qualifying certificates. I think the teachers were judged on the results of their students. This particular teacher was worried I wouldn't pass, and he used to harass me so much that when I was sitting the final exam I cheated on a maths sum. When I got the results back I saw that the only question I got wrong was the one that I'd cheated on. I had it right myself in the first place! I mistakenly thought this other kid knew more than me.

That experience taught me an important lesson. So cheating was something I only did once in my life, and it was only due to the pressure from this teacher. He used to say to me, 'You'll never pass, O'Brien. You'll give me a bad mark . . . and I haven't got time to teach you.'

From Payneham school we used to go to East Adelaide Primary for woodwork, which is in St Peters. Not too many Aboriginal kids would have gone to that school, but some of my own kids went there when I got married and we lived in Hackney, including my eldest lad, Stephen.

I eventually went on to technical school to finish third year, which was called Intermediate in those days. It was very unusual for an Aboriginal kid to go that far at school then. In fact it was unusual for an Aboriginal kid to be in high school at all. I went to LeFevre Technical School, which is on the peninsula just north of Port Adelaide, and sat for my Intermediate in 1946.

Most kids who lived around the Port only completed primary school, so when LeFevre Technical School started in 1942, it was quite a new concept. Most kids left after primary school to go and work, so someone thought it would be a good idea to give technical skills to kids before they went to work. It was only because of the progressive headmaster Mr Fred Vicary, at LeFevre, that we poorer kids were able to afford to continue to go to school.

We used to get three pounds each from a government allowance for our schooling, but that wouldn't cover all our costs to go to technical school – it wouldn't cover costs for all your metal work, woodwork, books and everything. The only reason we got to stay at school was because of Mr Vicary's innovation. He thought that rather than us buying our books he would hire them out to us. It was a rather clever and innovative idea for those days. So he'd buy these books on consignment, and we'd just pay him so much from each class. Eventually he managed to pay them off over a number of years. We'd give the books back at the end of the year, and he just had to replace the ones that wore out. He was a very astute principal to think up that scheme. But it was for his own survival as well, because if he hadn't thought of it he wouldn't have had any students, would he? LeFevre was a poor area.

I remember my mother taking me to LeFevre Technical School to enrol. That must have been just before she passed away, when I was still at Ethelton Primary. I think she was pretty chuffed about me going to high school, because it was so unusual for an Aboriginal kid. Some people didn't know we were Aboriginal though, because of our light colouring. But most people knew and didn't say much about it. We did get remarks sometimes though. Unfortunately people acted like that in those days.

A few years later, for example, when I got an apprenticeship with the railways, this bloke said to me, 'You're different to all the other kids.' See the state government had signed this agreement with the railways that allowed me to be indentured as an apprentice. So I used to get all these funny quips behind my back, and people would make these little remarks on the side.

So from an early age, particularly when we moved to the city, I learnt that we were different from all the rest. I soon found that there were actually very few of us Aboriginal people living in the city in those days. Most people were still living on remote missions and reserves. It wasn't really until the 1960s that Aboriginal people moved to live in the city.

Back in those early days, the Aboriginal people who did live in the city were living in different suburbs. A lot of them, I suppose, were hiding their true identity and denying their Aboriginal heritage, because of the discrimination they would have suffered otherwise. Many were exempted people, who were living as 'honorary' white people. They had received the right to be exempted from the government legislation that controlled the everyday lives of other Aboriginal people. So those early days in the city were a really awkward period for many of us.

Fortunately, after my stint at Felixstow, I finished up back in the Port Adelaide area living with a widow named Mrs Pues[4]. This meant I could attend LeFevre Tech. Mrs Pues lived in Company Street, Semaphore. She was not very well off, so taking in a boarder was seen as a sensible way to supplement her pension. However, the amount paid by Welfare was not adequate, and Mrs Pues was continually writing letters complaining that her allowance was nowhere near enough to clothe and feed a boy of my age. Eventually they came to some arrangement whereby Welfare paid for my clothes, and Mrs Pues just had to feed me. However, it was still a struggle. Eventually Mrs Pues' health failed and I had to be placed somewhere else.

During the Christmas school break the department would send me off on holidays with other foster families while they tried to work out where to place me the following year. One

4 This name is a pseudonym.

year I went to stay with the Little family at Penneshaw on Kangaroo Island, just off the tip of Fleurieu Peninsula. That was quite an adventure for me, but the holiday was overshadowed by the worry of where I would be sent to next.

After Mrs Pues, Welfare found me another foster family – this time an older couple, who I shall call the Betts[5]. They lived in Russell Street in Ethelton, so I was again back in familiar territory. The Betts were German people, but I think they changed their name before the war. It was common for Germans to do that because there was ill-feeling and prejudice in the community against them. I thought it was funny because during the war time they rounded up many of the Germans, but not Mr Betts. He had been made a special constable in the police force. How I knew this was that he showed me his special little silver revolver that he'd been given for the job. I don't know if he was left alone during the war because he changed his name or because they knew him so well in the community. I remember Mrs Betts' first name was Annie, but I forget the old bloke's name. I just used to call them Mr and Mrs Betts.

While I was at LeFevre Tech, and living with the Betts, I used to captain the school cricket team. Our team used to go down to Hart Street and be coached by Clarrie Grimmet, who played for Australia in the 1930s. I also captained the basketball team, and played footy for the school.

By the time I moved in with the Betts, the war was over and I was attending LeFevre Tech. I didn't know it at the time, but Mrs Betts wasn't too happy about having me. I only know this now because I have all my records from the welfare department. I've been able to read all the correspondence and communication that went on between my foster parents and the department. Maybe I knew *some* of the goings on then, but

---

5 I am using a pseudonym, instead of their real name.

I tended not to remember some of the more negative things that happened in my early life. I think I blocked them out.

Like Mrs Pues, Mrs Betts struggled to keep me on the money offered by Welfare, and complained about the state of my clothing. It was up to the department to clothe me and I remember Mrs Betts used to tell me all the time that I was eating like a horse. Reading my file from Welfare now, all the letters from the foster families said the same thing basically – that they wanted more money to keep me. Mrs Betts was trying to scrimp and save on what she got because she had her own family to keep as well as a husband who wasn't well. At one stage she wanted me to go out and get a job so I could pay one pound a week for board. She perhaps thought it was odd that she had to look after an Aboriginal kid who was still going to technical school at the age of fifteen, when none of her kids still attended school. Getting an education wasn't in her line of thinking, and her husband was no different.

Welfare actually wrote to the principal of LeFevre Tech, Mr Vickery, asking him whether he thought there would be any value in me staying on at school to complete my Intermediate certificate. Fortunately Mr Vickery knew the value of education, and he strongly urged Welfare to allow me to remain at school.

It's funny the details you remember from that long ago, because I remember having this strange conversation at the kitchen table one day in the Betts' home. I think it was at breakfast time and old Mr Betts, a pretty clever bloke, said to me, 'What's all this *a* and *b* stuff you do in maths at school?' I guessed he was talking about algebra. But I wondered why he wanted to know about algebra. I wasn't used to answering those sorts of direct questions, so I didn't quite know how to answer him. To me algebra was like mental exercise, so how could I explain to him what it was all about? I thought it was strange that Mr Betts, who could fix any machine in the

Schembri's factory next door that made cool drinks and ice-creams, was worrying about what the *a*s and *b*s in algebra meant. I knew he could fix anything because I used to go with him as a helper.

I used to go out to Mr Betts' workshop in his backyard and cut out and make wooden models with his wood lathe. He also had a large number of spanners and other tools and used to keep up with the latest inventions. It seemed to me that he had missed out on a lot of schooling. He was the type of bloke who should have been encouraged to stay on at school – just like me. So he was genuinely asking what on earth these *a*s and *b*s were all about in algebra.

I suppose Mr Betts was not only questioning the value of algebra – he was also questioning the value of a kid like me going on in school. With all the grumbling from his wife about me not being out there working like other kids my age, I suppose he wondered why this Aboriginal kid's going to school, and my kids aren't.

But he was missing the point. Opportunities in life shouldn't be limited by where you come from or who you are. It's who you are as an individual that counts. See people in those days, and even today, want to generalise – they want to say one group's better than another, or some individual is better than the rest, or some people deserve a better education than others.

So for Mr Betts the algebraic concepts of *a*s and *b*s were a hurdle for him. Whether you explained it to him properly or not, he couldn't understand it and he couldn't get beyond it. I see algebra as a metaphor for him and his understanding of life. Not many people he knew had gone to secondary school, and their understanding of life was pretty basic. Everybody and everything had their place and value and there were no variables, while *a* and *b* are variables. Mr and Mrs Betts accepted their place in the world as working-class people. As far as

Joe Edwards, champion
Point Pearce sportsman
and captain of the
football team.

My aunt Ethel Simpson,
Alice Smith, and my
grandmother Julia
Simpson (right) in
about 1918.

May Adams nee Edwards,
Lewis Adams' wife, 1939.

Lewis Adams, my grand-
mother's brother, 1939.

Auntie Gladys Elphick, my
mother's first cousin, 1939.

My mother, Gladys O'Brien,
and her sister Vera Smith,
probably at Moonta in the
1930s.

With my brother Lawrence (right) in about 1933.

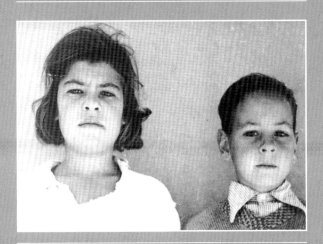

With my cousin Jean Smith at Point Pearce, 1939.

I'm in the Ethelton primary school band, aged perhaps ten.
I played the flute.

Fifth engineer on a Shell tanker in the Pacific, 1953.

With my wife, Pauline O'Brien, in the 1990s.

With my fellow South Australian winners of Australian of the Year awards (for 2003), in 2002. From left: Peter Smith (accepted for Lleyton Hewitt), Professor Barrie Vernon-Roberts, Dr Marie O'Neill, me, and George Slattery.

Giving a Kaurna welcome in recent years.

Here I am in the entrance to the State Library, with the feature artwork by internationally renowned textile artist Kay Lawrence AM, in collaboration with local graphic designer John Nowland. The work is inspired by the use of string games to indicate one way that knowledge is communicated – through gesture and observation – in Kaurna culture. The circular sculpture on the floor near the door is engraved with information on this process, along with an acknowledgement that the State Library was rebuilt on Kaurna territory at the beginning of the 21st century, and my words of welcome in 2003: 'First I welcome you all to my Kaurna country, and next I welcome you to the State Library of South Australia. My brothers, my sisters, let's walk together in harmony.'

they were concerned, the sooner their kids could leave school and get out and earn money, the better. They couldn't accept that a kid like me should be bettering himself through education. To them my place in life and my value to the community was set the day I was born an Aboriginal kid to a mother who was deserted by her white husband.

One of the Betts' kids was the same age as me and he had already left school to work for Bronson Drycleaners. You see the legal school-leaving age in those days was much younger than it is now. It's sixteen years now in South Australia, after the Labor government increased the minimum age from fifteen in 2003. But most kids in those days living in the Port Adelaide area left school after grade seven in primary school, if they found employment, when they were just twelve or thirteen years old. For the Betts family, being Germans, they believed in hard work. They'd often say *'Arbeit macht das leben sü'* meaning, 'Business is the salt of life'.

Besides hard work, they also liked music, so they got me to join the ex-naval band while I was living with them. Another lad who was also living with them joined too and became the drummer. I played the tuba, which was a brass instrument almost bigger than me. The Betts took their work ethic and their music very seriously, and if we didn't practise they cut crook at us. Mr Betts wanted me to bring my instrument back to the house to practise. So I used to play back at home, and the whole place seemed to rattle, which I used to get embarrassed about.

I must have been pretty insecure about things then, because I didn't want to upset them or disturb them with my music practice. I was at the mercy of the foster families who took me in and let me stay on at school. The Betts didn't mind or worry how loud my music practice was, but I didn't know that. That was the thing – I didn't know what they worried about, and whether I was bothering them. I only

119

wanted to feel safe and to be able to stay living in the one house. So I used to worry that the tuba was too loud – 'boom, boom, boom, boom' setting the whole house vibrating.

But Mr Betts actually wanted me to play and practise. He was proud of my playing. Even the band leader loved my playing, because he seemed to think that I was able to play at the right time. He thought the tuba gave the band balance. But when I told him I wanted to give it up, he said, 'Why?' So I explained that I couldn't read the music, and I didn't know when to come in.

He told me, 'Don't worry about that; you'll know what to do.'

I thought this was pretty funny, because I just couldn't understand what was on the page. He wanted me to just come in and play when I felt I needed to come in. He reckoned the band sounded terrific and that my instrument gave depth to the other instruments. But I was just embarrassed.

He used to love it, this band leader, standing up the front waving his baton and looking at me to signal the 'boom, boom, boom, boom'. Yeah, I guess it was terrific.

One tune we used to play was called 'The Protector'. Once I asked the leader what the protector was and found out that the *Protector* was the biggest battle cruiser in the country. I was in an ex-naval band so naturally we were playing a march written in memory of this big ship that used to guard us. In the 1870s the South Australians had this thing about the Russians coming, so this big battle cruiser used to chuff up and down the gulf with these guns. Eventually the guns were put in front of the old clock down on the beach at Semaphore. We used to sit on them when we were kids. Its amazing to think that these guns were off that big old ship the *Protector*. Sometimes you find out about your history through the strangest means.

I gave away the band-playing because it was too embarrassing. And I couldn't fathom the music. Band was another hurdle that I didn't want to deal with. I had enough trouble in my life without worrying about quavers and crotchets. I could play the scales and understand them, but all the other jazz involved in reading music was too much. To me reading music was like the algebra that stumped Mr Betts. I needed someone to explain it to me, but I was too shy to ask. I could play the tuba, and come in at the right time, but I didn't understand the written music.

When I was still at LeFevre Tech, I had this niggling feeling that the teachers never expected me to do well – this was in spite of the encouragement and support I used to get from the principal Mr Vickery. All my life, whenever I did things well, I had the feeling people were thinking, how the hell does this kid do this? I have this theory that I was always learning from my own people, like Auntie May and Uncle Lewis, and transferring what they taught me across to what I was doing at school. Yet there were certain skills that I needed for school that continued to elude me.

I was struggling in English at LeFevre and I started thinking to myself, how come those two boys are better than me? So I decided to watch what they did, and to do exactly what they did to see if it would help me with my English. I noticed that they were reading the *Champion* comic series, so I said to myself, right, I'll read those books – they seem easy to read and short. So I did, and to my surprise it seemed to help. My grades actually improved, and some kids even wanted to copy my work. I reckon it was the extra reading that helped.

I also worked harder on my homework. With some other kids in the class, I worked out a homework scheme that turned out to be really terrific. At one stage there were a number of us who caught the train to school, so we used to swap notes while we travelled. It wasn't cheating, we were helping each other. Word got around, and everyone wanted to join our homework group, so we started to arrive early at school to help each other before classes started. There were thirty-eight kids in the class, and nearly all of us were there in the morning, working on our maths homework, or whatever else we were having trouble with. You see, homework done at home often only works for kids whose parents have the wherewithal to help. Whereas people coming from a disadvantaged position, like me and many other kids in our class, just didn't have any support or help at home.

So there we were, almost the whole class early to school doing our homework together. Yet the school didn't change its homework policy. There we were actually demonstrating to the teachers that there was a better way to handle homework for disadvantaged kids, but they still continued to set us homework, and expected us to do it by ourselves at home. Our teacher wasn't too pleased about us helping each other – he thought we were cheating.

Change takes a long time. Today they have homework centres set up in a lot of disadvantaged schools, and they bring tutors in to help the kids do their homework after school. Back then our teacher let our morning sessions go on, but we didn't get too much encouragement. And there was definitely no change of policy. It was so ingrained that homework was to be done at home, no matter what your circumstances. Maybe the teachers knew all that and just didn't expect us disadvantaged kids to do well. Who knows?

8

Leaving school and doing an apprenticeship

When I was about to finish my third and final year at LeFevre Tech the school counsellor gave me a questionnaire to fill out about careers. When I'd finished he said, 'I don't know what to suggest to you, O'Brien. You've ticked everything on this paper.' He suggested the best thing for me might be to sit for the South Australian Railway's entrance exam. I thought that was an interesting suggestion, so I went to Brookman Hall, in the School of Mines on North Terrace[1], and sat for the exam with 400 other kids. Out of the 400 kids I think 100 kids were interviewed, and out of the 100 kids interviewed 67 got apprenticeships. So it was really only a sixth of the original group who got apprenticed. It was quite competitive to get a job with the Railways in those days.

I was lucky and I was offered an apprenticeship as a fitter and machinist. To do my fitter apprenticeship I had to go to Islington, where they trained the apprentices in the metropolitan area. The Islington rail yards are north-west of the central city square of Adelaide. We had to learn how to work with finely tuned machinery and I was amazed how the tools we used could measure to a millionth of an inch. At first it was mind boggling, because I didn't know these kind of tools and machines existed. We had to learn to work in thousandths and hundredths.

---

1 The School of Mines later became the Institute of Technology, and is now the City East campus of the University of South Australia.

I was fortunate because Islington was one of the better places to train. They had the technical school on site, where they offered special classes in maths and drawing, mechanics, science and heat engines. We also did another subject called trade theory, but to do that we used to have to go to the Trade School in Kintore Avenue in the city. They had some pretty interesting teachers there. One I'll always remember was Mr Wood. In our first year we had this old bloke who was a tradesman, but he wasn't a very good teacher because the kids used to muck up and he didn't know how to handle it. They used to say that we were bright, but we were also active as well, and rather difficult to manage sometimes.

But for our second year we got this Mr Wood, who was American and had been a wrestler – he was a huge man. One day we were mucking up a bit, so he started storming up and down the front of the classroom. He was getting upset with us and bellowed, 'I'll break an arm!' That made us quiet.

At the time I had this little fad of writing poetry, so the next week I went into the classroom about half an hour before Mr Wood's class started, and I wrote a poem on the blackboard. It was the sort of blackboard where you have two boards, one sliding up behind the other. So I wrote my poem up on one board and then slid it behind the other. I wrote:

There was a man called Wood
Who'd break an arm if he could
For days and days we'd utter this phrase
I wonder if he would if he could!

Mr Wood came in and started his lesson. We had an agreement with him: to make our lessons more bearable, he agreed that he'd start the lesson by telling us jokes and stories about his days as a wrestler and grid-iron player. And then for the last half an hour he'd teach the subject and we'd write like mad. When people would walk past the class and hear the carry-on, they'd say, 'Oh, that's the Islington kids,' because we'd be all rowdy and laughing. But we used to come out of class with our fingers aching because we used to go like mad for the last half hour copying notes down at full speed. It was a good agreement.

Anyway on this particular day, we were in this second half of the lesson and into this work zone, so there was silence. We were working furiously and Mr Wood was writing on the board, and telling us about the theory of something-or-other, when suddenly he pulls the board down, and there's the poem up there for all to see. We all started laughing, then he laughed because he appreciated the joke. After that, I used to go in early every week and write a poem on the board. Halfway through the lesson he'd pull the board down and see the poem of the week. One week he said, as he saw the latest poem, 'Ah! The phantom poet strikes again!' This went on for weeks, with me thinking of a new amusing poem each time.

The kids all used to laugh because it was pretty funny, but no one knew who the phantom poet was; no one had picked it was me. Anyway, one day Mr Wood came in and pulled the board down, and as expected there was another bit of poetry, and he said, 'I've had it, that's the end! The phantom poet's written for the last time! I'm going to get the principal and iron this out.' And so he went to the door and walked out. Meanwhile I'm sitting there in my seat feeling panicky. I thought, well, the best thing to do is get rid of the evidence, so I rushed to the board to rub it all out before the principal arrived. But all of a sudden Mr Wood sneaked back through the door to catch the phantom poet destroying the evidence. Now remember, he was a big man, so he came up and stood behind me and called out, 'Gotcha! So you're the phantom poet!' I nearly pissed my pants in fear!

Everyone got a real shock when they saw it was me, because they didn't have a clue who it was. When Mr Wood retired that year, the one thing he wanted was all the poems to be written up in a book. I couldn't remember them all myself, but the other kids could so they helped me make the book for him. Mr Wood was rapt.

I had another memorable encounter with Mr Wood before he retired. At one stage he was getting fed up with some of us boys arriving late for class, so he told us that anyone who came in late would be sent straight home. Now as I said, I used to come in early and write up the poem, then duck out again and come back later. So one day in 1947, I went to the classroom and wrote up my poem and then ducked out again to look at these flower displays they had along North Terrace between Kintore Avenue and King William Street. They've got all these statues along there now, and other sorts of encumbrances, but at this time there was lawn and flower displays, and a bridge that you could stand on to look at the flowers. The bridge was on the corner of Kintore Avenue, just in front of the War Memorial. They've taken the bridge away now. On this day I got distracted looking at these flowers from the bridge. I'd heard this new lateness rule but I got so engrossed looking at these flowers, and the gardeners laying them, that I forgot the time.

Suddenly I realised how late it was getting, so I raced down to the Trade School and poked my head around the door of the classroom. The lesson had started and there was this hush in the classroom, because they knew what was going to happen. I was about to be sent home. But I guess you learn to be quick-witted when you have to be, because I didn't want to be sent home. So I started to play the idiot, and charged into the classroom making out I had just had an encounter with the warrior Horatio. 'Sir! I met Horatio on the bridge and I fought him back with my sword!' And I ended up going through this nonsense, with my ruler as a sword, and saying things like, 'Get back you fools!' while pretend sword-fighting across the room. Everyone was cracking up watching me but all Mr Wood said was, 'Sit down!' He must have thought it was amusing, because he didn't send me home!

The two well-known Aboriginal identities, Charlie Perkins (now passed away) and John Moriarty, both went through the same system as I did, but later. They went to Ethelton Primary and then LeFevre Tech. Unfortunately they weren't at LeFevre in Mr Vickery's time, because he was a good influence on kids like me, but it's interesting, isn't it, the history you share with some people. Charlie and John weren't locals like me, they were sent down from the Northern Territory for schooling. John was one of the stolen generation living at Croker Island in Arnhem Land, while Charlie was from Alice Springs. They both ended up staying at Glanville Hall, which was called St Francis Boys' Home then, and run by the Church of England at Glanville in the Port area.

There were three sorts of homes for wards of the state in the Port area in those days, mostly along the seafront. There was St Francis Boys' Home, Sutton's Boys' Home on the corner of Union Street and the Esplanade on Largs Bay, which was run by Mr Sutton[2], and also St Joseph's, run by the Catholics, on the corner of Harrold Street and the Esplanade, Largs Bay. This building later became the Kura Yerlo community centre in 1986. Before that it was the Aboriginal Community College.

Although I was on a bit of a merry-go-round in those days, moving from place to place, I never did end up in a boys' home in the Port area. Instead I was sent to the Glandore Boys' Home and another foster home. When I left school and started my apprenticeship, I guess they realised it was better for me to be closer to the city and my work at the Islington rail yards, so I was then sent to Kumanka Boys' Hostel.

2 Mr Sutton ran the boys' home independently.

Once the Second World War was over, there must have been more money around, and all these other homes were established to get kids into schools in the city. Some Aboriginal girls were sent to Mitcham Girls' Tech, and they boarded at the Salvation Army home on Fisher Street in Fullarton. Later others boarded at Tanderra Girls' Home in Parkside, and they attended Unley Girls' Tech in Wattle Street in Malvern[3]. So all these other homes were started and things were slowly changing. Australian authorities were starting to realise that educating Aboriginal children was a good idea. See this was the era of assimilation. I think it's disappointing that the Aboriginal kids were always sent to the technical schools though. The government assumed that the best thing for all Aboriginal kids was to prepare them to learn a trade. It took Charlie Perkins to show them that it was possible for an Aboriginal person to study at university. He was the first Aboriginal person to study at a university and he got an arts degree from Sydney University.

Technical schools offered a good education to those who wanted a trade, even though it was also possible to study subjects there that were publicly examined (PEB subjects). So some technical schools were on an equal par with other high schools – Mr Vickery proved that when I was there at school. See to get into university, or teachers' college, you had to sit for the PEB exams. Mr Vickery had seven students from LeFevre sit for their PEB exams, and they all passed with credits.

At one time when I was living in Hackney, the lad next door was going to Norwood Tech and his mother used to send him across to me for help with his homework. When he finally sat for his exams at Tech, he missed out on getting his Technical Certificate and he said to me, 'What am I going to do now?'

---

3 Unley Girls' Tech later became Unley Primary School in Malvern.

I said, 'Well, you can go and sit for the PEB.'

'No, that's harder,' he told me.

I explained, 'No, it'll be easier.'

'How do you work that out?'

'Well, when you go to Tech there's only 200 kids, so you've gotta be in the top hundred to pass. But if you go and sit for the PEB there's thousands, so it's better odds to be one of thousands rather than one of hundreds.'

He replied, 'Oh! Well I'll try.'

In the end, he got all but a supplementary right, so he just sat for the supplementary and eventually passed his PEB exams. Years later he became a school principal, so it just goes to show that through knowledge of the system, and with a bit of encouragement from others, many things are possible. He rang me not that long ago to congratulate me on getting the Local Hero Award on Australia Day here in South Australia in 2003.

You know, one thing that has helped me in life is the good advice I have been given along the way. What Mr Vickery told me when I was a lad was very sensible. Everyone needs that in life – good advice. Mr Vickery said to me, 'Whatever you do, lad, make sure you do three years of high school. What you do in your three years here will carry you through the rest of your life. It won't be all the education you'll need, but it'll give you the basis to build on.'

I found that he was right, and I did build on those three years. I became a fitter and machinist, through an apprenticeship with the Railways, then later I became an engineer at sea with the Merchant Navy. Eventually I went to Sydney and got Part A of the second-class engineering ticket, which allowed me to sail around the Australian coast. With that certificate I was also able to go to Papua New Guinea. Later I

---

4 This barge was a 100-ton motorised landing craft.

became first engineer on a barge[4] and travelled around Papua New Guinea, north of the Australian coast – and that was a heck of an experience.

The disappointing twist to all we have learned from schooling over the years is that the government, in all its wisdom, decided to abolish technical schools. They reckoned that high schools were better than technical schools, and could do a better job. I think they're finding out now that that was not quite right.

Two other people who gave me good advice in this period of my life were Mr and Mrs Lyndon. They ran Kumanka Boys' Hostel at 206 Childers Street in North Adelaide. Once I left the Betts in Port Adelaide, I was sent to live at Kumanka, just north of the city centre. When I was in the hostel I thought the Lyndons were excellent people, the way they looked after us kids. They both had nice ways about them, and I appreciated that.

Mrs Lyndon would call us in the morning to get out of bed, knowing we'd have to go to work. I wasn't used to having someone watch over me like that. She'd call out, 'Come along boys!' It was a nice place to live – a big, old two-storey house, with a tennis court next door and a gym. We had a boiler at the back that we used to stoke for the hot water system for showers.

As a ward of the state, when you turn eighteen years of age, you are meant to become independent and fend for yourself in the world. I was still at Kumanka when I was getting nearer to my eighteenth birthday, so I thought I would have to leave. I was in this real predicament because I was only earning twenty-seven shillings a week on my apprenticeship, and I knew I couldn't possibly live on that. I really wanted to complete my apprenticeship but most board in Adelaide at that time was thirty shillings a week, so I knew I didn't earn enough. I was very worried about my future.

I remember clearly, ever since mother died, feeling insecure and always worrying about where I would live. My life was always in someone else's hands; at the mercy of the Children's Welfare Department as to where I would live and whether I could continue my schooling or training. So when I was seventeen, I went to see my Auntie Gladys Elphick, who was living in the city at this stage. She was my mother's cousin. I wanted to talk to her about my predicament. Later Auntie Glad became a well-known activist who worked tirelessly for Aboriginal rights in this state. I went to see Auntie Glad to talk to her about always being moved and not feeling settled. Unbeknown to me, Miss Newman, who was a social worker from the welfare department, had already come and spoken to Auntie Glad. Miss Newman was a good person, and she had told Auntie Glad that my brother Lawrence wanted to come and live with her. Miss Newman was also Lawrence's social worker and she had earlier had a chat with him. Lawrence was always crying, so he made it quite clear to her that he wasn't happy. Mrs Newman asked him where he wanted to go and Lawrence said he wanted to stay with our aunt. So Auntie Glad said she was willing to take on Lawrence, and before long he moved in with her. But Auntie Glad already had her own family, so there really wasn't enough room for me as well. However, when I came to see her, she agreed that she would take me in too. But she said she'd need some time to get the sleep-out built on for us, so Lawrence and I could sleep there. She said it would take six months before the sleep-out was ready.[5] Sometimes I think I should have learnt to cry a lot like Lawrence – then I would have ended up with Auntie Glad a lot earlier.

So it was during this uncertain period that I sat down and had a long talk to Mr Lyndon at Kumanka. He had noticed

---

5 A 'sleep-out' was a common feature of many Australian homes. They were enclosed verandahs on the back or side of cottages that were used as an extra bedroom. They were notoriously cold in winter and hot in summer, being made of corrugated iron and windows of louvers, or in some cases just fly-wire.

that I was out of sorts and he wanted to help. I asked him if I could stay on longer at Kumanka until my aunt's sleep-out was ready. Mr Lyndon agreed that I should stay on for another year. But it was Welfare who was in charge, not Mr Lyndon, so I had to write to them and ask them if I could stay on there. I explained that after a year I'd be getting a better wage and would be able to contribute a little to my board with Auntie Glad. From her place, I'd just have to catch the train to North Adelaide to go on to Islington – so it seemed an ideal arrangement. And I'd be with family again too.

Unfortunately, Welfare didn't agree. So I got upset again, and thought that I would just have to leave my apprenticeship and go and get a job as a seaman. I had always had this dream of going to sea. The Lyndons noticed I was upset and so I told them that I thought I'd have to leave my apprenticeship and go to sea.

Mr and Mrs Lyndon sat me down and talked to me for four hours. They said, 'Look, it'd be better to get through this difficult time and finish your apprenticeship. Then you'll be able to fulfil your dreams of one day being an engineer and going to sea.' Mr Lyndon said he would write a letter to Welfare asking for me to stay at Kumanka until I could move in with my aunt. I also wrote them another letter and Welfare eventually gave permission for me to stay on at Kumanka Boys' Hostel for just two weeks after my eighteenth birthday. The day before my birthday Welfare wrote to Mr Lyndon declaring that I was no longer under the legal control of the department.

Eventually, Welfare agreed to pay my aunt ten shillings a week toward my board until I earnt enough to cover the cost myself in the third year of my apprenticeship. I contributed one pound a week from my own small wage.

This period of my life was a real battle financially, and very unsettling. But I listened to the Lyndons and thought what they told me made sense. Even though my brother

Kumanka Boys' Hostel
206 Childers Street,
North Adelaide
7th Nov, 1947

The Secretary
   Children's Welfare Dept.,
      Adelaide

Sir,

   Re Lewis William Arthur O'Brien
(your memo MB/KM of the 6th Nov.)

   I desire to submit the following report.

   Lewis is apprenticed as a fitter at the Islington Workshops. His present rate of pay is £1/2/9 per week: I believe he will obtain a rise of 5/- weekly next year.

   Lewis is a fine lad, and should establish himself in a good position at the end of his training.

   In view of his small earnings and the fact that the Board have apprenticed him, it is strongly recommended that consideration be given to obtaining an extension of his sentence until he attains the age of 19 years.

   Lewis and I have discussed the matter at length and the boy fully appreciates the position. Unless he received some assistance he could not possibly maintain himself.

         Yours faithfully,
            Harold S. Lyndon
               Supt.

L.W.A. O'Brien
206 Childers Street
North Adelaide
3rd Dec 47

The Secretary,
    Children's Welfare

Dear Sir,

I sat down to write this letter
two nights ago, but I was unsettled in my mind what I would
do. I did not know whether to keep my present job or go to sea.

I did not rush into any hasty decision, instead I discussed
the matter with Mr and Mrs Lyndon. Then the following
morning I went to my boss and talked to him about it.
Strangely enough what he told me was similar to what Mr
and Mrs Lyndon had already said. That it was silly to give
up my apprenticeship also I had every possibility of becoming
a First Class Tradesman.

I thought the matter out taking into consideration what I
had been told and have decided to carry on with my
apprenticeship. In my second year I will receive £1-13-0
and also I will turn 18. At 18 I will be free from the
Welfare. But I find I will not be able to support myself on
this small wage. If the Board can extend my time or do
something which will help me finish my apprenticeship I will
be greatly pleased. As I am quite certain that I wish to
continue my trade namely Fitter and Machinist, I trust my
application will be favourably considered.

Yours Sincerely
Lewis W. A. O'Brien

Lawrence was working and getting paid more (he used to get five quid a week) I knew that if I finished my apprenticeship I'd soon earn ten quid. Apprenticeships are hard. In those days, you needed to be in a family who could support you financially while you got your qualification. The low training wage didn't work for kids like me who weren't supported by their families. So I was disadvantaged from the start.

Anyway, I stuck it out and fumbled through but it was a very hard time. I used to go out with my brother Lawrence and his mates sometimes, and they knew I had no money. So they would think, 'Why's this bloke coming with us? He's got no money, and he doesn't support the group.' I used to get upset and stomp off. I had to ride on the back of their motorbikes as a passenger, and I found it embarrassing because they thought I was a bludger. I didn't put much money in because I didn't have any to put in. I'd tell them that, but they just used to say, 'Well, that's not our problem, it's yours.' So eventually I dropped out of things they were doing, which meant there were very few things I could do. After a while I nearly gave up my apprenticeship again.

Then one day I asked the kids doing the apprenticeship with me, 'Is there anything I can do that doesn't cost much?' They suggested this and that, but then one kid said to me, 'You ever thought of the library?' When I found out it didn't cost anything to go to the library I ran the two miles from North Adelaide to the State Library, on North Terrace, and joined up there and then and got some books out on loan straight away.

Libraries changed my outlook from a disillusioned seventeen-year-old to someone occupied and entertained by the adventures I found in books. I became an avid reader of books on a wide range of topics.

I soon found that a lot of people I knew didn't like reading books – yet they always wanted to ask me questions about what I knew from books. I discovered books more or less because of my situation, but I didn't realise that I would love reading so much. See, when I was younger I had a bad eye, and I found it hard to read for long periods of time because it would strain my eyes. I'd read for half an hour and then my eyes would ache, so I'd put the book down. It wasn't until I had my eyes tested in 1947 to join the Railways that I got glasses. Then I could read for any length of time without getting a headache.

I find it interesting how you can turn trials in your life around to work in your favour. Even though I was disadvantaged financially, I managed to take advantage of free books in libraries, which in turn provided me with extra skills and knowledge. I invented a game to play with myself. Most people go to the library and get books they like reading, but I got tired of just getting the books I liked. Eventually I'd read almost all the adventure books they had in the library so I read the classics like *Tom Sawyer*, and the comic series *Phantom, Speed Gordon* and *Dick Tracy*. Then I thought, I think I'll try reading books translated from other languages. So I read some German books and French books and a Polish book called *Quo Vadis*. The authors I liked were Thomas Mann, Andre Maurois, John Steinbeck and George Bernard Shaw. I used to read all the Nobel Prize for Literature winners.

Then I decided to challenge myself and read different subjects. I'd go to the psychology section and the philosophy section and then I'd change my tack again and try autobiographies and biographies. In the end I found that I knew that library backwards, and I learnt an awful lot. I even read a book called *The History of Mathematics* in four volumes. I'm sure Mr Betts would have thought I was completely crazy reading a book about numbers, and all about *a*s and *b*s, but really there wasn't much maths in them at all!

Most people that work in libraries are literary people, and they tend to only know about literature. They don't know much about the other sections such as the sciences and all the rest. I used to ask them for certain non-fiction books and they wouldn't have them. So I'd ask, 'When are you going to order them?' And they'd say, 'Well, we won't be.' So that was a bit annoying, and sometimes I used to have arguments with them about what they ordered.

The only place I could get some of the books that I knew were coming out was in the university library next door. The University of Adelaide is further along North Terrace, and it has the Barr Smith Library, which has a huge range of topics. Then next door again in those days was the library at the School of Mines, which also had all these other books that were useful if you were studying a trade. In those days the School of Mines was in the big old building on the corner of North Terrace and Frome Road, and people went there to get their certificates for their trade. The institutions have changed a lot over the years, but the building with Brookman Hall is still there.

It may seem unbelievable to those who know me now, but during this stage in my life when I was doing my apprenticeship, I actually stopped talking. These days, I have the reputation of being able to talk the leg off an iron pot, but I didn't always talk like hell. I'm not really sure why I stopped talking then, but I think I was becoming a bit of a loner, spending too much of my spare time by myself in libraries reading books. I think I was also feeling the discrimination that was around then against Aboriginal people. I remember talking to this lad once who was also doing his apprenticeship. After I'd been talking to him for an hour he asked me where I came from. Without thinking too much about it, I told him I came from Point Pearce.

'What are you, the missionary's son?' he said.

And I replied, 'Nah, I'm Aboriginal.'

He immediately got up and just walked away, and I was left sitting there stunned.

Then I started thinking to myself, every time I mention this word 'Aboriginal', people just walk away from me and don't want to know me. So in the end I found it was better to not say anything. I decided I just wanted to get on with what I was doing, because I really wanted to finish my fitter's apprenticeship. I thought, if I start speaking up, I'm not gonna achieve my goal.

Even the Master Apprentice used to say to me, 'You're not like the other kids; you're different.' I thought, heavens, you've got to be someone you're not, or they single you out as being different. I soon woke up to the fact that if I wanted to achieve in life I would have to be anonymous. So I used to sit with a group of kids and just listen as they chatted away about themselves.

One day one kid said, 'So what have you got to say about yourself? You know all about us but we know nothing about you.' I was scared witless of being put on the spot like that, and I didn't know what to say. The only thing that saved me was some old bloke who was listening in. He said, 'Oh, leave the kid alone, he's alright.'

After a few similar incidences, I stopped talking. Every time I talked I felt I'd get into strife, or there'd be someone to put me down. So I just found it was easier not to say anything. I looked European so I thought I'd just let people make the assumption that I *was* European.

So I went through this funny stage of not speaking, just nodding or using body language. And it wasn't just with the other apprentices that I stopped talking, it was in the boys' home and with my family too. This went on for quite a while. Even my Uncle Fred Elphick noticed. So when I was visiting Auntie Glad's one day my uncle banged his fist down on the table and shouted at me, 'It's about time you spoke!'

Suddenly I realised what had happened. It wasn't just that I wouldn't speak – I'd stopped speaking for so long I'd got myself into this dilemma of not being *able* to speak.

I found that when I did try to talk again, and wanted to say something, I couldn't. I suddenly realised that speech is a practised art and there's nothing logical in it. You have to practise saying 'g'day' every day. So I had to start practising saying things before I actually had to say them. I couldn't make off-the-cuff comments like people normally do. I had to make sure what I was going to say was right, and not let it come from the top of my head. When you're speaking all the time you just say things as they come out, and you don't have to think. Whereas for me, I found I had to start thinking about what I was going to say before I said it. Otherwise I'd end up saying something stupid.

So I went through this harrowing time of learning how to talk again. One thing that did help me was this book I was reading at the time about speaking. It was encouraging for me to read about some Chinese person who went through a similar experience. Then in contrast, I read about the French philosopher Rousseau who wrote about the boy Emile who talked too much. Rousseau said Emile should spend less time talking and more time thinking. So really I think we can learn from both situations. We learn that life is really about balance. We have to think about what we're going to say, and we should only talk when we need to. We should also learn to shut up when there's no need to talk. I guess I should listen to my own advice because, as I said, now I talk like hell!

Despite my financial and social problems, I stuck it out with the Railways and managed to finish my apprenticeship after six years. I became a qualified fitter and machinist, who was trained to work all the machines, such as milling machines, grinders, lathes, shapers, planers, boring machines etcetera. As a fitter I was trained to make and repair machines and line up gearboxes to motors, among other things. Once a person has got all these skills the Railways ends up with a multi-skilled person. With all my skills I was able to eventually join the Merchant Navy and go to sea, which was my dream.

But it took me six years to finish an apprenticeship that normally took only five. Because I earned so little money in the first years, I couldn't afford to buy clothes or anything. Luckily the blokes who were in charge of our training let me go up to the wine-growing areas on the Murray River to earn some money picking grapes. I used to get five quid a week and I thought I was a millionaire. But the time I spent earning extra money extended the time I took to finish my apprenticeship. I used to go up there for three months at a time to make a few quid. When I went back to the Railways, I'd tell them about my situation and they said, 'Oh yeah, we understand. It's OK to start again.' I did that trip away about four times.

Besides grape-picking, I used to go rabbiting, and bag-sewing on farms, or I worked in a fruit factory. I'd do anything and everything to make a few shillings. I'm really grateful to the Railways. They knew of my circumstances, and they knew I was dead keen. I wasn't the only one of us in these odd situations, so they made allowances for a lot of us kids. It was a very pleasing thing.

Sometimes when I think about my family, and all we went through in those early years, I find it pretty amazing that we turned out the way we did. We were on the move all the time with my mother, and then we were all separated when she passed away. I wonder how we all managed to turn out okay. People often ask me how I have managed so many varied and satisfying careers in my life after such a bad start. I put a lot of it down to the stability I found with Auntie May and Uncle Lewis, who were such wise people. I also had Auntie Glad in the city when I was older. They were all good people and a great moral support to me. But not all my half siblings had that contact, because I was the eldest in the family, and they never went to Point Pearce or knew Auntie Glad. Lawrence, for example, used to visit Point Pearce in those very early days with our mother, but he was probably too young to remember Auntie May or to be influenced by her. Unlike me, he probably wasn't so interested in his Aboriginal side in later years either. He knew Auntie Glad though because he moved in with her before I went there.

I've often wondered about how we survived the difficulties and I've realised that we were lucky to inherit some really useful skills from different members of our family. See, our mother was a pretty cluey person, but circumstances led her to live this unusual life. But she used to tell us principles, which we tried to live by. She used to see me playing with these different boys, and she'd say to me, 'Don't you listen to what they tell you to do; you do what I've taught you to do. They'll just tell you to do silly things.' And she was right. I soon realised it was better to listen to what the older people were saying, because they were there to help me and to teach me from their experience and knowledge.

But when you look at all my half siblings, and how they survived, I think we each inherited different skills that made us very resourceful in every stage of our lives. If you consider the disrupted beginning we had being left all on our own, we really had to become resourceful. But I also notice we each developed specific skills, and I think that's unreal. Lawrence and I both became machinists, and I became a fitter as well. Joy later worked in a warehouse and became very skilled at remembering and analysing all the coding. The manager used to have to take her with him when doing the ordering deals – she'd just look at the coding and if the bloke offered him ten shillings and six pence, the manager would just look at Joy and she'd say, 'Well, it's a good margin.' And she learnt to play the piano really well, which is a kind of coding.

Then there's Angelina who became a skilled seamstress, and could sew up coats and trousers just like that. She was good with her hands, just like our mother. As I said before, mother had very good knitting hands – she could knit twice as fast as anyone else, and everyone who knew her used to give her their difficult knitting patterns to finish off. She'd do it in no time, without any trouble. She only needed to look at the knitting pattern book once or twice, and then she'd remember the stitches and just go like hell. She could crochet, too, just the same. So Angelina picked that up from her. Then the next brother, Angelo, he had a hearing problem, yet he became a skilled clicker. People often don't know what these old specialist trades are anymore, but a clicker is someone who cuts out the upper leathers for boots and shoes. The youngest brother, Lee, became a computer whiz. So you can see the whole family picked up these technical and specialist skills.

I shouldn't forget Merle, who is the youngest girl in the family. She became a shorthand typist and receptionist, and then went to sea with the Merchant Navy. Merle is a very skilled researcher – in fact I know a lot of the detail of my family history because of Merle's meticulous research. She's very clever the way she finds things out so quickly. Merle was quick to locate our youngest brother, Lee, in his adult life. He was just six months old when he was taken into care, and Merle wasn't much older. Merle didn't even realise she had a baby brother until I told her years later, and we had all lost contact with him. So she immediately did some research to find him and that's how we all came to meet up forty-odd years later.

I think the key to us all surviving as individuals was the resourcefulness and resilience we inherited. I know I also got some help and advice on the way from some very wise and supportive adults, such as Auntie May and Uncle Lewis at Point Pearce, Auntie Glad in the city, Mr Vickery at LeFevre Tech, Mrs Newman from the Children's Welfare Department, and Mr and Mrs Lyndon from Kumanka. I am very grateful to them all.

9

Joining the Merchant Navy

I always had this boyhood dream to run away to sea and travel the world. I don't know why, but whenever people used to ask me the inevitable question: What do you want to do when you grow up? I would always answer that I wanted to go round the world. Some people never get to realise their dreams and goals in life, while others do. So I am one of the lucky ones, because when I joined the Merchant Navy I did get to travel the world.

I'd talked about my dream when I was going to LeFevre Tech, but I became even more determined about going to sea when I started my apprenticeship with the Railways. There were lots of us lads doing our apprenticeships saying that after we did our time we'd go to sea as engineers on ships. Initially there were twenty, I think, when we started talking about it, but then we saw the numbers gradually dwindle away. In the end there were only five of us who went to sea, and even then I nearly dropped off myself. I'm glad I didn't.

So when I was twenty-two years old I joined the Merchant Navy and went to sea for three years. The first two years were spent with the Shell Petroleum Company as an engineer on their big oil tankers. I travelled all over the world with Shell and have many lasting memories of my travels on those big tankers. One time that stands out in my mind is the time I went to Japan. It was there that I was forced to decide who I really was.

They often say that to truly understand and appreciate your own identity and culture you need to meet other people and experience other cultures. Well, so it was for me, and going to sea gave me that opportunity. When you travel, you are inevitably asked where you are from and where you grew up. So for me, I had to decide how to answer those questions. I was fair-skinned, and when I told people I was from Australia, they simply thought I was a white Australian. But I knew different.

As I said before, when I was doing my apprenticeship, I often struck prejudice, so I had decided it was easier for me to let people assume I was a white Australian than to cope with the inevitable discrimination. It wasn't fun having people move away from you if they knew you were Aboriginal, and leave you to sit by yourself to eat your lunch. So at that stage in my life, it was easier for me not to admit I was Aboriginal. Because I was so fair, it was easy – in fact it would have been harder to act otherwise. So I guess I decided to offload this so-called 'burden' of being Aboriginal in order to make my life happier and to succeed in my apprenticeship. All Aboriginal people had to deal with the discrimination in their own way in those days, so that was my way.

My Auntie May at Point Pearce used to tell me that if people say nasty things about you, just go 'Hrrmmpphh!' and walk away from 'em. You've got to forget what they say, and you've got to forget they're talking about you.

It's like that old philosophy: if you don't hear gossip, a thousand evils will pass you by. But it wasn't that easy for me as a young boy living in the city, when everybody around me was white. I couldn't run away from it all and escape back to the mission. So if people assumed I was white, I was happy to go along with that. But these things tend to catch up with you and when you come to travel overseas, and you need a passport, your identity becomes very technical. Put simply, the issue of my identity caught up with me.

As I mentioned before, the day I arrived in Japan, we had just arrived at customs, and I had to show my passport to a

Japanese official. He looked at me and asked, 'What are you?' I replied that I was Australian. But when I said it, for some reason I went really red and felt very uneasy.

Even though I was telling this custom official the truth, I wasn't telling him the whole truth, so I felt awkward. It might have been because I suddenly saw the page on my passport, which had the place of birth as Point Pearce written on it.

This incident happened back when Aboriginal people weren't legally citizens of Australia, unless they were 'exempted' from the *Aborigines Act*, and made honorary whites. But none of my immediate family were legally exempted, not even my mother. Even though my mother was born in Edithburgh hospital on Yorke Peninisula, and lived for most of her life off the mission, she never applied to be an exempted person. If she had it would have meant she could no longer visit the mission without seeking permission from the mission super-intendent. She used to visit or stay at Point Pearce often, so exemption was out of the question. The only family member who applied for exemption was my Auntie Gladys Elphick[1], and she only did this because she wanted to visit her son Timmy Hughes when he joined the army in 1939. Otherwise she wouldn't have been able to see him off at the railway station when he left to serve overseas.

So my passport was saying indirectly (by mentioning my place of birth) that I was Aboriginal, yet there I was telling this custom official that I was an Australian citizen – not an Aboriginal person. Technically, I held this passport that stated that I *was* an Australian citizen, and appearance-wise I didn't look Aboriginal. But deep down I felt I wasn't an Australian

---

1 Auntie Gladys Elphick married twice. Her first husband was Walter Hughes of Point Pearce, and the father of her two sons Tim Hughes and Alf Hughes. It wasn't until she moved to the city as an exempted Aboriginal person that she married again and took on the name Gladys Elphick. Despite being exempted, she was a tireless campaigner for Aboriginal rights.

citizen, because I was an Aboriginal kid from an Aboriginal mother, and I had never been exempted to become an Australian citizen. So there were a lot of contradictions on that page in that small book.

When I declared to that Japanese customs official that I was an Australian, it was at a time in my life when I needed to affirm my identity. I felt uneasy denying it. I immediately thought of what the Bible said about Peter denying Christ, and knew how he felt. By denying my true identity, I was really denying my people.

When I was younger I didn't understand the system. I was too busy surviving and trying to stay on at school. But by the time I visited Japan I was older and things were different. I ended up saying to different custom officials that I was an Australian three times on three different occasions. Just like Peter in the Bible. Then one day I suddenly decided I wasn't going to call myself an Australian anymore. So from then on I started to say that I was an Aboriginal person.

Then people used to get shocked when I'd say I was Aboriginal. The only time I looked Aboriginal was when I was in shorts and you could see my skinny emu legs. So when I'd tell them I was Aboriginal, the white people around me would say, 'What are you on about? Why aren't you happy to be one of us?' They couldn't work out why I wouldn't want to be part of the dominant culture.

So it seemed as though my moment of truth came to me on that visit to Japan, when I realised that I could no longer deny my real roots and heritage. Up until then I had let the white people I mixed with assume I was a white Australian just like them. I decided that to deny being Aboriginal would also be denying where I grew up, and denying all the people who influenced me in my life, like Auntie May and Uncle Lewis. I said to myself, My people are an honest and spiritual people, thank you very much, and I'm not going to deny them anymore.

But you can't have it both ways in life. When I started to identify more openly as an Aboriginal person, I still got into a lot of strife. People would say, 'You'd have precious little Aboriginal blood in you,' or 'You don't look Aboriginal.' So I couldn't win, no matter which way I went. But these reactions got me thinking about what a funny world we live in. I felt like the odd one out. I grew up as an Aboriginal kid, yet I looked European, and eventually I found myself living and working among people on ships who knew nothing about Aboriginal people. So I was in this odd position through circumstance.

I decided I had to be who I really was, even though it caused all these funny comments. People would say things like, 'Why would you say you're Aboriginal? Why would you deny that you're Irish?' All I could tell them is that I didn't know my Irish father, so how could I be Irish in that sense? It was my Aboriginal mother and her family that I knew.

It was hard for people to understand. What I say now is that I can only be what I've grown up as, and I grew up as an Aboriginal kid. I learnt the stories, and I learnt to speak the language – to a limited degree – and I also learnt to think in the mode of my Elders. I can only be what is inside of me. The Scots have a nice saying: no one can be blamed for their parentage.

I am the only one in my family who identifies as being Aboriginal today. I was the only one who had to make that choice. My younger brother Lawrence was too young to remember much of Point Pearce mission. And the younger ones didn't stay there at all. I was the eldest so I remember it most.

Later on in life I became really interested in my culture. But even from an early age Auntie Glad used to quip, 'Even though that kid looks fair, he knows all about Aboriginal culture.' She used to be surprised at what I knew and remembered about the old days on the mission, because she didn't think I stayed there long enough. I think I was there more often and longer than she realised. See when I used to stay with Auntie May, I was often out of sight because of all these circumstances I've talked about before. Things like other mission kids throwing rocks at me because I was fair, and me hiding to keep out of harm's way. I think they thought I was an insignificant, frightened little kid, but I wasn't. I was just keeping out of trouble – it was easier to stay out of their way. I also learnt more by spending less time with other kids and more time with adults. And I did go to school off and on during my stays on the mission. So as a young man, I just couldn't deny that Aboriginal heritage, which I have come to value even more as the years have gone by.

But I should get back to telling you about my travels and where I went as an engineer with the Merchant Navy. Altogether I had two nine-month stints at sea with Shell, and one year in Papua New Guinea with Oil Search. I began my sea life by sailing on an oil tanker from Port Adelaide – the *Elix*, my first ship. This ship was returning to England after being diverted to Albany, in Western Australia, to let two Australian engineers off. From there I was flown to Fremantle and then caught my second ship, a Dutch tanker, to Singapore. Then on my third ship I travelled around the Pacific going as far north as Japan (already mentioned) and Sarawak and Java and Borneo. After these travels this ship was recalled to England. There was a company policy to keep the Australians in the Pacific because we could cope with the heat, but rather than me disembarking in Eden, at the beginning of the Suez Canal, I was able to continue to England. This was due to the current political situation with the handover of the Suez Canal, so it was recommended I go to England. After a couple of days in England, I caught my fourth ship to Curacao in the Atlantic. Then I joined another ship that toured the American eastern coast. The sixth and last ship was to go through the Panama

Canal to Sydney, so completing my first nine-month trip around the world. The second nine months was spent around the Pacific. After each nine months at sea I spent three months leave ashore back at home with Auntie Gladys at Ferryden Park in Adelaide.

I saw some magnificent sights while at sea, and some pretty stunning things happened during my travels. Once, as we were sailing on the Mediterranean Sea, I stood on the deck of the ship, open-mouthed as I watched this amazing sight before my eyes. The sea was incredibly still, it seemed as if we were sailing on glass – not a ripple to be seen. And not only that, as we ploughed through the water there was so much phosphorous coming off the water that it was lighting up our ship. We could see other ships in the distance doing just the same thing. I just stood there marvelling at the brilliant shine of the phosphorous as it lit up in the water. Then to top it off, all these dolphins came jumping up out of the water ahead of our ship. It was one of those one-off unforgettable moments that remain in your memory forever.

When I was in the Pacific, on our way to Japan, we got caught up in a typhoon. It was frightening. When you tell people the seas were sixty metres high, they think you're pulling their leg, but I swear the waves reached that height on this terrifying occasion. At one stage our tanker was sitting up there on the crest of a wave with our propeller sticking out of the water. We had to shut the engine down, because it started to make this terrible noise, as if it were a plane trying to take off. And then all of a sudden we dropped down the big dipper, the ship felt as if it was almost vertical, and all we could see was water all around us – it was a hectic and terrifying experience.

At night during the storm we had to strap ourselves into our bunks, otherwise we would have been tossed straight out. And as we lay there, listening to all the crockery smashing as it jumped out of the racks when we hit yet another bump, we started to hear the gas bottles hitting together. Then the ship started to creak. This went on for four days. It honestly felt like we were travelling at a sharp angle, side-on to the sea. Of course we couldn't sleep. Being strapped to our bunks didn't stop our stomachs from rolling – sleep was impossible. We soon realised why some sailors prefer to sleep in hammocks – they let you roll with the ship, so it makes sleeping in a storm easier. We also discovered that your body can only sleep if the ship is rocking in the same direction as your body is lying (from head to foot). So you need to steer into the sea. In the middle of this typhoon, we crawled up to the captain's cabin and pleaded, 'Cap'n! Can you put 'er into the wind so we can get a bit of sleep?' By the end of the storm we were exhausted because we couldn't sleep. That typhoon must have been two hundred miles wide and we must have been on the outer-edge where it was much rougher. It lasted four days too long for us!

Being an engineer, I spent my time in the engineering room in the aft (stern) of the ship, the back end. But on these tankers the sleeping cabins and the dining room were in the middle of the ship, so to get to them we engineers had to walk along this gangplank to get to the middle of the ship. Tankers move very low in the water and waves would come crashing over the side of the ship and you could easily get swept overboard. So we had to learn how to pick up on the wave patterns each day, and count the sea, so to speak.

One particular day we were heading for a feed in the dining room. We looked around the side of the ship to count the sea and worked it out that there were three short waves and then one long, high wave. We knew we had to run like mad *after* the fourth wave, which was long and high. The long waves can be so high (up to ten metres, or thirty feet, above the deck of the ship) that when they splash down on the deck you could get blasted over the side of the ship. So we looked around the end of the bulkheads, counting and taking turns to cross the gangplank.

On this day, one bloke mistimed his crossing and got caught. I'd already crossed, so I looked back to see what was happening and I remember thinking, Jeez, he was lucky. To save himself from getting swept overboard this fellow ran like hell up the mast. He was the second mate and I don't know how he got caught. Anyone else with less experience and he'd have been over the side and never seen again. So you can see it was risky work at times.

We also had to watch out for sudden bounces the ship made when we were running across the gangplank to midship. You hope like hell it never happens to you, but I saw it happen to one bloke. The ship bounced at just the wrong time and he got thrown up so high he hit his head on a beam, like a crane, that runs off the mast. It sure knocked him out. After seeing what happened to him, we all remembered to keep our heads down before we got to the midships. You might laugh about it later, but not at the time.

There is a distinct culture on board ship. It's a very unusual social situation – all these blokes at sea together for nine months at a time without their wives or families. When we went ashore, we would go and have a few beers together, and some would find some girl to go out with. When we came back on board, we'd sit at the table and some bloke would tell us he'd gone out with a sheila[2]. If he named her, the old chief engineer would THUMP! on the table and say, 'Gentlemen! Sitting at my table you are not to mention any names. You'll respect who you've been with and you won't say anything about anyone. Understood?' We could talk in general, but he didn't want specifics to be mentioned. We had to respect positions of rank, and respect each other's feelings and obey all the rules.

---

2 *Sheila* is a colloquial Australian term for a 'girl' or 'girlfriend'.

Sometimes the captain's wife came on a trip, and the first mate's wife, and the chief engineer's wife. They only took one voyage at a time, like a short trip, which is just as well, I think, for their sakes. The chief's wife used to share jokes with us. The second engineer's wife came once too, but she used to wear these little shorts and go out onto the midships, walking around like it was a Sunday afternoon at the beach. The blokes down in the smokeroom half-looked at her, thinking, she shouldn't be allowed to walk around like that. As if they were all puritans! But they were right. We were all living in an unnatural situation, and there she was thinking she was queen of the walkway on some luxury cruise ship. The blokes were disturbed and tried to start a petition to stop the second engineer's wife wearing these skimpy shorts on deck.

Some of the men I spent time with at sea were pretty cluey. I was pleasantly surprised to find myself working with such men and to spend so much time at sea with them. It was a good education for me, and I grew up quick. When I first went to sea I was a country kid with very little experience in the outside world, and to go to sea was like entering a new world, a real eye-opener. I got to see all these new and exciting things. But it wasn't playtime – it was full-time work, and hard work too. We worked two regular four-hour shifts a day, seven days a week for nine months.

During my first nine-month stint, I was on this ship running up and down with supplies from the island of Curacao on the northern coast of South America near Venezuela. Curacao was once the home of Captain Morgan – a famous pirate who they've made films about. This island was hard to find because it was so low-lying. We used to all have to go up on deck to help the second mate look for it at night. Once we found the island, we had to go through a channel to get to the landing wharf. The channel was guarded by two forts, on either side of the opening, which were originally built by Captain Morgan. He was pretty smart to base himself on such a well camouflaged and easy-to-guard spot. Morgan could easily attack any ships on their way into his inland harbour. They could not anchor because the sea was too deep around the island.

Anyway, we used to pick up bitumen there, which was pretty interesting because it had to be pumped on hot. Then once it was pumped into the hold it had to be kept hot, which was a feat of engineering. We had miles and miles of steam pipes that we had to keep functioning in order to keep the bitumen hot. This meant that the deck of the ship was also very hot. So I spent a considerable period of time on this very hot ship. But what was strange was that we found we had to wear shoes with special soles because if we wore normal leather shoes the soles would be ripped off. These specially soled shoes were made of an unusual composition we got in America and they were brilliant. They had a special moulded sole, and the tar couldn't stick to it. They only cost about seven bucks a pair and were such good shoes they lasted for years. They were styled like moccasins. I wore mine for ten years, then my uncle wore them after me for another ten years.

Things got tricky when we had to hand the ship and its hot cargo of tar to another crew in a hurry. The second engineer couldn't see how he and the rest of the crew could learn the workings of this complex system of steam pipes and valves, and the operations in the engine room, in such a hurry. So he said to me, 'We haven't got much time to learn all this. So from now on you're the second engineer and I'm the fiver.' He was handing the reins to me and designating himself as the so-called fifth engineer, or the lackey who just did what he was told. When I thought about it later, it really was a clever way to get the job done properly and to learn the operations of the engine room in a short time.

When I sailed up the eastern coast of America, we had to go through the infamous Bermuda Triangle. It is a strange place and when we sailed through there I realised why it has such a mysterious reputation – the sea suddenly changes temperature. The Gulf Stream current runs down the east coast of America, travelling down through the Caribbean and through to the south. When you're shipping in this region, you know you've hit the Gulf Stream because suddenly the water temperature changes by ten degrees.

When you're in that vicinity the officer on watch rings up and asks, 'Have we hit the Gulf Stream yet?' See they're trying to check their position on the charts, and work out where they are. So sometimes we'd assist with navigation.

The Bermuda Triangle is dangerous because warm water hits cold water, and that means disturbance – changing sea temperatures and strange current movements. The Bermuda Triangle is just *one* of these fascinating things you find when you're at sea. Then there's the risk of typhoons of course. We got stuck in New York once because there was a typhoon just off the coast. We were all happy about staying put, right there!

Another time while at sea, we suddenly saw an empty lifeboat go past. I guessed it had fallen off a ship, but it was a bit of a concern. No one had admitted to losing a lifeboat. At sea you have a responsibility to save anyone in distress.

After two years with Shell, I decided to join another petroleum company, which allowed me to travel throuhout Papua New Guinea on a large landing barge. Papua New Guinea at that time was still under the governmental control of Australia. I had some hair-raising experiences that year because, as you can imagine, we travelled to some fairly remote locations and we were completely dependent on the tides to both land and depart. See, on a barge, you don't pull in at a wharf to unload your cargo – instead you depend on the tides to bring the vessel up to the landing.

When you are in the business of shipping, particularly with barges, you get to know the importance of tides and the movements of the sea all over the world. When you are heading for a particular place, you have to find out about the tidal movements – when the tide is high, and when it is low. While I was in the southern waters of Papua New Guinea, I went to this very unusual place where you can't tell if the tide is turning until it hits you. And when it did, it was a king tide, which is a very high tide.

And to complicate things, it was very hard to navigate the waters around this particular part of Papua New Guinea, because of the tidal changes and the way the appearance of the coast would change according to the tides. There was one river entrance that we had to go through that was only sixty feet wide. It is near the border, west of the famous Fly River, called the Morehead River. We were at sea heading for the Morehead River's entrance with plenty of depth to carry the fully laden barge. I was at the stern on top of the wheel-house with the captain, taking sightings to make sure we knew where we were, and everything seemed to be going to plan, with the water depths just right. Then all of a sudden he calls out, 'Lunch!'

So I headed downstairs to the galley. You wouldn't believe it, but it was just ten seconds from that first lunch call, and I was only halfway down the stairs, when I felt this almighty BUMP! We'd hit the seabed.

So I rushed down the stairs to switch the engines off fast. I stopped the engines and headed back up on deck to look at our predicament and couldn't believe my eyes. There was not a drop of water in sight! I just stood there bewildered. I kept asking myself, where the hell did the sea water go? It was there just ten seconds ago!

When the captain called lunch we were doing eleven knots in about nine feet (or three metres) of water. How nine feet of water could just disappear in ten seconds seemed miraculous.

So we found ourselves high and dry. We couldn't believe it, so we hauled ourselves over the side and walked around the barge, scratching our heads. It was as if the sea had disappeared into a sinkhole.

One of the explanations we heard later was that that particular spot is a meeting point of all the seas, and at times one sea takes over from the other. But then, where did the water go? It bamboozled us. There are high-water tides around the northern parts of Australia too, and there can be twenty-foot drops with the out-going tides. In tropical waters there is room for considerable movement of the seas.

Another sight that I will never forget during my travels around Papua New Guinea was a tree full of fluorescent glow-worms. The tree was at least forty feet tall and it was absolutely full of glowing worms. Looking at that tree one particular night was the most magnificent sight I've ever seen. I just stood there open-mouthed and couldn't believe what was before me. After we passed it I thought, why didn't I go and get the camera? I could've taken a picture and had a world scoop!

When we saw this tree, we were travelling down the river at night. We didn't have to travel by night, but we were doing it as a kind of game to show these blokes back at the camp that we could out-manoeuvre them. See, it wasn't an easy thing to navigate some of the waters of Papua New Guinea, and everybody working in the area knew that. So we were out to prove to these blokes who were watching us from the nearby seismic camp that we could outdo them.

So it didn't matter where I went on my travels with the Merchant Navy, I always managed to see these oddities. My life was packed for a period with seeing amazing sights while travelling the coastal waters and rivers of Papua New Guinea and the rest of the world. But after all my many adventures at sea, I was finally ready to come home and be a 'land-lover'.

10

Becoming a 'land-lover' and settling down

After spending three years at sea, I decided to come ashore and get rid of my sea legs forever. Or so I thought – it wasn't long before I found myself at sea again on my own fishing boat. I bought a sixteen-foot fishing boat called the *Golden Cruiser*, but everyone else called her the *Golden Bruiser* because she was as heavy as hell to push out to sea. Me and my cousin Alfie Hughes went fishing for nine months off Port Victoria in Spencer Gulf, not far from Point Pearce mission.

One particular day it was a king tide, and the boat broke anchor and drifted down the head of Port Victoria Bay. When the tide went out, it ended up beached and we had to wait for a moon-lit high tide to move it. Then we still had to push the boat a hundred yards to water. With five of us pushing we still had to work like hell to get into enough water to float her. While we were pushing, Alfie quipped, 'This isn't the *Golden Cruiser* it's the *Golden Bruiser*!' And that's how she got her nickname.

Alfie was always quick-witted. Years later I'll always remember the way he used to call Hanson Road at Mansfield Park in Adelaide 'Saigon Road', because it had so many Vietnamese shops and restaurants – even the chemist shop was Vietnamese. And when Alfie worked in the Aboriginal Community Centre in Wakefield Street, he always used to tell his boss that he was going to the Far East for lunch. Of course we knew he was just going to the Orient Hotel for a quick beer.

Anyway, getting back to fishing, Alfie and I went to sea one day and caught twenty pounds worth of fish, which was equivalent to two weeks wages then. That was our one day of glory, and one day when the *Golden Cruiser* lived up to her name. On most days we didn't make much at all – just enough to get by. I wasn't much of a success as a fisherman, but I did learn a lot of lessons. After making twenty pounds in one day, I went on a weeks holiday, but when I came back it was blowing a gale for four days and I couldn't get out to sea for a week. So I learnt that when you're a fisherman the weather is your boss, and you have to listen to it.

It was at this time that Pauline and I got married, so I got myself a new boss! We married in June 1957 at the registry office in Flinders Street, which is in the middle of the city of Adelaide. The day I went to Point Pearce to ask Pauline's father, Eddie Sansbury, for permission to marry his daughter, was the first time I really got to meet him. He was a lovely old bloke. He had a lot of knowledge, and we would talk about many interesting things. He kept up with all the latest events and was always chatting. He had his little philosophies about things, so we soon got on well. When I asked that old man if I could marry his daughter, Pauline, he said, 'I don't mind if you marry her, me boy.'

Pauline grew up in the city, even though her father was from Point Pearce, but she also moved all over the country a fair bit with her mother. When she moved to the city to work I used to go out with her sometimes. She worked as a waitress in a Chinese restaurant in Rundle Street called the Oriental Cafe. She sometimes invited me to the restaurant to have a meal, but I'd say, 'I don't eat any of that rubbish, thanks. Just give me steak and eggs!' And she'd smile. Now I eat Chinese food all the time and love it. Later Pauline got a job as a cleaner at St Peters College, which was really handy when we moved to Hackney. To get there she just had to hop through the boundary fence (where there was a missing picket) at the end of our street.

As it turned out, Pauline's father, Eddie, lived with us in the city for the last few years of his life. He had moved around a bit, but he lived at Point Pearce a long time. Some say he was well over eighty years old when he came to live with us, because he was there right at the beginning when Point Pearce started in 1868. He would have been born before they started the births register on the mission. So that makes him pretty old, doesn't it? If Point Pearce started in 1868, and he was still there in 1957, well, that would have meant he was nearly ninety. You can see him in old photographs tending the sheep on Point Pearce mission in the very early days.

As well as at Point Pearce, Eddie worked all along the Peninsula – on farms and in many of the towns, such as Minlaton. On farms he'd put in posts, do fencing, shearing, lumping wheat and barley bags and bag-sewing. But he'd also worked in factories in the city – labouring and cleaning up all the mess made by machines, grabbing all the shavings and putting them in bins and sweeping floors. My father-in-law was a well-respected man, and he did all sorts of work. He was pretty adaptable. A lot of blokes had to be adaptable about finding work, because their families couldn't survive on just the rations they were given on the mission. There wasn't enough work for all the men on the mission, so they had to go off and find work. Eddie also played football for Point Pearce; he was a very fast runner.

Pauline's mother's name was Jessie Sansbury. She was a Newchurch before she married Eddie Sansbury. I got a surprise in later life when I found out that she had Kaurna beginnings too. I thought the Newchurches were Narungga people, like the Sansburys and other Point Pearce families. But according to Doreen Kartinyeri, Jessie Newchurch was a descendent of this Russian Finn by the name of John Wilkins. He was the sealer who abducted the Kaurna woman Nellie Raminyemmerin. He must have had two 'wives', because he had a daughter to another so-called 'full-blooded' Kaurna woman, who was called Lizzie (nicknamed 'Bumble Foot'). Their daughter was called (Jessie) Elizabeth Wilkins, who later married Eli Bewes. Together they had a daughter named Edith Bewes, who married Dick Newchurch and they were the parents of Jessie Newchurch, Pauline's mother.

When Pauline's sister Dulcie showed me this bit of paper with the genealogies of all these Kaurna women, she pointed out Jessie Newchurch. I immediately thought to myself, well, I'll be blowed, we're both descendants of Kaurna people. Even Pauline didn't know she had Kaurna ancestry until her sister showed us that bit of paper.

The old people on the mission sometimes hid things from us. See, after the Adelaide Plains were colonised, all the Kaurna people started disappearing, and those who remained were sent to missions like Poonindie. Then the missionaries in charge paired people off, so there was a fair bit of intermarrying within the different groups. So it was hard to know who was who anymore, and where you came from. But, amazingly, it was still possible to find out that my background is both Kaurna and Ngadjuri and Pauline is Kaurna and Narungga.

When Pauline and I got married in 1957, we decided to live in the city where there was more work for us both. As I said, we found ourselves a little place in Hackney, not far from the city centre, and very near Pauline's work. And it wasn't long before my father-in-law came to the city to live with us. He didn't want to leave Point Pearce, but he was pretty old and couldn't look after himself. In those days there weren't old age pensions for Aboriginal people who were living on the mission. To get his pension he had to leave the mission and he wasn't too pleased. He used to say, 'Why should I have to leave my home to get a pension? I don't want to be a burden on anyone ... and now I've gotta leave my home.'

He was over eighty years of age and had worked all his life and never been a burden to anyone. So here was this well-respected gentleman who had to leave the mission to get his pension. So you can see the dilemma he was in.

Our people always seem to have to face difficult choices. Life is never straightforward. We always seem to be disadvantaged. The minute we try to gain some sort of advantage, others get jealous and say that we get everything. It's like double jeopardy.

I think that those complainers should try living like Aboriginal people did for years. Try getting locked out of society and serving time living under mission conditions. We had to earn the right to the few advantages we now have offered to us, after many, many years of disadvantage.

Eddie didn't come to live with us in the city at first. He initially went and lived in an old folks' home. But he pleaded with us, 'You have to take me out of this place!' and ended up walking all the way from Felixstow to us at Hackney. He didn't know which street was ours, so he called out Pauline's name in each street. It was lucky a woman in our street heard him. She came and told Pauline that her dad was looking for her. We couldn't object to him coming to stay with us after that, because we were fond of that old man.

It was so good having Eddie with us for those last few years. It was during the era of the Russian space explorations, and we'd sit together and watch the Sputnik satellite way up in the sky. He'd say to me, 'We gotta watch this tonight!' I thought that was terrific – this old Aboriginal man worrying about the launch of the Sputnik, and watching it coming across the southern sky every night. He'd been brought up watching the stars at night, so he'd notice the satellite coming up, and he'd say, 'Come on, me boy, it's coming across the sky.' This Sputnik was different to anything else he'd seen before, so sometimes he'd say, 'Oh, I don't know about this.

I'm not sure whether we humans should be up there.' But that didn't last long. He soon changed his mind and kept watching. He felt at home with his family, and he felt happy with our food and his daughter's cooking – all that made him feel happy and contented.

Eddie was very interested in what was going on around him because that's how he was brought up – to observe. He'd look at the sky, and he'd watch the kids as they started to arrive. My daughter used to sit at the table and play with her food. And Eddie used to tell Pauline, 'Get that kid away from the table. If she don't wanna eat, don't let her sit there!' They were very strict, the old people, and he didn't like to see kids playing with food. I remembered that from when I was on the mission – all the old people being very strict, just like old Eddie.

One day I found him out the back polishing up this dirty old tap that he'd picked up. He said, 'You could use this.' So there he was out there polishing this tap so hard he made it like brand new. But then all that night he was coughing and spluttering because working so hard had upset his asthma. So we found ourselves up all night taking care of him – well, you know, it was the wife doing it, but I was awake too because I was worried about him. I told Pauline, 'Why don't you tell your father not to be doing these things? He doesn't have to do anything to live with us.' But helping us was how he got his pleasure. It was a sad day when we lost Eddie Sansbury.

Eventually Pauline and I settled with our young family in Taperoo, a new suburb of Port Adelaide. I managed to get a job for the Adelaide Brighton Cement Company working in their factory at Birkenhead near Port Adelaide. I ended up working there for twelve years. I met some tough blokes in that factory, and some of them were pretty racist. However, I always tried to remember what my Auntie May had told me: 'You've got to walk away from these people, and you've got to forget that they're talking about you.' I found it was one thing to say that, but another to actually do it. When you're caught up in it all, it's not so easy to walk away, because some things people say can get to you.

But it wasn't always nasty in the factory, there was also a lot of good-hearted ribbing and joking among us. Work in the factory was dirty, hard and tough, so we'd try to balance it by having a bit of fun. One source of amusement was giving each other nicknames. There was this one old bloke they called Ox-head. Once when we were sitting down having a smoko break, I asked why. My mates looked at me as if I was stupid and said, 'Well, look at the size of his head. Can't you see he's got a big head?'

One day Ox-head came up to us during smoko to have a yarn and to help himself to some lollies another bloke, Seth, had bought. See, Seth and the rest of us would take it in turns to buy a bag of lollies from the lollie cart each day. So Ox-head comes up and says, 'I see you got lollies.'

Seth says, 'Do you want one?'

'Yeah!' he says as usual, so Seth offered him one.

Secretly Seth was getting pretty cranky at Ox-head because he'd noticed he never bothered to buy any lollies to share.

So on this day Seth said to me, 'That bludger. Every time I buy lollies he thinks he's pretty smart getting something for free. I'm going to fix the bludger!'

The next day when the lolly cart came round, Seth bought two bags of lollies, and when Ox-head came up during smoko for his lolly Seth said, 'It's alright Ox-head, I've got a whole bag for you!'

Ox-head says, 'A whole bag? But I ain't got no money!'

Seth replies, 'It doesn't matter – you're good for it.' By this he meant that Ox-head could owe him. So the next day, and all the days after that, Ox-head never asked Seth for any more lollies.

Working life at the factory was full of all these games and tricks we'd play on each other to make the day more bearable. It's in factories and work places like this that the larrikin side of men's personalities come through. I met and worked with some real characters in that place.

But we also had some real work challenges in that factory. There was the time, for example, when the cement kiln was lit and we found the cooler on the fan was overheating, but we just couldn't work out what the problem was. The gauges told us the cooler was far too hot, even after we'd opened up all the valves to get the water flowing through all the cooling pipes. We even put cold water on it with the hose. No matter what we did, we just couldn't get the cooler temperature down. In fact the temperature kept going up and up. It can get very dangerous for the operation of the fan when problems like this arise. As it turned out, we discovered that we shouldn't have had all the valves open, because the water was going around in a circle and getting hotter and hotter. We should have had one of the valves closed.

We always learnt from these puzzling experiences. At one stage one of the bosses, who was actually the boss engineer, said to me, 'Lew, sometimes you and I know that the weather affects these machines. But we don't dare say that.' And he was right. I was working as a maintenance fitter for a time and every year without fail one of the many pumps in the factory just wouldn't pump no matter what we did to try and fix it. This happened one day every year for all the twelve years I was working there. But it wasn't always the same pump. Do you know we never ever solved the problem or worked out why it was one day each year?

We'd ring up the experts and ask them to come and have a look, but they wouldn't come. They said they knew that if we couldn't fix it they wouldn't be able to either. So there we were – the experts knew they couldn't fix it, and we knew we couldn't fix it, so we just had to live with no answer to our problem. We'd do all the repairs we thought it needed, try a few of our experiments, then wait a couple of days. After that we'd just press the button and up it would start again.

Even Henry Ford, the famous car magnate in America, got caught by these anomalies. He once said it was because we just don't know enough about materials. Every so often his company would have to throw away a whole Ford car because they just couldn't get it to work. This was back in his day in 1914, but even today they experience the same phenomenon. I've been out to the Holden factory here in Adelaide where I've seen them put whole cars aside because they just can't get the doors to close – even after they've tried to repair them. I don't think they even worry about trying to get them to work now, because time is money. If they come across a bummer that won't work they just get it off the line and toss it away, or melt it down and start again. They know it's not worth worrying about because the car will never be right – there's just something wrong with it.

You know from all that hard yakka I did in the factory, and all the different jobs I've done as a fitter, I've developed very strong forearms. But the funny twist is that my hands are really soft, which I reckon must be from the grease I put on my hands every morning at work. This grease had lanolin in it, from sheep's wool, so it did my hands some good.

I also cottoned on to the benefits of limestone when I worked in the factory. See, when I was a kid I read that people who worked in limestone quarries suffered fifty per cent less lung disorders than other people. I decided that I would try to get some of the same benefit from working in a factory that had plenty of powdered limestone around. Every day I would throw a handful of limestone up in the air and walk under it. I don't know what the other blokes in the factory thought, but I reckon it did the trick because I've never had any lung problems, and there was a time in my life when I smoked quite a few cigarettes.

Pauline and I went on to have six kids together – five boys and one girl. I reckon they've all turned out okay and done us proud. I'm not sure if there is any great secret to being good parents, or to bringing up kids, but I've learnt a bit over the years. Through my work with kids in schools, and through my own experience as a parent, I've learnt that all kids need adults to guide them in life. More specifically, they need what I call an Overviewer, a Mentor and a Checker. All of these roles are important.

First, kids need an Overviewer. It's their job to monitor the child's overall health and well-being, how things are going and where their hurdles are. Second there is the Mentor, who the kids can turn to for help with certain problems. Finally there's the Checker, who has to check how well they are progressing. They also need to see their kids are not watching rubbish on TV, or doing other things that are unhealthy or harmful. These roles can be taken on by either parent, or any other adult who is influential in the lives of their children. Ideally the roles should be shared. Pauline, for example, was very good at checking our kids didn't watch rubbish on TV. She was also very capable at looking after the well-being and health of each of our kids. She's still very good at looking after young children today, and minds our grandchildren quite often.

In bringing up children you also need to have standards. You have to have moral standards, educational standards and caring standards. In caring for them and nurturing them as they grow, you need to demand that they do their best. But they have to do their best to their level – you can't demand a standard that is way beyond what a kid is capable of. My kids, for example, knew they should be better than their parents in their schooling – simply because they had more opportunities than we did. We had to watch our kids intensely, to see they were making the most of their opportunities, and to watch for anything going wrong. Some parents don't understand the implications of what they do to their kids, or what they fail to do.

It's important that both parents watch their kids carefully, and talk to them when necessary. But kids don't like to be asked too many questions, so you need to know *when* to ask. Otherwise they think you're picking on them. Sometimes mothers ask too many questions, but fathers know the silent world, and they know how annoying it is to be nagged and asked lots of questions. So men and women are different, and that's why it's important for mothers and fathers to work together as a team, because we bring different skills to the important job of parenting. But we should celebrate our differences and not berate each other, so the important thing is for the parents to talk and communicate with each other about these differences.

Fathers can't get away with certain disciplinary actions that mothers can, simply because mothers are often closer to their children. They not only spend more time nurturing them and caring for them, they seem to have this innate ability with children. Just a couple of simple examples are the way women understand the different cries of babies. They also have a very good sense of smell and can tell when a child has a dirty nappy long before the father does. So this closeness that women develop with their children affects the way we discipline our kids. Mothers can get away with a lot more because they have this special rapport with their kids. So when fathers take on the role of the disciplinarian, they can't act spontaneously, and they have to be very careful. They must be calm and collected, and speak quietly without any anger, and most importantly they must have no smell of drink on their breath. Then the kids will be more accepting of their disciplinary actions.

One important way that fathers can get involved with their kids is through sport. Time spent taking their kids to their various games and watching them play can be rewarding to both the parent and the child. Kids can also learn many important lessons in life through sport – and these are often hidden lessons. They learn things like the importance of training, and how you can get better with practice. You learn how to listen to your body and know when to stop with different pain barriers – you have to know when to push on and when to stop. Kids can also gain a lot of confidence as they feel themselves improve week by week, and learn different strategies and achieve their goals. They also learn discipline and how to play in a team and do what's required as a team member. It's also important to learn how to take instructions, but also to develop initiative and not wait to be told every move. Another lesson sport can teach is how to cope with being put on the bench, and watching their team-mates play while they're left off the field. Kids can also learn a lot about maths through timing and also scoring in games. They soon learn how to look at the clock too, so they get to each game on time. So there's a huge amount to be learnt and gained from playing sport.

I was a pretty keen sports person when I was younger, and Pauline was very capable at sport, especially athletics. Pauline was told by teachers at Sturt Street primary school in the city that she could have gone to the Olympic Games with her ability. She even won the 100 metres at this picnic race after she'd had her six kids. I think she inherited her fast legs from her dad, because she wasn't that tall. Eddie Sansbury, her dad, was a powerful 200-metre runner, as well as a very good footballer. Anyway, I think our kids inherited some of these sporting genes, because they all did well in sport. Besides watching my kids play sport over the years, I also got a great deal of pleasure from coaching their football and cricket teams.

I don't like to brag too much, but what my kids achieved

in sport made me a proud parent. First there was Stephen, who was captain of the Taperoo school football team, and a champion athlete. He equalled the hop-step-and-jump record for Under 13 at thirty-nine feet for Taperoo. He won the high jump at six foot one inch for interschool, and won the 100 metre and 200 metre sprints for interschool sports. He later played football for the Port Adelaide league team. Stephen now runs his own business in the steel industry and is a good salesman.

Next there is Jennifer, my only girl, who was captain of the Taperoo school netball team. She was also a good softball player and hit a home run in the final of a school game which they won. She worked in a haberdashery warehouse here in the city for a long while, responsible for the orders and keeping the books and doing all the typing and sales. Jenny is presently an Aboriginal Education Worker (AEW) in a school in Canberra.

My next boy, Rodney, was captain of the cricket and football team at Taperoo Primary. His cricket team got the highest score in the state – a batting record of five wickets for 429 in 1972, which was written up in the local paper. Rodney was asked to go out for state cricket training. He also won the district championship for football and played in the finals in the schoolboy championship, but unfortunately lost. Rodney was also captain of the Taperoo High football team, and he played cricket too. He was in the Under 19 team for the Port Adelaide Football Club when they won four premierships in a row and he also played in the state Under 16 football team. Even though he was short, Rodney could run all day because he had so much power in his legs – just like his grandfather. Rodney is presently a project officer with Family and Youth Services (FAYS).

Trevor, the next one, eventually played grid-iron (American football) for Australia, and went over to America and England.

Back in Australia he played for the Razor Backs grid-iron team and they won the state championship. Trevor also played baseball for the Port Adelaide team and was captain of the squash team at Semaphore Squash Club. Trevor is now a security guard and an electrician by trade.

The next boy, Michael, was a wizard at athletics, and he won the 100 metre and 200 metre sprints at the interschool sports day held at the Kensington athletics grounds. He was also a great footballer and played in the state primary school team. Then in high school he played football in the Under 16 state team, the Under 17 Teal Cup state team, and the Under 19 state team. He later played league football for Port Adelaide. Michael currently works for the Department of Aboriginal Housing.

Mark is the youngest lad and lived in the shadow of all his older brothers and sister. But despite the sporting reputations that preceded him, he's done well. He was captain of the Under 9 Taperoo Football Club and ran for the Western Districts Athletics Team at Kensington. He was well-liked, and a bright kid. He is a natural leader and now works as a manager for Telstra.

I now have eleven grandchildren and two great grand-daughters. Most live here in Adelaide, except for Jenny's four in Canberra. Three of the grandchildren are presently at university, including Dennis who has graduated with a Bachelor of Arts in anthropology and linguistics. He is currently doing Honours in anthropology. So the O'Briens are not just a sport-happy family – we believe in study as well!

But you can see, it would have been pretty hard not to be keen on sport in our household! However, it wasn't all plain sailing. You can cop a bit of ribbing when you do well in sport. I learnt *that* from when I was younger myself. I used to cop some rubbishing from my own team-mates. Once I got my photo in the paper, and they said to me, 'Oh, look who's got his photo in the paper!' And that was from my own team-mates!

I didn't have anyone to help me understand all this ribbing and I often couldn't cope with these hurdles. Those sorts of taunts would beat me. I hope I've managed to help my kids learn how to get through being given a hard time. I've warned them about the taunts they may get from people – especially from people they don't know. Facing this on the sporting field helped them be stronger and more able to cope. People taunt you largely to put you off your game. But it's not only on the football field that you get the taunts. Unfortunately, it goes on in all spheres of your life – it's part of growing up.

We had a lot of fun times living at Taperoo as a young family. I remember one time when I bought a shed from a bloke around the corner. My lads and I went and pulled the shed down ready to rebuild it in our backyard. But when we saw the runners on the ground, we saw that they had all rotted away. So I said to the bloke, 'Those ground timbers are no good.'

'Oh,' he said. 'Come down the Port and I'll get you some more.'

So we went down the Port to see this bloke called Harry, who was to supply us with some loose timber. When we got there I saw the wharfinger and asked for Harry, and he said, 'You mean the Judge. You'll find him over there sitting on a case!' See, this Harry had a reputation for doing an awful lot of sitting on that wharf – and usually on a packing case. Eventually the Judge directed us to where we could get the wood that we needed and we headed home with our supplies, and built our shed. We learnt a lot putting up that shed, because the trusses were made from jarrah and were very heavy, so they weren't easy to put in position. We had to hold them upright with ropes while we anchored them with struts. It was a big shed, and we used one end as a billiard room and the other end as a work area with my tool bench and all my tools.

The beauty of all these experiences – both negative and positive – is that I have been able to pass on what I have learnt over the years to my kids. I've been able to play the Overviewer, Mentor and Checker roles for my kids and cushion some of the blows they've received in their own lives. It was because of my experience with my own kids that I was offered a job with the Education Department of South Australia as a Liaison Officer, working with Aboriginal kids in the southern area of the state.

11

Reflections on working in schools and university

In 1977 George Tongerie came to ask me to apply for a job with the South Australian Education Department. Uncle George was one of the stolen generation and a Colebrook kid (or Tjitji Tjuta[1]). He went to live at the Colebrook home when it was set up by the United Aborigines Mission (UAM) at Oodnadatta. He was originally from up that way. George was working for the Department of Community Welfare as a Welfare Officer. He was one of the first people to train in community development with the task force at the Institute of Technology on North Terrace where the School of Mines once was.

George told me he wanted me to apply for this Aboriginal Home Liaison Officer's job with the Education Department, because he said I had the experience for the job.[2] He said, 'You've been to high school yourself, and you've got kids who have all done alright at high school, so you'd be ideal for the position.' So that's how I got started working in the field of education after thirty years working as a fitter. Now I believe it was inevitable that I end up working in schools, and eventually in the university, because all my life I have had a thirst for books and knowledge.

I had the job as the Aboriginal Liaison Officer with the

---

1 *Tjitji Tjuta* is the term used for the kids at Colebrook Home. It means 'many children' in the Pitjantjatjara language of South Australia.

2 I was officially called a 'Home/School Visitor', rather than 'Liaison Officer' because I wasn't a registered teacher.

Education Department from 1977 to 1986. It was my job to support the Aboriginal students in schools in the southern half of the state, which was a huge job. At the time, Lowitja O'Donoghue had the northern half of the state to take care of. She went on to become the first head of the Aboriginal and Torres Strait Islander Commission (ATSIC) and later Australian of the Year in 1984. She was another Colebrook kid, a Yankunytjatjara woman originally from De Rose Hill station. She was 'removed', along with her siblings, and taken to Colebrook at Quorn when she was two years old.

In this new job of mine I got pretty involved with the schools in the Port area in particular. There were a lot of Aboriginal kids in that area, and I knew many of the families already through my own kids and from coaching footy and cricket. I used to visit Alberton Primary, Taperoo Primary, Taperoo High, Largs Bay Primary, Largs North, LeFevre Tech, LeFevre Primary and then further along the LeFevre Peninsula to North Haven Primary. I think that's how I first met Rod Sawford, who is presently the Federal Member for Port Adelaide. He used to be the principal at Taperoo Primary. I'd also make trips to visit other schools in the rural areas of the state such as Burra, Kadina, Meningie and Penola.

It's a well-known fact that Aboriginal kids aren't staying at school as long as non-Aboriginal kids, and when they *are* at school, they are not achieving at the same levels as non-Aboriginal kids. It was my job as Liaison Officer to support the Aboriginal kids in schools and help them achieve more. This meant becoming involved with the awareness programs that helped teachers to understand the problems and issues facing Aboriginal kids. I used to talk to teachers about individual students to try and get them to understand the Aboriginal kids more – particularly those who were having problems. One of my primary roles was to counsel individual children in schools. I saw this role as important because I knew from personal experience what it was like to feel out-of-sorts at school.

I remember going through a stage at primary school when kids used to harass me by passing me nasty notes. I used to get upset and push my chair back in frustration. But as soon as I pushed my chair back the teacher would notice the disturbance and pick on me, shouting, 'Is that you again, O'Brien? Sit down!' I started to get aggro at these kids but after a while I realised that the only one getting in trouble was me. So I stopped reacting and tried the silent response.

I sat in class silently for three months, without responding to the kids who were trying to tease me. I'd sit there and do nothing, but the teacher would *still* turn around whenever he heard any disruption and say, 'Is that you, O'Brien?' I had to put up with that nonsense for a long time before this teacher woke up to the fact that it wasn't me anymore. I'd figured that it was best if I stayed quiet and got on with my work, but it was not an easy road! So I knew first-hand where the kids I was counselling were coming from.

I've already mentioned how I stopped talking for a period when I was doing my apprenticeship. Well it also happened a couple of times when I was at school – I just forgot how to communicate. People would come up to me and ask me a question, and I wouldn't be able to answer them. It wasn't that I didn't know the answer, I just didn't know how to say it. They'd say, 'What are you, ignorant or something? What's wrong with you?' And the longer I remained silent the worse I got – so I lost the ability to talk spontaneously.

As I said before, what helped me during the difficult stages in my school life was the support of key people, like the Lyndons. That's why school liaison officers and counsellors are so important – they can help kids get through difficult times. I hope I was able to help Aboriginal kids having trouble at school, just as others helped me.

My speaking problems were helped when I became the cricket captain as well as the basketball captain at school. Part of my job was to get up and make speeches about the team. It used to embarrass me, but it was good training. Even though I mumbled and made errors, I was just a kid, so it was good for my confidence. I learnt good lessons from these responsibilities because I was forced to speak in public. So every sports week I had to give the scores to the whole school assembly. I'd say, 'Well, we made so many runs today and so-and-so was the best batsman, and someone else got three for twenty and he was the best bowler. And in basketball we won 120 points to 110.' It was a nerve-racking exercise, but it was just what I needed to get me going. Now I talk in public without any difficulty at all, and people would think I've been like that all my life, but I haven't.

One thing I have never lost in my speech is my Point Pearce accent. On the mission they spoke a different dialect of English, which had a number of local Indigenous words. These days they call this dialect Nunga English[3], and teachers are told to be respectful of this dialect when it's used by Aboriginal kids. But at Point Pearce we also pronounce our English words differently – particularly words with an 'r' sound. We actually pronounce the 'r' sound in words, such as 'girl' and 'bird'. This is the same way the Cornish miners who settled at Moonta and other mining towns near the mission used to speak. I think I'll always round all my 'r' sounds like a Point Pearce person – it's like an identity thing.

Unfortunately, a lot of kids look at schooling as a chore. When I see that I smile and think to myself, they just don't know. There were a number of kids who used to muck up in class, so they would be sent to stand in the corner. But I had

---

3 Nunga English is the southern South Australian dialect of Aboriginal English. It contains some Narungga and Ngarrindjeri words, plus some words from the west coast.

to fight hard to be able to stay on at school, so I was keen to make the most of my opportunities.

I believe that in order to have a successful life you need to stop acting like a victim. By acting the victim, you're condemning yourself to a life of always carrying your wounds. I think it's important that we know about the past, and that other Australians learn and understand about the way this country was taken from Aboriginal people. But we Aboriginal people can't dwell on the past forever, and continually see ourselves as victims. Otherwise we spend our time licking our wounds, and never get on with our lives and make a go of it.

When I was counselling Aboriginal kids in schools, I would have conversations with them about their behaviour and why they were mucking up in class. Many of them were angry about something going on in their lives. They were lashing out at something or someone, and always blaming something for their predicament. They would often see themselves as victims. I will always remember this one kid I counselled in the Port area. He used to act up and be disruptive, but then he stopped. I asked him why he had stopped acting up and he told me, 'It was like my arm was cut and it would never heal, and I was carrying this wound around.' I thought to myself, wow. I asked him if his wound had healed. He replied that it had. It's a nice story that one. It shows that you can reason with kids if you give them support and a listening ear.

My liaison job was meant to be just with the Aboriginal kids, but there were other troubled kids in the schools. Once a teacher asked me if I would counsel a white girl. This one time I agreed and sat and listened to her talk for a long while, without interrupting. Then I tried to help her work through some of her problems. I would go to different counselling workshops myself, where I would learn all these useful counselling skills. A lot of what I found most valuable though I learnt through bringing up my own kids.

Once my own daughter declared she wanted to leave home. She wasn't very old at the time – I remember she was definitely too young to be leaving us. Her brothers must have done something to annoy her. Anyway, she told me she was leaving home, so I thought I'd use a bit of reverse psychology and helped her pack her bags. Pauline thought I was really losing it, and wasn't too pleased with me. But I knew Jennifer wouldn't actually leave and my little technique would work in the end. It wasn't long after she walked out the front door that she realised leaving home wasn't such a good idea. I'm sure she was also wondering why Dad seemed so keen to get rid of her! When she came back and knocked on the door, I opened it and she said, 'I don't think I'll go today.'

'Good!' I said, and let her in.

I know many people in this country don't fully understand what happened to Aboriginal people in the past. Some of the laws that were imposed to control the lives of Aboriginal people were quite barbaric. One I always think about is the law against *consorting*, which many people are unaware of.

Some non-Indigenous people say to me, 'How come in all these years I never met an Aboriginal?' Well, Aboriginal people weren't allowed to talk to Europeans, it was against the consorting law. The only Aboriginal people who could talk to white Australians were those exempted from the *Aborigines Act*, and were therefore no longer considered Aborigines.[4] The penalty was jail for *six months*! That's a heck of a price for such a little thing – and both unjust and racist. We could actually get arrested under two laws – the *Police Act* and the *Aborigines Act*. Fancy being put into jail for six months for talking to a European.

It might be true that things were bad for us in the past – but

---

4 This exemption to the Act came in in 1939.

it's not healthy to keep looking out from this negative position. It's important to have a positive outlook on the future and the possibilities it holds for young Aboriginal people. If you continually hear adults whingeing about how we never got any government assistance on the mission, and how we were governed by superintendents, you risk imposing a victim's attitude onto the kids. I know you've got to talk about such things at times, especially if you need to get it out of your system, but the trouble with off-loading it onto the young people is that they can also start to carry the load and become embittered.

It's important that we give kids hope for the future and encourage them to move beyond being victims within an unjust system. Many young Aboriginal people these days don't seem to have any hope for the future – in fact it sometimes seems a lot of them have given up hope of ever getting a good job and a house and all the other things that white Australians dream of. Many kids only know the welfare system and don't have any adult role-models who work and own their own home.

If kids think of themselves as victims, it's like they're half living in the past. When these kids hear stories about how their older relatives were treated and what happened to them, it's a big load for them to carry. They feel the misery of it all and think there's no hope for them either.

It's understandable that some older people who were treated harshly can't get it out of their system. Some Aboriginal people were never even given the opportunity to go to school, particularly high school, so they feel bitter about what they missed out on. But my message to parents these days is not to forget the past, but not to be bitter about it either. Get over your grieving, get over the anger and sadness. Move on. You need to support your kids as we move into the future, especially now that your kids have so many more educational opportunities. It's important that parents encourage kids to get a better education than they did. If parents still need to grieve about the past, they need to grieve among themselves with their own age group. And if we are to teach kids in schools about the past, we have to be very careful the way we teach it. It's so easy for the kids to get all aggro!

Teachers have to be prepared for the reaction and understand how to deal with the anger, and the grieving process. My daughter Jenny, who teaches in Canberra, has talked to me about this. She's got a program she teaches to her own students, and I think she does it well. She says, 'You've got to let them get angry; they've got to get it out of their system. If you don't they just become a victim of their own anger.' As that young lad told me, you've got to heal your wounds.

It's a very complex issue, dealing with our past, yet looking to our future. You really have to have someone with expertise to teach it properly in schools and universities, especially when the students are Aboriginal.

We can't tell our kids to go to school because the government says they have to or because you say so. We've got to ensure that they understand *why* they need to go. They have to realise for themselves that if they don't get an education they are limiting themselves and what they can achieve in life. I used to tell my kids that they would have far more options in life if they were well educated. If you can do the sums, and can read and write and can work the computer, you're employable. A lot of kids seem to have this idea that what they learn at school isn't relevant to the real world, and once they get a job the boss will show them what to do. They don't seem to understand that schools are a gymnasium for the mind, exercise for the brain. School is meant to teach you *how* to learn, so that when you start work you only need minimal instruction.

Unfortunately many kids get disillusioned with school, and it's these kids who create a discipline problem in schools. Schools need to realise that they have to change and make school more interesting and relevant for these kids. They've got to talk to kids about what they're interested in, and make the curriculum more interesting for them. As I said before, I believe that abolishing technical high schools, and making all schools into academic institutions, means kids who want to get an apprenticeship can't specialise in the subjects that prepare them for the trades. It also means that many kids find the compulsory academic subjects that they are now forced to study 'boring'.

I think schools also have to put their more capable teachers with the kids who find school boring, because it is these teachers who have the ability to make their lessons more relevant and interesting for students who would otherwise drop out of school. If you put your cleverest teachers with some of the battling kids, they also have more chance of academic success. These smart teachers know how to teach the difficult concepts in a straightforward and understandable way. When you look at it, top students don't need the best teachers. All they need is the curriculum, they can do the work themselves because they're pretty cluey. Unfortunately many schools put the worst teachers with the kids who are struggling the most, because they have given up on those kids. The best teachers understand that there are different ways of teaching and learning, and that they have to adopt the most appropriate method for particular kids. Maybe changing the wage structure for teachers will help change the way teachers are allocated to different schools and different groups of kids. This is particularly important in our state, now that the government has increased the compulsory leaving age for high school students from fifteen to sixteen years of age.

Another problem is that some teachers don't bother to find out where their kids are at academically before they start teaching. They just have in their minds that there is a set curriculum, they've got four terms to teach it all, and there's no time to cover the basics. They assume that the basics have been covered already. But what our kids are saying about all this is interesting. They say that their teachers should know where they're at and give them work they can do. But many teachers just follow the curriculum. If you challenge the teachers about this, they say that the kids should ask if they don't know something. What I tell them is that when you come from a disadvantaged position, how can you ask questions when you don't even know which questions to ask? These kids should be taken from whatever level they're at, and then work with the teacher to a level where they can manage the work, and only then move on in the curriculum.

I know from personal experience that with a good teacher it is possible for disadvantaged kids to achieve at high academic levels. When I had been at sea for nine months, I came ashore for three months' leave. I had been on a British ship, as a fifth engineer, which I was able to do without an engineering ticket. I only had a tradesman ticket at that stage. If I wanted to sail on the Australian coast as an engineer, there was a requirement to have Part A of the second-class engineering ticket. I wanted to advance, so I decided I needed this ticket.

So I headed off to the Sydney Institute of Technology to get my Part A ticket. Three of us had been sailing on the same ship and we all wanted our ticket. In our first class, one of the lads asked the lecturer how long it would take. The teacher told us two years. We nearly had a heart attack, because we only had three months, so we got up and left there and then. We searched around to find a place that could teach us a bit quicker, and heard about a private engineering school run by a Mr Cotteman on Circular Quay. Unfortunately it cost a hundred pounds, but we didn't have much choice. That was twenty weeks' wages for an ordinary labourer on a ship, and ten weeks of a fitter's wage. As we were to find out, it was well worth it.

I completed the course in just six weeks and passed the

exam! There were two of us who did it in this time, but the third bloke took longer. This teacher Cotteman was brilliant. He asked each person in his class where they were up to and then started teaching to bring us all up to the same level in mathematics. Then he said, 'Righto, now that we're all at the same level, we'll all go and buy a slide rule.' He spent one day teaching us how to use a slide rule, then he said, 'There's the book, now I want you to go right through that book, and do everything.' And we did.

So you can see how you can progress when you're motivated. It might have been partly because we were paying so much for the course, and we had limited time, but we were able to work through the course by ourselves and we did it real quick. We worked like mad to do it – six days a week, nine to five. We'd do four hours on a Saturday morning, then homework on Sunday. Even when we went home on the tram we'd look at our study cards with formulas written on them. So we were living and eating these formulas, it was intense. Without this Part A ticket we weren't allowed to sail the coast and my ultimate aim was to sail the coast of Australia and Papua New Guinea in the Merchant Navy.

I don't think kids should be put through this kind of pressure at school, but it shows what's possible when young people are highly motivated. I think the key to our success was having a skilled teacher, our hard work, and being highly motivated to get through the course.

Schools these days should also teach students self-discipline and to respect others, as well as good manners and how to dress correctly and talk properly. That's what society and the workforce expects. It may seem surprising, but many kids these days don't know how to dress and perform for a job interview, and they don't know how to speak and behave in the work place. They think, oh, they should just accept me as I am. But that's not right. Kids have to learn that there are standards, rules and community expectations. The dress code and manners they have to adopt are not those of their own community but those of the work place they wish to enter. They soon learn that pleasantries can help open doors. We saw that with the kids from disadvantaged homes on the movie *To Sir With Love*, starring Sydney Poitier, which was set in the rough west end of London.

Sometimes I think our people have got to stop listening to so much country music with all those cowboy lyrics lamenting about life – your dog's dying and your wife's just left you, or some other tragedy. I think we've got to start moving away from all that negativity. We've got to listen to more positive songs that are about singin' in the rain. You know what I mean? It's a matter of balance. We've got to learn to dwell more on the pleasantness of life. Sure we need songs about the sad things, but we also need songs that can brighten your day.

These days it's easy for kids to get caught up in the money world. They think they need money to have fun – for the movies, videos, DVDs, CDs and computer games. But many parents have limited resources. I had to discover entertainment that was free when I was a lad. I discovered walks in the National Park, going to the beach, visiting the Art Gallery and, of course, borrowing books from the public libraries. We had no choice. A group of us used to play cricket – we'd go to the parklands or the hills, make a scratch team and play another group of kids. We'd bring a bat and someone else would bring a ball, and someone would bring the stumps. It was terrific.

Now though, the public commons or parklands are disappearing to developers, and we don't have free access to large grounds as much as we used to. They've cleared them all and built housing estates on them. There's less and less places for kids to go now, especially in the suburbs. That's why we need these skating rinks now in the inner city. It's a new era, which is good, but it costs dough to buy a skateboard!

I believe schools need to re-think the setting of homework as well, particularly for kids from disadvantaged backgrounds. As I said before, homework is a stupid idea for disadvantaged kids. It really only works for kids whose parents have been to high school and have got books at home and access to computers. Where are kids from disadvantaged homes going to get the help they need to do homework? Their parents often can't help them. That's why homework centres have been set up in some of the schools in the western suburbs of Adelaide, to help kids who don't have the learning support they need at home.

It's also important for kids to be able to help each other with their homework. Teachers shouldn't accuse them of cheating when they are just helping each other out. If they let kids talk to each other and help each other, they'll get through the hard stuff more easily. I told the story about how I used to come down on the train with three other lads and we used to go into the classroom early to talk to each other about our homework. Once we'd had a talk about the bits we didn't know, we would sit down and do the questions ourselves. We didn't cheat, we just shared information with each other so we could do the work.

Kids need to learn to speak up when they don't understand. Everyone comes across stoppers and hurdles and it takes guts for kids to admit they can't do something and that they need help.

There are some young Aboriginal kids these days who don't want to jump the hurdles, and would rather give up. We've got to motivate these kids not to give up, and to believe that it is possible to jump those hurdles. Maybe we should produce more books about Aboriginal people who have succeeded in fulfilling their dreams, and achieved their ambitions. Kids need role models who demonstrate they *can* be successful. Unfortunately the only place that we tend to see successful Aboriginal people these days is in the sporting arena. Kids see successful footballers and think they don't need an education to be a good footballer.

What these kids don't see, or don't get told, is that after ten years of football, when their bodies are all worn out, what can they do? I believe you have to be educated to make your mind flexible to learn other things. An education teaches you to read and to enquire. You need to be able to read in order to understand forms and how to follow instruction books, for example. If you don't have reading as a skill, how can you read and follow the instructions of some complicated machine that you need to operate? How are you going to fix an error in your computer if you don't know how to look it up in a book or read about it on the internet? So you've just got to learn to read.

You've also got to learn to write. That's another essential. And of course you need some maths. But there is now a fourth element that is essential to a good education, and that's computers. You've just got to be able to use a computer these days to get a good job. It seems that each generation has more to learn, and it's snowballing. Adolescents have to come out of school these days with a lot of skills, and if you haven't got those skills to start your working career it's going to be very hard to fit into the workforce.

This is what I used to explain to kids when I was working in schools. I also used to tell them about what I saw when I was studying – all these blokes my age out in the workforce, getting five quid a week, while I was living on next to nothing. They could dress well on their reasonable wage, and they went out with their girlfriends and went dancing. It all looked good to me, but the funny thing is that I saw these same blokes when they got to forty, still labouring as unskilled workers, and their girlfriends (now their wives) weren't so impressed anymore. They got disillusioned, and then divorced. Then you suddenly find out that they've become derelicts.

You can't limit yourself in life by being jazzy now and not looking to the future. Work can be hard enough without being limited to a boring job all your life. You might be able to last at it for a certain number of years but ideally people need to be interested in and knowledgeable about their work. So I tried to encourage kids to wake up and think, I can do what *I* want to do in life. I don't want a dead-end job.

That's why I worked so hard to get the qualifications I needed to go to sea, because when I was doing my apprentice-ship I was almost living like a derelict myself. I thought the only way I could get out of this poverty trap was to go to sea as a seaman. But then I realised that if I completed my appren-ticeship, I could go to sea as an engineer. Then I would get a higher wage, a uniform and more respect. As an engineer I had more responsibility, such as running watches, whereas the seamen had to do what they were told.

We need to inspire our kids to aim high in life, to be engi-neers or doctors or lawyers. They need to know that they can go far beyond working in a factory. They need to know that it is possible to break the poverty cycle and get off welfare – if they only get themselves a decent education. Unfortunately, some Aboriginal families have been living on welfare for a couple of generations, and so they have no thought of ambi-tions or extending themselves in life. They simply don't know anyone who has gone on in their studies or gone to university.

Even though it's important to encourage kids to achieve, it's equally important not to put too much pressure on them. In my day, boys had this terrible imposition put on them. We were told we had to do well because we would have to support a family later on. I felt that was one of the heaviest burdens I carried in my life. It was a hell of a prospect for a young lad. Adults kept reminding us that we'd have to carry the whole weight of our wife and family – and we weren't even married yet, we were only kids! I thought that was terrible. I used to look enviously at the girls. They were told to find a good husband to look after them. It seemed to me the girls had the freedom to pick and choose, and they could read books and do what they liked. I thought to myself, that's an easier life than this boy thing! In reality marriage should be a partnership and the pressure to earn money shouldn't be on either one or the other.

I think some blokes thought, I don't want to do that, I'm not gonna get married. So we really need to be careful in what we say to kids. We can be supportive and encourage them to achieve – but at the same time not put too much pressure on them. It's a fine balance.

I've found that my own kids sometimes criticise me for things I said or didn't say to them. But I think it's possible to make some general rules, such as: don't put your kids down and don't talk to them in a negative sort of way. And as I have already said, men have to be particularly careful in the way they discipline kids. They should be calm and rational and not use their physical strength.

You don't get any training for one of the most important roles in life – being a father or mother. I think I was lucky in what I learnt from Auntie May and my Uncle Lewis. I know my mother hit me once when we were staying on the mission, and Uncle Lewis yelled out, 'Who's hittin' that child? There's other ways to deal with it.' They knew she was hitting me because Lawrence was crying all the time with colic or something, and she was frustrated. In those days it was more acceptable to smack kids: spare the rod and spoil the child. It was thought you've got to smack kids when they do something seriously wrong – to remind them that they mustn't do it again. These days you're in trouble with Welfare if you hit your kids.

Looking after teenagers is a different business. You must

never hit a teenager. You've got to talk to them as they grow bigger, because they're going through turmoil. Teenagers are growing physically with their bodies changing dramatically, as well as developing mentally. Their whole world around them is widening, and they're wondering where they will fit into it. Sometimes they have negative thoughts about themselves and their looks, and think they're hopeless. They may go for a job interview and get refused, and think it's the end of the world. But they have to learn that going to an interview is all part of the experience, and you learn from each one you have. It's not pleasant to go through all these things, but that's life and there are no shortcuts. We've all got to go through the pain and the anguish of growing up. But we can help make the journey a little less rough for them.

I know I've learnt a great deal about counselling kids through experience. It's important to be able to give kids sound advice. But sometimes you have to help kids work out what is right, and what is the truth for themselves. You need to empower them to make their own decisions.

So after nine years working as a liaison officer in schools, I changed roles and became the Coordinator of the Aboriginal Education Workers (AEWs) in the Pennington District Office of the Education Department. My role there was to train AEWs and place them in the schools where they were most needed. I worked alongside Howard Groome. He was terrific to work with and has done a great deal for Aboriginal education in general. He dug out and printed the first facsimile edition of the Kaurna wordlist and grammar that was originally compiled by the two German missionaries Teichelmann and Schürmann.[5] It was originally published in 1840. That little publication has opened up a whole world for me and the Kaurna community,

---

5 It was entitled *Outlines of a Grammar, Vocabulary and Phraseology of the Aboriginal Language of South Australia, Spoken by the Natives in and for Some Distance Around Adelaide.* It was self-published.

and made it possible to reclaim our language. Howard also produced a little booklet called *The Kaurna People*.

During my twelve years working with the Education Department, I decided to enrol to do an Associate Diploma in Aboriginal Studies with the South Australian College of Advanced Education. I studied internally at the Underdale campus[6] and it took me eight years part-time. I actually did more subjects than I needed to do but I found it was worth it because it was very beneficial to me in my work. They kept changing the course all the time, so some of the subjects I did weren't even counted in the end.

Some of the subjects I studied were Media Studies, Cross-Cultural Studies, Action Research and Aboriginal Studies. I nearly didn't finish the course because they were insisting I do the core subjects which I argued I had been practising all my life. I was supposed to go and do work experience with an Aboriginal organisation, but I had been on fourteen different Aboriginal committees for years, since the 1960s. I'd also been on the Curriculum Committee with the Education Department and on the Aboriginal Community College Council. In 1985 they eventually awarded me my Associate Diploma.

In 1990 I finally resigned from the Education Department after twelve years of service and joined the staff at the Kaurna Higher Education Centre at Underdale as a Resource Centre Manager. I managed all the books and teaching resources on Aboriginal Studies. By this stage the Underdale College of Advanced Education had become part of the University of South Australia. I enjoyed that work, because it gave me the opportunity to interact with the students and to assist them in learning how to use the computers in the Resource Centre. Eventually the Resource Centre was closed down, but before

---

6 The Underdale campus of the University of South Australia has now been sold and demolished to make way for housing development.

that I moved on to Kura Yerlo, out at Largs Bay, as the director in 1993. Previously I was the founding chairperson, beginning in 1986.

So life can be a funny road to walk down, but you learn invaluable lessons along the way. I must say, when life is a hard road, you can get a certain strength from overcoming the hurdles. I know I gained real strength from overcoming my problems. As they say, life's the best teacher of all, isn't it?

12

Sharing our space

Yertarra Padnima Taingiwiltanendadlu
If we walk across the land, we gain in our strength.

One of the reasons I wanted to write this book was to set the record straight on the past regarding Aboriginal people in this state, particularly on the Kaurna people. I believe it's important not to ignore what has gone before and it's only by recognising our bad experiences that we can move on to a better future. That's what reconciliation is all about.

I also think we can learn to share the land in this unique state of ours. As a Kaurna man, I believe it is particularly important that we learn to share this city of Adelaide. If we learn to listen to each other and to hear each other's stories we will see the importance of 'sharing the space' – sharing this country.

A good place to start with reconciliation is to listen to Aboriginal stories about this country, particularly Kaurna country. By educating people about Kaurna country maybe we can all learn about the past and learn to share the land. Take for example the Kaurna land north of the city in the Clare region. As I said before, this land was taken from my ancestors – not just once, but over and over again. When Kudnarto was granted the lease on her land at Crystal Brook – Block 346 of Skillogalee – it was really already her land and it was just being given back. And then when she died, it was taken away yet again. Much that belongs to Aboriginal people has to be owned several times before we get it back.

In South Australia some of those early governors were sympathetic to Aboriginal people, and when the land was surveyed they set aside reserves for occupation by Aboriginal people. Unfortunately they didn't realise that Aboriginal people prefer to live on their own land, not land belonging to some other group. That's why the Kaurna people weren't happy about being shipped off to Poonindie on Eyre Peninsula. That was someone else's country.

But not all white people wanted to take the land for themselves and ignore the rights of the local Aboriginal people. There are several cases in Adelaide, for example, where newly arrived settlers wanted to share the land with local Kaurna people. The family of John Adams, a shoe-maker, arrived on the first ship the *Buffalo* with Governor Hindmarsh, and John made personal friendships with the two Kaurna men Kadlitpinna (nicknamed 'Captain Jack') and Mullawirraburka ('King John'). There were also a few other colonists who were Quakers, including John Hack and Robert Cock, who tried to befriend, protect and provide for the local 'natives' through their Society of Friends. They offered to pay rent for their land into a fund to be set aside for the use and benefit of local Kaurna people.[1] That's true reconciliation! But unfortunately they were the exception, rather than the norm. The Quakers still financially support Kaurna people today, in different ventures, particularly in reviving our language.

In the very early days of South Australia's colonisation, first under Governor Hindmarsh and then Governor Gawler, and later Governor Grey, there were actually quite a number of blocks of land, or reserves, retained for Aboriginal people within the Adelaide city boundaries. This was during the times when respected Kaurna men like Mullawirraburka, Kadlitpinna

---

1 An opera *Dancing Ngutinai*, which tells the story of these families on their arrival in Glenelg, has been written by the local musician Chester Schultz, and was performed in Adelaide in 2002.

and Ityamaiitpinna were living in the city. Once, in 1840, Mullawirraburka stood up and spoke to the people of Adelaide about getting some of his land back.

The idea of preserving land for the 'native inhabitants' of South Australia was actually what the British government had declared in their charter: that ten per cent of the land should be set aside for the 'natives'. And so in 1840, 1200 acres were allotted to the Aboriginal people, which is equal to 430 or so hectares today. So the land was given out, and the local Kaurna were expected to settle down on it, to build a house and establish vegetable gardens or farm the land – just like the white settlers. But because they didn't settle down, all the land was taken back.

One thing I read, during my research in the archives, was about Hindmarsh Town, which was in the vicinity of the present day suburb of Hindmarsh. It's along the River Torrens where the West End Brewery is today – at the western end of the city centre. They used to do a lot of wool-washing there in the river. At one stage, around the late 1860s, there were 186 Aboriginal people living there in Hindmarsh Town, so the local council informed the state government authorities that they should establish a reserve for the Aboriginal people to live on.[2] So they set aside a reserve for them at Ridleyton – on the south-eastern corner of South Road and Torrens Road.[3] Aboriginal people lived there for a number of years. It used to flood a bit because it was on the flood plains. Then someone complained that these poor whites didn't have anywhere to go,

---

2 This information can be seen in the Hindmarsh City Council History book *Hindmarsh Town*, written by Roland Parsons (1974). This council area is now run by the West Torrens Council. Hindmarsh Town became The District Council of Hindmarsh in 1853.

3 More recent research by J.M. Burke & S Weaver, *Former Aboriginal Reserves in the Adelaide Region* (1999), found this reserve to be placed at neighbouring Renown Park, bordered by Lamont Street and Torrens Road.

so they decided to set this Aboriginal reserve aside for white people. So the reserve was cut up into eighty-acre blocks called 'workers' blocks' and the reserve disappeared. The reserve land was taken back by the crown by 1870.

I was surprised when I read that there were so many Aboriginal people living on the one site in the city then. I also found there were a number of Aboriginal reserves along Torrens Road; one where the huge Arndale Shopping Centre is now, in Kilkenny, and another further back towards the city on Goodall Avenue. So there's three that I know of. The curator of the Unley Museum, Marie Boland, did some research on the reserves. She found there were a total of forty-five, at one stage, within the Adelaide city boundary. Yet within five years they were all taken back.

What made me realise that this giving of land and then taking it back again, was all a game, was when I realised who got the reserved land in the end. See, the people who were in the know eventually got the land. Many of the blocks were taken over by people high up in the bureaucracy, and their friends. So it became a game played by people in power for their own benefit.

So there you go. The founders of this state back in England initially had good intentions, but these underlings or bureaucrats took the law into their own hands and altered things. They listened to the cry of the public and ended up giving the land to the white people. It's ironic really because all the land that Aboriginal people own today in this state is mainly out in the bush. A large percentage is the Anangu Pitjantjatjara Lands, in the far-north-west desert country of the state. And the few other Aboriginal reserves are also way out on marginal land, like Raukkan – which is on saltpan country on the shores of Lake Alexandrina. It wasn't until nearly one hundred years later, in 1966, that some of the wrongs in this state were righted when Don Dunstan, premier of South Australia, formed the Aboriginal Lands Trust. This enabled him to claim all this Crown land as Aboriginal reserves for Aboriginal people.

Remember, we Aboriginal people owned all the land in the beginning, then they took it off us, then they gave it back, and then they took it away again. Why does the government seem to give the productive land to whites and only the waste land to Aboriginal people?

There's another intrigue that I found when I was researching this Hindmarsh Town. I'm not sure why, but I have noticed that surveyors seem to make significant Aboriginal grounds into a triangle shape. Maybe it's just a coincidence with the way the main arterial roads are planned in Adelaide, but it seems to be a pattern. See Hindmarsh Town is in a dead triangle. Similarly, if you go down to Warriparinga[4], which is another important Kaurna site, it's also located on a triangle – Laffer's Triangle – on the southern side of the city of Adelaide.

So all these triangles got me thinking. Hindmarsh Town was actually a Kaurna burial ground, and Aboriginal people used to go down there to bury their dead. I was asked once, by this Hindmarsh gardening group, to work out a Kaurna name for this place they were developing at Hindmarsh. I suggested the name *Karrakundo*, which means 'high chest'. How the heck I came up with this name I don't know, but I think it was because it was a place where you bury or lay down the dead, and you pile dirt up over the chest on the grave. Actually, *karra* is an intriguing word because it has three meanings: there's *karra* meaning 'high', *karra* meaning 'redgum', and it also means 'on high, heaven'. Now, *kundo* means 'chest', so together *karrakundo* means 'high chest' or maybe 'high ground'.

I consulted the Kaurna dictionary, prepared by the German

---

4 *Warriparinga* actually means 'Windy Creek', and is located on the Sturt Creek, *Warri* means 'wind', *Parri* 'river' and *-ngga* means 'at, in, on, by'.

missionaries Teichelmann and Shürmann in 1840, because they listed some Kaurna place names. For Hindmarsh Town they had *Karraundo*. So then I checked with the linguist Rob Amery, and he said, 'You've come up with the same word!' He explained that when you put two words like *karra* and *kundo* together you drop off the second 'k' sound, and you get *Karraundo*. I thought to myself, well I'll be blowed. So there's a certain intrigue to me about Hindmarsh Town, particularly because it was a burial ground.

I don't know whether people realise it, but they've built the Hindmarsh Sports Stadium for playing soccer on that burial site in Hindmarsh. But even after spending a huge amount of money on it, it still can't hold the amount of people required for international matches. And then if they want to use it for local soccer matches, the clubs can't afford the hire fees. It's funny how comedies of errors seem to happen on sites like that. These big ventures don't finish up being practical, do they? It seems that site was doomed from the start.

The other intriguing triangle is Laffer's Triangle – the site of Warriparinga. It's on a triangle between South Road, Sturt Road and Marion Road, near the Flinders Medical Centre. Now because Warriparinga is such an important Kaurna site, the Marion City Council established a Kaurna Interpretive Centre there for us in the late 1990s, in collaboration with the Kaurna people. Warriparinga is a particularly significant site for the Kaurna people, because it is the place where the Kaurna Dreaming story of Tjilbruke starts. It's where the Dreaming ancestor Tjilbruke picked up the body of his nephew Kulultuwi, and started his journey south.

Warriparinga was set in a very peaceful corner where Sturt Creek meanders through the site, with these magnificent gum trees along the banks. At the new Interpretive Centre there are a number of interesting things to visit. The senior Kaurna woman and activist Georgina Williams runs Friendship Fires for Conciliation, on a regular basis there – she's been running them for many years. She won't use the word 'reconciliation' because she says, 'How can we have "re-conciliation" if there was never "conciliation" in the beginning?'

Some of the latest developments that have happened down at Warriparinga, however, have been disappointing. They've built this new Southern Expressway there for all the commuters heading to the southern suburbs of Adelaide. The expressway has cut right through the triangle. Furthermore, just off Sturt Road they built that huge Ansett Call Centre and concreted car park. But not long after they built the centre, Ansett went bust. I don't know what they're using that building for now. There's so little land in the city which is designated as Kaurna land, I don't understand why they keep encroaching on that important Kaurna site. Why don't people want natural country within the city area, where you can go and have some relief and meditation from the busy city?

There's nothing wrong with building houses in the city, but our people say that you've also got to have space for people. This country is designed like that, with its rivers and serene places and gums that are hundreds of years old. Tim Flannery, Director of the South Australian Museum, talks about how we need to work out how to live cooperatively in this country of ours. Unfortunately too many people have got this silly idea from Charles Darwin that life is one big struggle to exploit our environment, and survival is just a matter of the fittest, strongest and most powerful winning out. It's a silly notion! You can't do that in this fragile environment. If you don't cooperate with nature in this country you'll go bust. Just like Ansett – they were the last ones to build on Laffer's Triangle at Warriparinga. These big companies only worry about profits and forget to consider the social and environmental cost of their developments.

I'll tell you another story. Someone rang me up once and

said, 'Lewis, they're gonna put this drilling rig opposite one of your sites down the Gulf. What are you gonna do about it?' See they wanted to drill out at sea opposite Moana, which is a significant site on the Tjilbruke Dreaming trail. So I said, 'I'm not gonna do anything. I'll leave it up to the old people.' Anyway, it wasn't long before I heard that the leg had fallen off the drilling rig and they had to tow the whole thing away! I still can't get over that – our Kaurna ancestors sure took care of them. This is a steel rig we're talking about, and this is a low lying gulf, so why would the leg fall off? They had to get it repaired before they went somewhere else to drill. They never came back. So there's a lot of intrigue in this Kaurna country – this is no ordinary country.

The whole of the city of Adelaide is built on the site of our Red Kangaroo Dreaming. As mentioned before, we call the red kangaroo *tarnda* in our Kaurna language. That's where we get the name for Victoria Square from – Tarndanyangga, which means 'at (the place of) the Red Kangaroo'. Tandanya is also the name of the Aboriginal Cultural Institute on Grenfell Street. There was once a large rock in the city, named *Tarnda Kanya*, which was an important Kangaroo Dreaming site for the Kaurna people.[5] It was located alongside the Torrens River where the present day Adelaide Festival Centre complex now stands. It was a large limestone outcrop, which was mined long ago. Soon after colonisation, that whole area became a quarry. The limestone was used to build the Old Parliament House on North Terrace, as well as the Holy Trinity Church, also on North Terrace near the Morphett Street Bridge. So this sacred Kaurna site was erased from the landscape and replaced with a modern-day icon – the Adelaide Festival Centre.

---

5 *Tarnda* means 'red kangaroo', and *Kanya* means 'rock'. The word *Tarndanya* comes from these two words. You drop the 'k' when you put them together. The suffix *-ngga* means 'at, in, on, by'. The cultural institute Tandanya is spelt without the 'r'.

Now, if you look at the larger area where the city of Adelaide is located, as an aerial photograph, it is shaped like the kangaroo. The layout of the streets of Adelaide actually form the body of the kangaroo. Port Road forms the tail, which then goes up to North Terrace, which forms the back of the kangaroo. Botanic Road and the turn onto Dequetteville Terrace form one ear and the top of the nose. Wakefield Road forms the bottom of the nose. East Terrace forms the chest,

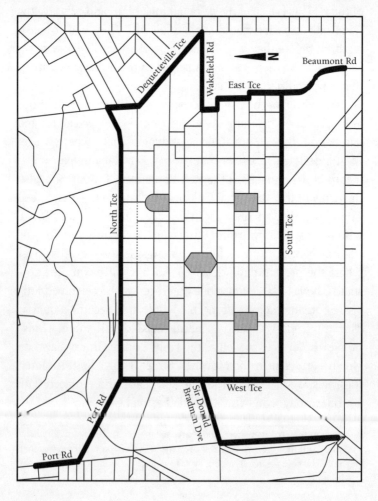

and then Beaumont Road the upper paw. South Terrace and West Terrace complete the body. Sir Donald Bradman Drive and along the railway tracks form the two main legs. Amazing!

North Adelaide is shaped like an emu, another important animal and Dreaming ancestor for the Kaurna people. We call the emu *kari* in the Kaurna language, and it features in the Tjilbruke Dreaming story. In North Adelaide, Mackinnon Parade starts the back of the emu, and then Finniss Parade and Sir Edwin Smith Avenue form the neck. Pennington Terrace is the back of the emu's neck and Montefiore Hill and Strangways Terrace form the back of the body. Mills Terrace forms the back end of the emu, and Barton Terrace marks the underbelly. Then it continues along LeFevre Road for the chest and up Kingston Terrace to form the underside of the neck. Park Road and Mann Road surround the head. One of the two legs is formed by Jeffcott Street, Torrens and Churchill Roads, and the foot is Clifton Street. The other leg is formed by Main North Road and the final foot by Nottage Terrace.

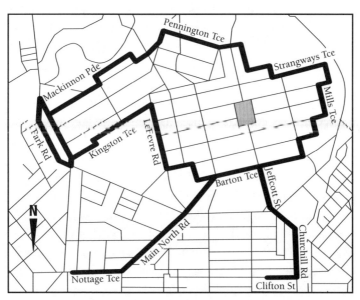

Some people mistakenly think that all the Aboriginal Dreaming sites in this country are way out in the bush, but that's not the case. Some Dreaming sites are right here in the middle of the city. I also think the non-Indigenous people in this country have developed the idea that all the 'real Aboriginal people' live in the bush, but that's not true either. We Kaurna people of the Adelaide Plains have got Dreaming sites in the middle of the city, as well as trails that go for many kilometres down the coast of Fleurieu Peninsula. The Tjilbruke Dreaming track begins at the Warriparinga site and goes all the way to Cape Jervis. Even non-Indigenous people haven't been able to rub it out over the years. That shows a certain power, doesn't it? Even though the Tarnda Kanya rock was destroyed, its spirit still lives on in the city of Adelaide too.

So you can see this whole country is spiritual and has more depth than people realise – it's not ordinary. Even the last Pope John Paul II said it when he visited here in 1986 – he commented on how it is a spiritual country. This spirituality stands out because everywhere you go there are Dreaming stories about the land. Not only that, there are old burial grounds and places that should never have been disturbed. We Kaurna people quite often get requests from people to perform smoking ceremonies on certain sites around Adelaide where unexplained things keep happening and bad feelings persist. These requests come from non-Indigenous people as well as from Aboriginal people. They ask us to cleanse these places of the spirits that are still in the area. One example is down at Seaford in the southern suburbs, where they built a new shopping centre and a new school. The developers didn't bother to do any anthropological digs before they started building in that area, and the people living there now are paying for it. They are feeling that something is not right when they are walking in one of the schools down that way, because they sense something is there – they don't feel at ease.

A different example of the past affecting the present is at the old Port Adelaide police station, which has been converted into an Information Centre. Those walking into the cells could feel the moans and groans of the spirits of earlier prisoners in the jail. Visitors didn't feel happy about going into the cells and the old jail area. These strange feelings and problems were felt among the non-Indigenous community as well as our own people – they could sense something. I tried to help at the police station, but didn't seem to solve the problem. So some Aboriginal women from Tauondi College were called in to help and they performed a further smoking ceremony. They also painted a mural on the wall before the people who ran the centre were happy.

So there's a lot of intrigue in this city. I've seen it all my life and have been involved in these intriguing things for many years now, all over Adelaide. When you're travelling and visiting people across the country as much as I do, you notice certain things, and see people acting strangely. You observe people getting upset at particular sites, and you say to yourself, jeez – there must be a burial site there.

But it's not all to do with burials. It's also to do with the positioning of new developments in relation to storylines and Dreaming trails. Sometimes it's even to do with past conflicts on particular sites. All these issues come up. Occasionally I stand in a place feeling bewildered, wondering what the source of the problems are. And not only our own people are sensitive to these feelings about this land, many non-Indigenous people feel the connection too.

There is no way that an important Dreaming trail can be ignored, or simply wiped out by whiteman's developments. Even if they change the landscape and remove all the trees, it is still there. Tarndanyangga is living proof of that – in the middle of the city at Victoria Square. There we have a major site of the Red Kangaroo Dreaming trail. It has always been a meeting place for Aboriginal people, and still is. Similarly, as mentioned before, we have the very important Tjilbruke Dreaming trail, which begins at Sturt Creek at Warriparinga, and runs all the way down the coast of the Fleurieu Peninsula.

We have geological evidence that sites along this Dreaming trail are six thousand years old, so this Dreaming story is at least that old. The middens at Moana Beach have been dated at between 6000 and 7000 years old. If it couldn't be rubbed out in 6000 years, then how could it be rubbed out now? We've got people today who still feel the strength of the Tjilbruke Dreaming, and the intrigue it has to offer both non-Indigenous and Aboriginal people at the springs and different sites along the trail. That's why people like Bill Reschke and the artist John Dowie formed the Tjilbruke Committee many years ago. They wanted to protect these sites. They eventually put up a monument at Kingston Park of a sculpture of Tjilbruke holding his nephew Kulultuwi, which is lovely. There are also cairns at all the significant sites along the coast to mark the different spots where Tjilbruke rested as he carried his nephew's body to his final resting place.

The Kaurna Dreaming story of Tjilbruke is probably one of the oldest recorded stories in the world – it's at least six thousand years old. The present coastline itself can only be seven thousand years old, because that's when the water came up onto the land after the end of the last ice age. So, you see, we can date the coastline, and so we can date the story. That's proof that the Tjilbruke story is old. There are probably older stories elsewhere in Australia, but they are hard to date. The Tjilbruke story teaches you about the geography of this country, and tells you where it is safe to walk, and where you'll get water for your journey, and where the easier low-lying country is along your path. It gives you directions to follow. It becomes a fascinating story because of all these multiple layers of meaning.

The Tjilbruke story is about our ancient Dreaming ancestor, Tjilbruke, the Ibis man. It tells of how Tjilbruke discovered the body of his young nephew Kulultuwi, who was killed. So he decides to carry his nephew's body all the way along the coast of the Fleurieu Peninsula to his final resting place at Cape Jervis. On the way, Tjilbruke stops to mourn the loss of his nephew, and in the process creates fresh water springs with his tears.

This is how the story goes. Our ancient ancestor, Tjilbruke, found out that his nephew Kulultuwi had been killed by his two half-brothers, Tjurawi and Tetjawi. They killed him because they claimed he had killed their uncle's emu – which was forbidden. However, Tjilbruke had actually travelled earlier with Kulultuwi and given him permission to pursue the emu, but the two half-brothers didn't know that. They saw Kulultuwi's foot prints, which were following the uncle's, and said, hello, he's taken his emu. See, the person who has the right to kill a bird or animal is the hunting leader – not the one who is coming second. So the half-brothers misinterpreted the tracks, and assumed Kulultuwi had broken the law.

So the story is full of intrigue. What seems a simple story actually becomes quite complex. When Tjilbruke was originally chasing this emu, Kulultuwi came up behind him and said, 'Oh, sorry Uncle, I'm taking your emu.' But then Tjilbruke gives him permission to spear the emu. But the half-brothers could not see this permission being given in the tracks – they were just looking at the footprints and seeing what they thought was Kulultuwi breaking the law. So they killed him.

This is just one of the layers of this story, which tells us about the technicality of law, how people can jump to the wrong conclusions and fall into the dangers of taking the law into their own hands. These lessons aren't explicitly stated – the story just develops in a way that encourages you to think about these issues for yourself.

Now after Kulultuwi was killed, his body was left lying

there at Warriparinga, by Sturt Creek. Before long, his uncle Tjilbruke got to hear about it, so he went down to Warriparinga and picked up Kulultuwi's body. Then he walked with him on a long trek, all the way down along the coast of the peninsula, creating springs along the way. When he arrived at Kingston Park (where the monument to Tjilbruke now stands) he put his nephew's body across his knees and cried bitterly. His tears fell at his feet, and in that very same spot a fresh water spring emerged. That spring has kept running for centuries. So another layer of this story tells you which path to take as you travel down the coast – if you follow Tjilbruke's trail you will be safe and always have fresh water to drink.

As Tjilbruke travelled further along the coast, he came to other sites that are of significance to our people, including men's and women's sites. There is Red Ochre Cove just south of Moana, which is a very important site for men. It was also a very important source of ceremonial ochre for the Kaurna people. There is also yellow and white ochre in the same region. We were lucky in this country to have our own ochre, and other Indigenous people used to come from miles to trade with us for it. The ochre was mined at one stage for paint, by a mining company, because it was very good quality red ochre. But it's not mined anymore.

So Tjilbruke travelled further along the coast, past Moana, stopping regularly to mourn the loss of his nephew, with the tears flowing freely. Several more fresh water springs mark the places where he stopped. After Kingston Park, there's one at Sellicks Beach and another one at Aldinga Beach. The one at Aldinga is right in the sea, and you can only reach it when it's low tide.

When Tjilbruke finally reached Cape Jervis, on the tip of Fleurieu Peninsula, he held his nephew's body aloft, and pointed him towards Karta, the Kaurna name for Kangaroo Island. Karta is the land of the spirits of the dead, and it was to there that Kulultuwi's spirit travelled. From Karta, the spirits of the dead either go to *karra* ('heaven') or to *pindi* ('the grave'). So that is where Kulultuwi's journey ends.

You can learn something new every time you hear the Tjilbruke story. Some of the sites along the coast are unbelievable. At Maslin's Beach, for example, there is an amazing quarry of coloured sands. When I was a young lad one bloke told me how the rainbow serpent started there at Maslin's Beach.

Years later, when I was in my sixties, I found out more about this special sand quarry. I met this German artist named Nicholas Lang who came all the way out here looking for coloured ochre. Someone told him about the ochre site on the coast south of Adelaide. While he was here he came across the sand quarry and couldn't believe the range of different coloured sands. There's deep purples and every other shade of the rainbow – they run layer after layer. Unfortunately, a sand company has been mining the sand there for years, not realising the value of the coloured sands. They mine it as garden sand, mixing it all together so that it becomes red sand. Nicholas Lang was horrified at the mining and wrote to our government saying: Look, these are the most colourful sands in the world. There would be two hundred different shades of colours there. It took forty million years to create these sands – that's what the geologists can tell you – and non-Indigenous people have managed to mine the lot in a matter of thirty to forty years.

The amazing thing is that Nicholas Lang came from Oberammergau in Germany, and when I asked him about their famous Passion Play, he said to me, 'Ah, an educated man!' They have performed the Passion Play regularly at Oberammergau since 1633. So I asked him if he had ever acted in the play, and he said, 'Yes, I was Christ.' Here's this man who comes from a very spiritual place in Germany, travelling all the way over here to experience this special Dreaming place. It took someone from Germany to petition our government to protect this place. Eventually this bloke wrote a paper about the sands, and the government did meet us to talk about preserving the remaining sands before they all run out. We suggested the quarry be used as a ceremonial ground, with the spectacular backdrop of all the layers of sand – but you'd have to find some way of stabilising the sand. We could have plays and dances performed there, which would be nice to see, but it hasn't happened yet.

So you can see the journey along our southern coastline is a mind-boggling one. It's said that we even had caves at Sellicks Beach with underground limestone formations that were better than those in the famous Jenolan caves in the Blue Mountains, west of Sydney in New South Wales. And then they went and blew them up! That was when they were mining for gravel or something down there. This is only a couple of years ago. Sense tells you that we'd have been better off having the long-term tourist attraction of caves, rather than the short-term profits from mining the area. But now all the caves are destroyed.

At the start of the Tjilbruke trail, at Warriparinga, there is an old coach house that used to be owned by the transport company Cobb & Co. It's where they used to house their coaches and horses for their southern run. There is a place there where it was easy for the coaches to cross Sturt Creek on their way south. They called this crossing the Fairford[6]. There is also a house on the site named Fairford House, which is still standing. My Uncle Fred used to drive Cobb & Co. coaches. He had five horses pulling the coach, which was odd, because

---

6 A 'ford' is a low-lying and safe place to cross a river, so they called it the Fairford.

most coaches in those days usually had four horses. So Uncle Fred used to travel to all these places, stopping to water the horses on the way at the fresh waterholes on the Tjilbruke trail. These fresh springs were important stop-overs for many travellers. But the unusual thing was that they had to head right down to the beach to get water at both Sellicks Beach and Aldinga Beach. Normally you would think, heavens, what are they drinking down there? But there was fresh water there in the sand that the horses could drink. At Aldinga Beach there is fresh water right on the beach, which is unbelievable. When the high tide comes in the spring is covered. At Sellicks Beach the spring is a bit further back and there's a little stone wall around the spring to protect it, so it's more visible.

Another Kaurna site I should mention in this rich region is the important women's site. The Onkaparinga River is actually a women's river, just north of Moana. If you look up the 1840 Kaurna dictionary, compiled by the missionaries Teichelmann and Shürmann, you see the word *Ngangkiparringga*, which literally means 'at the woman's river'.[7] It took me six months of looking in the dictionary to work out this word. These days the river is spelt with an 'O' at the beginning, not like in the dictionary. I wondered why that was until I realised the British must have changed the way they say the word, because English speakers can't say an 'ng' sound easily at the beginning of words. My theory is that these white men also wouldn't have wanted anything named after women, so instead of starting the name for the river with *Ngangki* they changed it and began the word with *Onki*. If you remember the infamous Hindmarsh Island Bridge affair here in South Australia, you'll recall that people were pretty sceptical about the women's business. Well, here's an 1840 document that lists a river, named Ngangkiparringa, just south of Adelaide, that was the 'woman's

---

7 *Ngangki* means 'woman'; *parri* means 'river' and the suffix '-*ngga*' means 'at'.

river'. In this case, the site was special to Kaurna women, rather than to Ngarrindjeri women. So we know this site was not 'fabricated' – which is what the Ngarrindjeri women were accused of doing.

There's further evidence in a book first published in 1908, written by Rodney Cockburn, called *What's in a Name?* It was republished in 1984 by his son Stewart Cockburn. He also lists the Onkaparinga River as being the 'the women's river'. It's interesting that Moana, on the coast, is like a cross roads for Kaurna women and men. The women headed north to the Ngangkiparringga, while the men headed south just round the corner to Red Ochre Cove. I think it was lovely the way the women would go one way and the men would go another. Moana was the campsite, dead in the middle. They actually camped at Pedlar's Creek, which is by Moana. See, in the old days, the Kaurna women would go and perform their fertility ceremonies, and the men would go and perform their increase ceremonies.

You can see that the grounds in the Moana area were used for ceremonial purposes. Fortunately the land has been set aside now and is a reserve. They had stone emplacements there that are a hundred yards long and thirty yards wide – full of stones. They were probably used for increase ceremonies. It was an educational event – they'd learn all about the stones, explaining all about the designs and what they meant. A lot about life can be explained by those stones. The ceremonies they performed were all about the increase of life and the protection thereof. I think it's interesting that now we've stopped performing these ceremonies, there is a definite decrease of the species. It just shows that if you give up your old ways, there's a lot to lose for both the Kaurna and the white man.

If you look all around the world, Indigenous people have performed fertility ceremonies for centuries to maintain the different species. By contrast, it seems as if modern society is all about decrease, and population control. Who is more advanced? Modern society that is wiping out all these animal species? Or Indigenous people who lived in harmony with nature?

There are other significant Kaurna sites in Adelaide that many people don't know about, and one of them is Green Fields where there is a burial site alongside the Salisbury Highway, about ten kilometres north of the city. It's just before you get to Parafield Gardens on the left. In 1992 they discovered some Aboriginal bones at Green Fields when the site was being cleared for a car park. An Italian bloke owned an olive oil factory out there, and they were digging with a bobcat, when they dug up a whole lot of bones. So straight away they got the archaeologist Neale Draper to come out and look.

As the then chairperson of the Kaurna Heritage Committee I was asked to go out to Green Fields while Neale Draper was working on the site. Neale had a lot of Aboriginal people working there with him, and they were excavating the site professionally, with all these string lines laid down in grid formation. They were sifting the soil and finding the odd bone as they went. Then they discovered this large mound, which was very intriguing. It was about twenty or thirty foot in diameter. So they dug out a corner of it, and that's where they hit many more bones. When they started counting them they thought they'd dug up six people, but as they looked and separated the bones, they realised they actually had fifteen bodies. They realised then they'd discovered a large burial site, rather than a single grave.

So, as chairperson, I had to make a decision about what to do with these bones, because they were on private land. Neale told me that the Institute of Medical and Veterinary Science (IMVS) research centre were really interested in examining the bones, so we had to make a decision. Some Kaurna people were upset and started saying, what are you digging up all these people for? They wanted to start a protest and build a tent city, and all this sort of thing. So I had to go and talk to them. We had a meeting at one of the schools out at Salisbury, and I told them that the whole business was a rescue operation. We weren't digging up the bones, we were rescuing them from being lost and destroyed forever. Sometimes people can misinterpret what you're doing.

I must admit that my first thought about the bones was to put them straight back in the ground. But as you grow older, you learn to look around you and to trust your instincts in difficult situations. So during one visit, as I entered the Green Fields site, I saw a willy wagtail – what we call a *Tjintrin*. Aboriginal people consider this bird a messenger. So this little *Tjintrin* was sitting on the fence as I walked in, and I noticed he was sitting quite still. When you live in a city, you have to look hard for the signs of nature, and I had to think about this little bird. Why isn't he moving? Why isn't anything exciting him? He seemed to be just sitting quietly. Normally a willy wagtail is an active little bird, and when he comes to tell you of danger, or of a death, he flits around in an excited manner so you notice that he has come to you with a message.

As I walked closer to the site, I looked back at the *Tjintrin* still sitting quietly and thought to myself, he's telling me it's alright. I had to make a decision about these bones, so I decided to let them keep excavating.

Once they 'rescued' the bones from the site, the IMVS researchers got involved. I ended up liaising with this Dr Cornish on the bones, and went to meet him at the centre. He introduced me to some of the people in the medical centre there on Frome Road in the city. There seemed to be a lot of top forensic doctors from around the world interested in these bones, probably because they were found so close to the city. The first important job to be done was to date the bones. Neale helped with that and I think they finished up dating them at around 200 years old. So they weren't ancient bones, they were more from modern times, from just before the time of the first Europeans coming here. It could have been a grave-site from 1789 when the first wave of smallpox came over this way from Sydney and killed large numbers of our people.

As the medical analysis of the bones continued, I used to go and see Dr Cornish and he used to write me letters. Anyway, one of the intriguing stories to come out of all of this was that an x-ray of one of the skeletons showed this bloke had been attacked like Caesar! He had five stab wounds in his body – in his chest, one in each side of his body, one in his lower back, plus a wooden dagger in his upper back which had gone through his spine. We could tell because he still had this hole from the dagger in his spine. It was wood because it had rotted away and disappeared, just leaving a hole. Straight away when we saw the hole in his spine we knew he was a paraplegic. But, as Dr Cornish told me, the most surprising part was that alongside the stab wound was a growth of bone about three and a half centimetres long which meant that this man must have lived for six months after being injured.

So this Kaurna man survived all that time with those terrible injuries. This means that Aboriginal medical care must have been far more advanced two hundred years ago than the Europeans were back then. This fact was reported in the news-papers after the findings at the Green Fields site. So we have learnt more amazing things about the Kaurna people through research work done on the bones. But how the hell did the Kaurna keep this man alive for six months?

I found the answer to this mystery soon after. I was talking to a Native American Indian bloke visiting from America once, and he said to me, 'Do you know, Lew, we teach our kids natural science in schools.' And he proceeded to tell me about all the things they teach their kids, and especially how they learn about natural bush medicines. He asked me, 'Where do you think we get citronella, tea tree oil, eucalyptus and all the other naturally occurring antibiotics from?'

And I thought to myself, bloody hell, we've not only given up our country for free, we've also given away our natural remedies as well.

So that's how this Kaurna man had been kept alive. Those old Kaurna people knew a lot about natural antibiotics. See, all Indigenous people around the world get to know their own plants and products and what they can be used for. They become astute observers of what remedy works and which plants to use. Over a long period of time the Kaurna became skilled bush-medicine doctors. Unfortunately, when foreign viruses like smallpox arrived, our mob weren't prepared. Our traditional doctors would have tried to treat the sick, but they would have got sick too, and then all the expertise in medicine would disappear when they died. New ailments like smallpox caught our people off guard – we had never had things like that in our thousands of years of existence. Similarly we had never had measles or mumps or influenza. All we had was rheumatism and a few other non-infectious ailments like injuries. Maybe we got a bit of food poisoning from eating foul meat, but nothing too nasty.

So when I eventually told our Kaurna people about Dr Cornish's discoveries they were very pleased. I don't think either Neale Draper or Dr Cornish have written about their findings in any academic papers, so you're getting to hear about all this through me instead. Maybe you'll read about it in books on Aboriginal people in the future, telling about how our people knew a lot about medical care in the old days. At least they reported this in the newspapers.

Eventually the bones were returned to the original site at Green Fields and given a proper burial. The IMVS researchers had wanted to keep them, because they were very interested in looking at the children's bones. But I said to Dr Cornish, 'Look, you can have the bones to study, but only for one year, and then we've got to put them back.' They nearly went into meltdown. See, they wanted to keep them. That's what tickles me about non-Indigenous people. They talk about Aboriginal people taking our time over issues, but they can also take time when it suits them. The researchers said, 'How can we do all this research in a year?' But when it came to the crunch, they agreed to our one year term and finished their research.

Originally the bones were buried under a mound, so we explained to the bloke who owned the factory that it was important to protect the mound. He said people had been driving their motorbikes over it, so he agreed to put a fence around it. I thought that was good of him, because when the bones were discovered it was a real nuisance for him. Eventually he changed his view and became very protective of that site. So there was a happy conclusion. It just shows that a lot of positives can emerge from a negative situation. After all the objecting and the different sides battling with each other, in the end the Green Fields site became fully protected – and there was no government intervention at all. It was a very positive outcome.

So there are different ways of approaching issues relating to Indigenous rights. If you talk to each other rationally and explain your point of view, other parties will be receptive to your needs. This factory owner was very obliging in the end because the whole issue was explained clearly to him. He also benefited by getting reduced council rates for having a significant burial site on his property. This whole story is an example of a good compromise and how we can all share the space in our city of Adelaide.

13

Achievements and celebrations

Although there has been injustice and hard times for Aboriginal people in the past, I want to highlight the positive things that have happened during my lifetime. I also want to acknowledge the contribution as well as the many achievements that other Aboriginal people have made over the years.

Aboriginal people have contributed a great deal to this country in many ways. Take the famous Ngarrindjeri man David Unaipon, from the community of Raukkan on Lake Alexandrina. He became a well-known public speaker, writer and inventor in his time. He patented eleven of his inventions, the most famous being an improved shearing handpiece. Unaipon's handpiece design can be seen on the Australian fifty-dollar note alongside his portrait. Unaipon was eventually awarded a South Australian Centenary Medal as well as a Coronation Medal, for his inventions and for services to his people. Another big contribution Aboriginal people have made to this nation is through the army. Many Aboriginal men volunteered to enlist and fought alongside non-Indigenous Australian soldiers in every war involving Australian troops, from the Boer War (1899–1902) to the modern Gulf wars. From Point Pearce alone there were at least seventy-two men who fought in the four wars: the First and Second World Wars, Korea and Vietnam. Their names are commemorated on a memorial plaque at Point Pearce, which you pass as you drive into the township.

The irony is that the Australian government was willing to accept Aboriginal men and women to fight overseas for their country, but on their return they weren't allowed to vote, and weren't counted as citizens of this country until 1967. That meant they couldn't drink in the Returned Soldiers' League (RSL) clubs on their return from war, and they weren't eligible for the returned soldier settler blocks. An exception was made for those Aboriginal people who were willing to renounce their Aboriginality and become exempted from the 1939 *Aborigines Act*, but then they could no longer visit their families living on the missions.

But life has many twists and turns. Who would have thought that in November 2002 I would be awarded the Local Hero Award (for the year 2003) within the South Australian section of the Australian of the Year awards. I had to go to Government House to receive the gong from an Australian of the Year representative. I was given the award for my services to the Aboriginal community, particularly as the inaugural chairperson of the Aboriginal Elders Council of South Australia. When I gave my acceptance speech on the lawns of Government House, I told the audience that I was honoured and surprised. I also told them what my Auntie May always told me: 'Someone has to do it, and it may as well be me!'

I guess that has become a philosophy of mine throughout my life, because I have always just got on with the job, and haven't expected the accolades. So to get all these rewards later in life has been a real shock.

I must say that I have found, over the years, that not all people are willing to put in the hard work to make a difference in this world. It's easier to complain. To ask someone to do voluntary work or to sit on a committee is time-consuming and can be a heck of a task. Some of us worry about future generations, and whether they will volunteer for community work. Sometimes the young can become disillusioned about the enormity of the problems in this world today, and ask 'why bother?'

When I hear such sentiments, I think of the story of the starfish. Once I read about this little kid who was walking along a sandy beach picking up stranded starfish, lying high and dry in the sun. He was throwing them back into the sea, one by one. An old man was watching him do this, and he went up to the boy and said, 'Sonny, if you look along the beach those stranded starfish go for miles. There must be a million of them. What difference do you hope to make?'

The little boy looked at the old man as he tossed another starfish back into the sea, and said, 'It makes a difference to this one!'

I've learnt from stories like this all my life, and this story tells me that it's better to do something than nothing, because you *can* make a difference.

I was also honoured in 2003 to be awarded the Centenary Medal, for further services to the community. The citation reads: 'For service to the Aboriginal people of South Australia, and in particular Port Adelaide'. That was a bit of a surprise really. To choose recipients each federal minister forms a committee from their electorate. I suppose they thought they had better give a medal to one Aboriginal from my area, so I was the one they chose. But I guess I have done a few things in the Port Adelaide area. If I think about them they soon add up. I was on the Tauondi College council for seventeen years. Tauondi is an independent TAFE college for Aboriginal students, now located in the old Port Adelaide Primary School facing Grand Junction Road. Tauondi was once located at Brougham Place in North Adelaide and was formerly known as the Aboriginal Community College. The word *tauondi* is from the Kaurna language, and means 'to break through'.

I was also on the Kalaya Committee, which established the Kalaya kindergarten for young Aboriginal children in the

Port Adelaide area. The word *kalaya* means 'emu' in the Pitjantjatjara language (from the north-west of South Australia). We finished up getting nice new kindergarten premises, freshly built in a lovely setting in the Port.

Another task I really enjoyed in the community was coaching the young kids in the Taperoo district at both footy and cricket. As I've mentioned before, I also got pretty involved with the schools in the area with my work as the Aboriginal Liaison Officer. I think that's how the federal member for our electorate, Rod Sawford, remembered me, because he used to be the principal at Taperoo Primary.

One major community project that I have been particularly involved with over the years is the establishment of Kura Yerlo. This project grew out of my involvement with Tauondi College and Kalaya kindergarten. We realised there was a need for an extra child-care centre in the Port area for Aboriginal children before they began at kindergarten. We thought they could learn all these skills that they need when they start kindergarten, such as playing happily with other children, and sitting still when asked to. We eventually managed to acquire this lovely big old building on the foreshore at Largs Bay. That's why we chose the name *Kura Yerlo*, which means 'near the sea' in the Kaurna language (*Kura* means 'near' and *Yerlo* means 'sea'). The building is on the Esplanade, just a stone's throw from the sea. Now it's grown into a much broader community service venture, and serves Aboriginal people of all ages in the Port area. It's a beautiful spot, where the kids can walk down to the beach.

It was a long struggle getting that centre established though. The people in the area weren't too pleased about it and the Port Adelaide Council took us to court over it. We had been offered these premises by the Sisters of Joseph – they actually call themselves the Sisters of the Sacred Heart. They were marvellous, because they were happy to forego the rent for two years while the whole venture was tied up in court. The Provincial Mary Reardon told us, 'We will stick with you.' The building was once the St Joseph's Orphanage.

At around the same time, Tauondi College had to move to larger premises from North Adelaide, so they were initially offered the orphanage. Then this other offer came up of the old Port Primary School for our child-care centre, but it was too big for our purposes, so we suggested a swap. Eventually Tauondi took the old primary school, and we planned on taking over the orphanage. However, this was all a long time in coming. But since all our struggles with the local residents and the council, things have turned out well, and the locals are now happy to have us as neighbours. They realise their fears of drunkenness and unruly behaviour were all ill-founded.

We originally began talking about the child-care centre in 1983, and we were still in negotiation three years later. But eventually Tauondi moved out and the Education Department made some adjustments to the building for us, and we moved in in 1986. I was the founding chairperson of Kura Yerlo, but the original idea came from the committee of Kalaya, including Tony Barrett, Nina Barrett and Angela Norris. I was also on that committee. After we finally got our building and moved in, I ended up being appointed as the director in 1993, but that was only for three years. My wife, Pauline, put a lot of work into Kura Yerlo too. She's marvellous with little children, and she worked for many years cooking for the children in the child-care centre. But we all had to work really hard to get the funding to get Kura Yerlo off the ground. Finding a venue was just one of our major hurdles. One person who did a huge amount of work for us was the St Joseph's nun Michele Madigan. She was very skilled in a lot of areas, particularly lobbying for us with the various charities we had to deal with. But there were a number of other people who did a lot of work too, such as the Kaurna women Mary Cooper and Alice Rigney.

As I've said, I also worked in factories in the area for much of my working life. Before joining the Education Department, I worked in the Adelaide Brighton Cement factory, which is still operating at Birkenhead on the Port River. Then I worked at the Harbors Board for four years. So I basically grew up in the Port, and have worked in the Port most of my life – well, ever since I came there with my mother in 1936 from Point Pearce, via Moonta and Wallaroo. I've also had all my formal education in the Port: at Ethelton Primary and then LeFevre Technical School. So having been in the Port most of my life, I guess I could say I really am a 'Portonian'! I suppose that's why they decided to give me the medal.

I've also been on different advisory committees, such as the Port Adelaide Council Aboriginal Advisory Committee, and been the Kaurna Heritage Committee representative who deals with heritage matters in the Port area. I was also in the Aboriginal Elders Council of South Australia Incorporated for three years. I've taken on a lot of different roles in the field of education. I used to be on a lot of curriculum committees and all that sort of stuff, so I guess I've had a pretty broad spread of things. It takes time and effort to be on these committees, and the results don't always come immediately. But you soon realise that you've got to be there for the long haul, and you have to put the effort in if you want long term results. Some of our people drop off because it's such a long haul and hard yakka – especially if you are trying to get funding and support for different ventures. But I realised in the early days that someone needed to do that, because if you don't, things just won't happen. It's not automatic, and the effort needed can wear you down. You also need to seek out people with the expertise for some projects, like we had with Michele Madigan in getting Kura Yerlo established. You rarely do anything alone.

Of course there have been a number of ventures in the Port Adelaide and Alberton area that haven't lasted. There was the

Sunday Club that Pauline was involved with, along with many other women such as Shirley Sansbury and Mona Tur. The Sunday Club was a social activity for Aboriginal kids. It was good while it lasted. Peter Bicknell used to be involved and now he's the CEO of Uniting Wesley Care at Port Adelaide. We also started youth groups at the Port, and at Alberton. But then they folded.

I keep telling people, we seem to get funding for a lot of these pilot programs, yet I'm still looking for the aeroplane! What I mean by this is, the government will fund these short-term programs, but they inevitably fall by the wayside because the government won't come good with the long-term support that these programs need.

One project that has been successful in recent years is the Port Youth program, now known as Kurruru[1]. This program provides after school and quality holiday activities for the youth in the Port area, but now is developing as a theatre and dance group, giving young people an opportunity to perform at different events. The Kaurna Elder Auntie Josie Agius has been very involved with this program for many years, working with the coordinator Diat Alferink. Together they seem to manage to get funding for their projects each year, but it's a struggle.

There are three recent projects that have been important for the Kaurna people here in Adelaide. One of them is the naming of the many parklands that make up the green-belt surrounding the city of Adelaide. There are twenty-nine public parks altogether, and they have all been given a Kaurna name in recognition of our prior ownership of this land. This has been a joint project between the Kaurna people and the Adelaide City Council. All twenty-nine Kaurna names have now been endorsed by the City Council, and many of the

1 *Kurruru* is a Kaurna word meaning 'to form a circle'.

parks have new signs showing their new names. Seven of these parks are dual-named, while the other twenty-two have been given names for the first time. Before that they just had numbers, not even an English name.

An example is Park 1, which is located alongside the Torrens River just north of the weir, by the par 3 golf course owned by the Adelaide City Council. This park has been given the official Kaurna name *Piltawodli*, which means 'possum home'; this was the site's original name. As mentioned earlier, it was the site of the Native Location, which was the fenced-off compound where the Aboriginal people of Adelaide lived in the very early days of the colony. They originally camped at the site of the Adelaide Oval, but were moved by the government to the Native Location. You will remember this was also the site of the first Aboriginal school in this state, which was started by the German missionaries Brothers Christian Teichelmann and Clamor Schürmann in 1839. Now there is a plaque at Piltawodli commemorating the site and the school, as well as the Kaurna Elders who lived there and shared their language with the German missionaries. Later Brother Sam Klose joined the team, and Schürmann moved to Port Lincoln. At Piltawodli, the missionaries taught the students to read and write in the Kaurna language for five years, until 1845 when the school was closed and relocated to Kintore Avenue. This second school was called the Native School Establishment, and was where the Migration Museum now stands. Here the Kaurna and other Aboriginal children were instructed in English only and, as mentioned earlier, it was here that my great great grandmother Kudnarto received her training.

The five parks that lie within the city centre of Adelaide have also been given Kaurna names. The park in the very centre of the city is Victoria Square, and as I've already mentioned, is named Tarndanyangga. The other four squares have been given Kaurna names in recognition of important

Kaurna Elders from the very early days when Adelaide was first established. Hindmarsh Square is named Mogata after Mullawirraburka's (King John's) wife. Hurtle Square is named Tangkaira after Ityamaiitpinna's (King Rodney's) wife. Light Square is named Wauwe after Kadlitpinna's (Captain Jack's) wife, while Whitmore Square is named Ivaritji. Ivaritji (or Princess Amelia) was King Rodney's daughter, and as mentioned earlier was the last living so-called 'full-blood' Kaurna woman when she passed away in 1929.

The other big square in North Adelaide, Wellington Square, is named after my own ancestor Kudnarto. She, of course, was the first Aboriginal woman to marry a European here in South Australia. The Torrens River has also been officially dual-named by taking on its original Kaurna name *Karrawirra Parri*, which literally means 'red gum forest river'.

Another project I was involved with was the re-landscaping of the area in front of the Adelaide Festival Centre. The Graham F. Smith Trust gave a reconciliation and educational gift to the Kaurna community, which was to take the form of an art installation. So in collaboration with Kate Brennan, the CEO of the Festival Theatre, and Leonie Ebert (the wife of the late Graham Smith), it was decided that a piece of artwork would be installed at the new Festival Theatre entrance. This resulted in some Kaurna art work in the form of carved sandstone from the River Murray – which we accepted as a gift from the Ngarrindjeri people. The stone sculpture was designed by the artist Tony Rosella and the two Aboriginal artists Eileen Karpany and Darren Siwes. The artwork features the words *kauwanda* 'north', *patpa* 'south' and the words *yertarra padnima taingiwiltanendadlu*, meaning 'if we travel the land then we become strong'.

The words of a letter, scribed in 1841 by a Kaurna schoolgirl, Ityamaii (Jane) and signed by eight other Kaurna children from the Piltawodli school, also appears within the installation.

It reads:

Murkandi ngadlu parnu kurlangga, padlo ngadlu numa nakketti.
Ngadluko yerlitta ba tikketti maiingga parnungga mutyertilla. Mai
mutyerta padlo ngadlu yungketti. Maiiyerta ngadluko padlonungko
kudlaityappi.

Lament we at his absence, he at us well did look, our father
he did sit regarding food, meat, clothing, food, clothing he us did
give, land for food he us back gave.[2]

The letter is a lament to the departing Governor Colin George
Gawler, who was very good to the Kaurna people, at the time
when he was being replaced by Governor George Grey. They
were sad that he was leaving and wanted to let him know.

An educational booklet was also produced in 2002,
entitled *Kaurna Meyunna, Kaurna Yerta Tampendi*, which is a
Walking Trail Guide of the River Torrens and the Adelaide city
area. It explains the significant Kaurna sites in the city, as well
as giving an interpretation of the Kaurna artwork at the Festival
Centre entrance.

A further project I have been involved with is an art installation at the entrance of the recent redevelopment of the State
Library of South Australia, completed in 2004. The art work
was designed by Kay Lawrence. Engraved in the pavement
immediately in front of the main entrance is a Kaurna statement of welcome:

Munara ngai wanggandi 'Marni naa Kaurna yertaanna budni.
Wortangga marni naa State Library of South Australilla budni.
Ngaityo yungandalya, ngaityo yakkanandalya. Padniadlu wadu.'

---

2 A more natural translation would be: 'We lament at your [Governor Gawler's]
   departure; our father who looked after us with food, meat and clothing. You
   gave us some land to farm.'

225

The English translation takes the form of another Kaurna installation in the new foyer of the library, and includes a large metal ring, reading:

> First I welcome you all to my Kaurna country, and next I welcome you to the State Library of South Australia. My brothers, my sisters, let's walk together in harmony.

I sigh with relief that we Kaurna are at last sharing the space in the very centre of our city of Adelaide.

One last group that I should mention that I particularly enjoy being involved with is *Kaurna Warra Pintyandi*, which literally means 'creating Kaurna language'. We are a language advisory group that meets once a month of an evening to discuss and consult on Kaurna language issues. The linguist Rob Amery, who did his PhD on Kaurna language reclamation, and the highly respected Kaurna Elder Auntie Alice Wallara Rigney and myself are the three signatories for the group. We now have our own web page on the University of Adelaide website if you want to look us up. The meetings are open to all Kaurna people and anyone who is interested in promoting and developing the Kaurna language. A large part of our meetings is taken up with the many requests we get from artists, musicians and other people or groups wanting to use the Kaurna language in some way, whether it be in an exhibition, installation, song or naming some institution or other. We give them permission to use certain Kaurna words or phrases, and correct anything they may have wrong in the language they are proposing. I guess it's good that so many people are interested in using our language in public places, but it is important that they consult our language group first. This also allows us to keep track of our language and its use in public. But this is just one of the reasons we set up our little group. Another is to keep our spelling and grammar standardised and to help make the Kaurna language stronger.

Sometimes I find it pretty ironic when I read about Aboriginal people in some of those early textbooks they used in schools. They say we were a primitive people who wandered aimlessly all over the country. I used to get confused when I was a kid, because I didn't know who on earth they were talking about – maybe there were these other Aboriginal people that I didn't know about. I thought I'd better do my own research because what was written in the books didn't make much sense to me.

I guess that's what started me on this quest of inquiry and research into my own people. I found that I knew very little about my own people. I guess when you're living under the government policy of assimilation, it wasn't easy to learn about your Aboriginal culture. We were no longer really in the proper setting and the proper surrounds. And with my mother's predicament of being a single supporting mother, we were living this ad hoc life, moving around in odd situations. I didn't have the understanding and the language to follow all that was going on in our lives.

But among the snippets I got from the Elders around me – which fascinated me – I started putting bits together, and suddenly started to realise what an in-depth system of beliefs and philosophies my own Aboriginal people had developed over a long time. It's really a very clever system. Hopefully this book has managed to convey and share some of it with you all. My people's beliefs are really more involved than some people can imagine.

I can now honestly say that Aboriginal society is built on a system of sound management. So it just shows how wrong those early books were that portrayed us as hapless wanderers. I say, the highest form of management is to teach the workers to do the jobs themselves and to manage their own affairs. So what Aboriginals are practising is actually the highest form of management. Some people might argue that we were not a structured society because we didn't have any so-called 'chiefs'. I argue that we did have Elders, but they didn't need to act like the bosses, because the 'Indians' were empowered by the Elders to make the decisions and were therefore happy to do the work. When the work force is empowered it is a far more efficient way of working.

Not only that, in the past Aboriginal people had the highest form of education in the world for their whole populace. To get to the top of the educational ladder is a very hard road in any society and culture. In the Western world, for example, not everybody gets a university education. There are limited numbers at the top – that's understood and accepted. But our people, on the other hand, believed that the whole of society should be educated to a reasonable level – so they were very good at educating the bottom layer too. They said, if you're gonna get your people to do the jobs and take responsibility for themselves, you must educate them and prepare them to do this. And that's what they did. They actually *all* had to be educated to a certain level because the Australian landscape can be harsh, and understanding it can be a matter of survival. In Australia we've got more poisonous snakes, more poisonous trees, and more poisonous animals than many other continents, so in effect it forced Aboriginal people to know and possess a lot of information – just to survive. So education was the only answer.

The English soon discovered that Australia is not an easy country to live in. They wanted to transform the country into another England because they were terrified of this new country. They immediately chopped down everything because they were afraid of these unknown trees, and wanted wide open paddocks. They wouldn't have survived in this country if they'd tried to eat the local plants because they couldn't differentiate between which ones were good and which ones were bad. They would have been poisoned by all sorts of plants. Working out what's safe to eat can be a very involved business, because you *can* eat certain poisonous things if you know how to prepare them. I know there was a particular fruit in Western Australia that the Europeans saw the local Aboriginal people eat, so they also ate them. But the Europeans died because they didn't realise you had to take the poisonous seeds out. It was the seeds that killed them.

So every Aboriginal person had to attain a fairly high educational level in botany, zoology, meteorology, geography and genealogies to survive in this country before Europeans arrived. They had to acquire this information in order to stay alive and govern their own lives. So education took the form of a very well-thought-out system. Another marvellous thing about Aboriginal society and Aboriginal culture is the fact that it lasted, and even thrived, for so long – that alone shows that it was built on very sound principles. *No* other culture has lasted as long and as continuously as ours has. Ancient history shows that other cultures have come and gone over thousands of years, but none has lasted tens of thousands of years like ours. These days they talk of Aboriginal culture having lasted forty or even sixty thousand years. It's the longest-living culture the world has ever seen. It's obvious from that statement alone that it must have been built on sound principles – and this fact should be celebrated.

One of the activities that I am most well-known for here in Adelaide is the giving of Kaurna Welcomes. I get to meet many people through being asked to welcome visitors and locals to conferences, workshops, seminars, openings and launches. People come and talk to me afterwards and ask if it is alright for them to call me Uncle Lew.

All this welcoming stuff began in 1989 when Professor

Colin Bourke asked me to give a welcome in the Kaurna language to people attending the inaugural David Unaipon lecture for the University of South Australia (then the South Australian College of Advanced Education). So together with the linguist Rob Amery, we worked out what to say in Kaurna, along with an English translation. The lecture about the Aboriginal inventor and writer David Unaipon was given at Brookman Hall on North Terrace by Doctor Eric Willmott. Then in 1991 Colin asked me again to give a welcome at the next David Unaipon lecture, but this time only in Kaurna, and not to translate it into English. This particular lecture was given by Mick Dodson, who later became well-known as the Human Rights and Equal Opportunity Aboriginal and Islander Social Justice Commissioner.

Then in 1992, the well-known crusader for the environment, David Suzuki, came to Adelaide to launch his book *Wisdom of the Elders*, and his publishers contacted me. So before the launch I met David at the Hyatt Hotel for a cup of coffee, and he asked me to welcome everyone to his book launch in Kaurna. Then he also asked me if I would say a few words extra as well, which I thought at the time would be a bit daunting in front of 5000 people at the Entertainment Centre. But David Suzuki said, you'll be alright. I smiled wryly and thought to myself, yeah, it's alright for you, but a bit much for me. I was nervous but I managed to do it, and as it turned out it went well. David was so pleased that he gave our Kaurna Heritage Committee $1000 towards our heritage work. In my speech I actually called David *Karnu Meyu*, which means 'mountain of a man', which he really appreciated.

Now every time David Suzuki comes to Adelaide he generally rings me to say hello. The last time he came, I had moved house and he had trouble contacting me. So he casually asked Premier Mike Rann if he knew me. Mike Rann said, 'Yeah, I know Uncle Lew. He's an old friend of mine,' and passed on my number. The premier's office is always ringing me to ask me to welcome people to different events and functions. So when David rang me he said, 'Hey, Lew. Even the Premier knows you. It's a pleasure to know you. You're famous!' To which I responded, 'Ease up, David. It's a small town here!'

So from then on, things started to escalate exponentially. By 1997 fourteen different Kaurna people had given a total of 100 Kaurna welcomes to Adelaide since 1989. Now there are some people who are giving up to 100 welcomes a year just on their own. A couple of years ago I actually counted the number of welcomes I'd given and was pleasantly surprised to find it was well over 100 welcomes in one year – amazing! Now when I give a welcome, I generally tell people during my speech that my own people used to meet for conferences (just like they are) for thousands of years. I tell them about the Kaurna word *Banba-banbabalya*, which means 'conference', and how we held conferences when the Nukunu, Kaurna, Narungga and Ngadjuri people used to meet for two moons. I also often put a little quip at the end – we probably had more to say than you people, because you're only meeting for a few days.

I think Mike Rann first got to know me when I was asked to give a welcome to the Constitutional Convention held in South Australia in our Parliament House in 2001. I gave the welcome in the Kaurna language and the late Auntie Doris Graham, then the oldest living Kaurna Elder, gave the English translation. Ever since 2002, I have given a Kaurna welcome each year to the governor at the opening of the sessions of Parliament. First I welcome the governor, currently Her Excellency Marjorie Jackson, and for the last two sessions I welcomed the governor's deputy, His Excellency Bruno Krumins. I conduct the welcome at the bottom of the steps of Parliament House, and then we go into the chamber where the governor presents the forthcoming parliamentary program to the government. Then I'm invited to hob-nob with all the dignitaries, as we go off for a good feed and a glass of wine at their official luncheon, which I thoroughly enjoy.

One particular event that I was very pleased to be involved in recently was the opening of the Regency Green Aged Care Facility in June 2004. I was one of the initiators of the project very early on when I was involved at Kura Yerlo. The facility was opened by Premier Mike Rann, who said it was the most innovative of its kind in the country, largely because so many different ethnic groups were involved.

This project all began when Aboriginal Elders from Kura Yerlo, and Marg Tripp from the Department of Aged Care, formed a partnership with Wesley Uniting Care. They thought the idea of forming a partnership was such a good idea they decided to invite eighteen other ethnic groups to be involved to make the whole plan workable. This is why it made for a unique program. So it just shows that I'm a bit more than an ugly face!

One of the latest celebrations that I was very happy to be a part of was a graduation ceremony held in the Festival Theatre for graduates of the University of South Australia in September 2004. They made me a Fellow of the University of South Australia, which was quite a surprise. I had to get all decked out in this fancy gown with all the trimmings, and stand up there on the stage as Professor Paul Hughes said all these nice things about what I have done over the years in the area of education. I must say it was quite an honour, and all my sons were there and my daughter came over from Canberra.

There's this myth that says that South Australia was different to the other states in Australia, and was settled in an orderly manner. But I think by telling my own family's story I have demonstrated that that was not the case. We Aboriginal people were pushed off our land, particularly in the urban areas, just as they were in the other states. But now I think it is a time to celebrate the fact that South Australians are coming together in different ways to reconcile our past, and to share this country of ours. And with Aboriginal studies being taught in all primary schools, our kids are learning more about the past, and coming to terms with the truth. What I have written here is about what I know, and what I've been told, and what documents I've read through my own research. Now that I've finished telling my story, I get a certain sense of pride from what I have written, and a great deal of satisfaction from what I have achieved – both in my life and in writing this book. And I'm very happy to have managed to put it all down in black and white for you all to share!

Appendix 1

I don't feel as if I have to prove this theory of mine of the Egyptians travelling to Australia 5000 years ago. But there are some signs that could be seen as evidence that the Egyptians did come here and learn from Aboriginal people. As far as I know the Egyptians started to believe in just one god 4000 years ago. The Jewish people also came out of Egypt with the same beliefs. And there are certain markings on rock paintings in Australia that are hard to explain – they could have possibly come from the Egyptians. There is other evidence as well, such as the symbol in Egyptian hieroglyphics for the number ten that looks like an upside-down boomerang. So I reckon the Egyptians could have taken some of our ideas and religion back to Egypt. I might be wrong, but it's something to think about.

Some people may think it's fanciful to believe that the Egyptians could manage to travel such a long way to Australia 5000 years ago, but they had the technology and the know-how to build seaworthy crafts that would stand the long voyage. This was demonstrated recently by modern-day adventurers Thor Heyerdahl and Vital Alsar. They both made similar long journeys across the oceans, just like the Egyptians, but in the last half of the twentieth century.

In 1947 the Norwegian adventurer Thor Heyerdahl travelled from Peru to Raroia in Eastern Polynesia in a balsa raft, a flat-bottomed craft that he called the *Kon-tiki*. He was able to travel such a long way because he took advantage of the

Humboldt current. This current runs like a river from Peru to Polynesia and gave his raft a free lift. In 1969 Heyerdahl attempted to sail across the Atlantic in a replica of the reed boats built by the Egyptians 5000 years ago. He actually constructed the boats at Giza near the pyramids on the Nile River and his aim was to prove that 'the oceans weren't the great barriers to early movement' across the world that they were thought to be. He considered the oceans to be 'the cultural bearers, serving as natural conveyor belts to carry man and civilisation from one part of the earth to another'. You can read about what Heyerdahl set out to do in his books.[1]

For Heyerdahl's second journey he built the reed boat the *Ra I* and sailed from Safi in Morocco hoping to make it to Barbados. Unfortunately it broke up after 3000 miles and sank just 200-odd miles before its destination. If he had added tar to the bottom of his boat it would have lasted longer and not sunk. Then in 1972 Heyerdahl tackled the Atlantic again in the *Ra II*. This time he did manage to successfully travel from Safi to Barbados, making it in fifty-seven days and covering a distance of 3270 miles. For this journey he was carried by the Canary current, which runs past the Canary Islands right across the Atlantic Ocean.

I think it is also significant that the Maoris travelled to New Zealand from Polynesia in the Pacific just over a thousand years ago, so they alone proved that it was possible to make long journeys across the oceans.

---

1 Thor Heyerdahl wrote *Early Man and the Ocean* (1978), Allen and Unwin. He discusses the early crafts of the Egyptians. He also wrote books of his own adventures: *The Ra Expeditions* (1970) and *The Kon-Tiki Expedition* (1950).

Appendix 2

Whether there is a connection or not between my great great grandfather, Thomas Adams, and the infamous Tichborne affair is still a matter for speculation. Nevertheless, the story of Roger Charles Tichborne is a fascinating one. His journey began when he left England as a wealthy British aristocrat heading for South America. A year later he sailed from the Brazilian port of Rio De Janeiro in the ship *Bella* but the vessel was ship-wrecked and Roger Tichborne was never heard of again – well, not under that name. A report reached England saying that some of the crew and passengers of a vessel called the *Bella* were picked up by another vessel bound for Melbourne, Australia. It was not known whether Roger Charles Tichborne was among the drowned or saved.

In the 1860s a reward was offered by Roger's French mother for information regarding the fate of her beloved son. Notices were placed in the colony's newspapers on 5 August 1865. A handsome incentive was offered to any person who could supply such information that would lead to the discovery of the fate of Roger Charles Tichborne. The newspaper notice said that at the time he went missing Roger Tichborne would have been about thirty-two years of age. He was supposedly of a delicate constitution, though rather tall and had very light-brown hair and blue eyes. Roger Tichborne was the son of James Tichborne and heir to all his estates. A notice also appeared in the South Australian paper the *Advertiser*, again stating that a most generous reward would be granted to anyone giving information about the fate of the missing heir. All replies were to be addressed to Arthur Corbit, care of the Missing Persons Office, Bridge Street, Sydney, New South Wales.

So you can see that these notices would have aroused a great deal of interest, in fact it stirred up the whole of Australia, as well as some people in England. Everyone likes riches, so this simple notice in the paper was to spark a long-running saga of false identity in Australia. It later became known as the Tichborne Affair. The first bloke to pick it up and run with it was Arthur Orton, alias Tom Castro, who claimed he was the missing Roger Tichborne. He had actually been to South America and managed to get all these different people to back him up in his claim to being the missing heir. His claim was challenged and it became one of the most expensive court cases of the day. You see, everyone in the Tichborne family was convinced that Tom Castro was a fraud – all except Roger's eccentric French mother. It was a very long and costly court case because there were a lot of people involved and they had to come from all over the place to testify. There were also detectives and researchers and all sorts of people working for the different sides to try to either build up the case or knock it down.

Roger Tichborne was born in Paris on 5 January 1829. He was the eldest grandson of Sir Edward Tichborne who was the ninth Baron of the ancient Tichborne family of Hampshire. Apparently his ancestor, Sir John Tichborne, Sheriff of Southampton, was made a Baronet by King James I in 1621. His descendants inherited great wealth and became one of the leading Catholic families in the south of England.

Roger's father was James Francis Doherty Tichborne, the tenth Baron. He married Henriette Felicite, the illegitimate daughter of English gentleman Henry Seymour of Wiltshire and a French woman (apparently of royal lineage). Henriette disliked her English family-in-law and was intent upon bringing up her eldest son Roger as a French boy. As a result, Roger, at sixteen years old, spoke little English and had little education. So his father sent him to Stonyhurst Jesuit school in Lancashire, England. From there Roger proceeded to Dublin and joined the 6th Dragoon Guards.

They say Roger Tichborne eventually left his regiment because he didn't fit in. He had a French accent and was somewhat sickly and eccentric, causing him to be the butt of many jokes. So he ran away to sea – something I can relate to, because I did the same thing myself nearly 100 years later! Roger arrived at Valparaiso in South America and eventually Rio de Janeiro, in Brazil. It was when he set sail on the *Bella* that tragedy struck. But was he one of the few survivors, and did he shed his former identity and continue his travels to the colonies of Australia?

The Tichborne case made big news in England as well as Australia. It cost over a million pounds, a lot of money in those days, and ran for 188 days. It seems everyone was fascinated by it because it was widely reported in the papers and many plays and books have been written about it since. I remember when I was living with my Auntie Glad she'd sing out to me when the Tichborne play was on the radio. She'd call out, 'That play's on the air!' We used to get the script too, but the script told us very little actually. So in the end I read different bits and pieces in encyclopaedias. Then recently I managed to get this book, which is probably the latest one about it, by Robin Annear called *The Man Who Lost Himself: The unbelievable story of the Tichborne claimant*. After reading this book, it seems this Tichborne claimant, Arthur Orton, had an awful lot of people convinced that he was Roger Tichborne, even Roger's mother, Henriette. I suppose they thought they'd get to share some of his huge inheritance.

For some reason, Roger's heart-broken mother, the wealthy

dowager Henriette, was prepared to listen to the claims of this Arthur Orton. Maybe because he too once sailed himself to Valparaiso and later spent time in Chile. In fact he acquired his alias name 'Castro' from a Chilean family he befriended before his sojourn in Australia under the name Tom Castro. When he arrived here in Australia he became a butcher in Wagga Wagga, New South Wales.

In order to stake his claim as Roger Tichborne back in England, he had to travel back there. When he finally met up with the eccentric Henriette, his supposed mother, she actually acknowledged him as her long-lost son. She even gave him the diaries and letters that Roger had sent her while he was in South America. These became a great source of information for him.[1] Unfortunately for Tom, when he arrived in England one of his real sisters, Mary Orton, recognised him and claimed his name was not Tom Castro, but Arthur Orton, the son of a butcher from Wapping. So that's when all the lawyers and all the investigators stepped in, trying to find out all the facts and where this Tom Castro was really from. By the 1860s Tom Castro was becoming a large obese man, quite different from the thin sickly description of the Roger Tichborne who sailed for South America many years earlier.

Tom Castro claimed to be Roger Tichborne because the title of Baron would have passed his way, through his supposed father. But there was not only the title at stake, the Tichbornes were a wealthy family who owned a lot of property. It seems amazing to me that even Roger Tichborne's mother was convinced this bloke Castro was her real son. In the end Tom Castro was accused of being an impostor after many days in the English court, charged with perjury in 1874 and sentenced to fourteen years of penal servitude.

---

1 Perhaps Roger Tichborne could write well enough to write to his mother in French, but did Tom Castro know French? See Robin Annear's book.

If Tom Castro didn't manage to inherit the family money, the rest of the Tichborne family would get it all. It seems Lady Henriette thought she'd rather let an impostor son have the inheritance than let the rest of the family have it back. She herself was running out of money, so she probably thought that at least Tom Castro would be nice to her. She might have thought that she'd give him the money rather than lose all the money to her in-laws.

Once a bloke pointed out to me that my ancestor Tom Adams couldn't have been Roger Tichborne because Roger Tichborne would have been educated. But Roger was brought up in France by his mother with little formal education. She didn't send him to school. Roger Tichborne didn't read and write in English because he was a French kid really. His mother taught him in French, and he had French tutors. So every time someone said something to me that seemed to prove there wasn't a connection, a strange explanatory twist came in.

The final twist for me in this whole Tichborne story is the long-standing ceremony known as the Tichborne Dole. This is a special event run by the Tichborne heirs on 25 March every year in England. Amazingly this day is the very same day as my birthday! The Tichborne Dole is held on the day of the Feast of the Annunciation (Lady's Day) and is a tradition that was started in the thirteenth century by Lady Mabella on her death bed. She appealed to her husband (another Roger Tichborne) to give a 'dole' of bread to any poor folk who applied for it on Lady's Day. Her husband, rather heartlessly, agreed instead to donate as much corn from his land that Lady Mabella could manage to walk around. Being bed ridden he assumed she would not be able to walk at all but the determined Lady Mabella managed to crawl around a twenty-three acre field, which is still called The Crawls to this day.

Lady Mabella then laid a curse on any descendents who failed to be charitable and distribute the promised annual dole to the poor. She declared the penalty would be for the ancient Tichborne house to fall down and for only daughters to be born, causing the family name to be lost. Perhaps the less charitable nineteenth-century Tichbornes, who failed to distribute the dole, caused the trouble that later came to the family, the loss of young Roger Tichborne at sea in 1854 and the eventual failure of the Baronet title to be passed on to male Tichborne heirs. The original ancient house also no longer stands on the Tichborne estate in Hampshire.

So who knows what really happened to Roger Tichborne? But one thing we can ponder on is the misfortunes of a young Thomas Adams who was transported in 1826 to Australia for stealing bread. If only Leicestershire were closer to Hampshire in the south, Tom could have received free corn from the annual Tichborne Dole and wouldn't have resorted to stealing bread and been shipped away. But then this whole story of mine would have had a very different twist!

Postscript

With most stories there is always a little twist at the end, and so it is with my story – it seems the clock has struck again! Through the diligence of my sister Merle, who has searched the family genealogies, new information on my ancestry has just been revealed. All my life I have been known as Lewis William Arthur O'Brien; on my birth certificate my father's name is Ernest James Patrick Holmes O'Brien.

I have since found out that his mother (my grandmother) changed his name to O'Brien after she became involved with an Irish man, Patrick O'Brien. My father's registered name (at birth) was actually Ernest Holmes Prince: he was only an O'Brien through his mother's association with Patrick O'Brien (although apparently he does have some Irish ancestry on his mother's side). He was English, not Irish.

So all these years, I thought I had Irish blood in my veins, only to discover that I'm also a 'Pom' on my father's side, and of course Aboriginal on my mother's.

After leaving Australia, my father had another family in England. I recently learned that he later returned to Australia with his second family. On 22 July 2006, I had the opportunity to meet with three of my newly-discovered half-siblings, which was great.

Wakefield Press is an independent publishing and
distribution company based in Adelaide, South Australia.
We love good stories and publish beautiful books.
To see our full range of titles, please visit our website at
www.wakefieldpress.com.au.